A Student's Commentary on Ovid's *Metamorphoses* Book 10

A Student's Commentary on Ovid's *Metamorphoses* Book 10

Shawn O'Bryhim

Franklin & Marshall College
Lancaster, Pennsylvania

WILEY Blackwell

This edition first published 2021
© 2021 John Wiley & Sons, Inc.

All rights reserved. No part of this publication may be reproduced, stored in a retrieval system, or transmitted, in any form or by any means, electronic, mechanical, photocopying, recording or otherwise, except as permitted by law. Advice on how to obtain permission to reuse material from this title is available at http://www.wiley.com/go/permissions.

The right of Shawn O'Bryhim to be identified as the author of this work has been asserted in accordance with law.

Registered Office
John Wiley & Sons, Inc., 111 River Street, Hoboken, NJ 07030, USA

Editorial Office
111 River Street, Hoboken, NJ 07030, USA

For details of our global editorial offices, customer services, and more information about Wiley products visit us at www.wiley.com.

Wiley also publishes its books in a variety of electronic formats and by print-on-demand. Some content that appears in standard print versions of this book may not be available in other formats.

Limit of Liability/Disclaimer of Warranty
While the publisher and authors have used their best efforts in preparing this work, they make no representations or warranties with respect to the accuracy or completeness of the contents of this work and specifically disclaim all warranties, including without limitation any implied warranties of merchantability or fitness for a particular purpose. No warranty may be created or extended by sales representatives, written sales materials or promotional statements for this work. The fact that an organization, website, or product is referred to in this work as a citation and/or potential source of further information does not mean that the publisher and authors endorse the information or services the organization, website, or product may provide or recommendations it may make. This work is sold with the understanding that the publisher is not engaged in rendering professional services. The advice and strategies contained herein may not be suitable for your situation. You should consult with a specialist where appropriate. Further, readers should be aware that websites listed in this work may have changed or disappeared between when this work was written and when it is read. Neither the publisher nor authors shall be liable for any loss of profit or any other commercial damages, including but not limited to special, incidental, consequential, or other damages.

Library of Congress Cataloging-in-Publication Data
Names: Ovid, 43 B.C.-17 A.D. or 18 A.D. Metamorphoses. Liber 10. |
   O'Bryhim, Shawn, 1960- Student's commentary on Ovid's Metamorphoses Book 10.
Title: A student's commentary on Ovid's Metamorphoses Book 10 / Shawn David
   O'Bryhim.
Description: Hoboken, NJ : John Wiley & Sons, Inc., 2021. | Includes
   bibliographical references and index. | Text in Latin, commentary in
   English.
Identifiers: LCCN 2020051150 (print) | LCCN 2020051151 (ebook) | ISBN
   9781119770503 (paperback) | ISBN 9781119770510 (epub) | ISBN
   9781119770527 (pdf) | ISBN 9781119770534 (ebook)
Subjects: LCSH: Ovid, 43 B.C.-17 A.D. or 18 A.D. Metamorphoses. Liber 10. |
   Mythology, Classical, in literature. | Metamorphosis in literature.
Classification: LCC PA6519.M9 S78 2021 (print) | LCC PA6519.M9 (ebook) |
   DDC 873/.01--dc23
LC record available at https://lccn.loc.gov/2020051150
LC ebook record available at https://lccn.loc.gov/2020051151

Cover image: Limestone sarcophagus: the Amathus sarcophagus, The Cesnola Collection, Purchased by subscription, 1874–76, The MET, Creative Commons Zero (CC0)
Cover design by Wiley

Set in 9.5/12.5pt STIXTwoText by Integra Software Services, Pondicherry, India.
Printed and bound by CPI Group (UK) Ltd, Croydon, CR0 4YY

C114113_240521

For Angela O'Bryhim
uxori optimae amicaeque

Contents

Acknowledgments *viii*
Preface *ix*

Introduction *1*

i. **Ovid's Biography** *1*

ii. **Ovid's Works** *2*

iii. *Metamorphoses* *5*

iv. **Summary of Book 10** *6*

v. **Scansion** *6*

vi. **Suggestions for Further Reading** *7*

Glossary of Terms *8*
Abbreviations *10*
Text of Book 10 *11*
Commentary *30*
Works Cited *134*
Index *144*

Acknowledgments

I began my study of Ovid's *Metamorphoses* while I was a graduate student in the Department of Classics at the University of Texas at Austin. The Near Eastern background of its Amathusian myths became the topic of my dissertation, which was guided to completion by the members of my committee: my Doktorvater G. Karl Galinsky, Michael von Albrecht, John Kroll, M. Gwyn Morgan, and Douglass Parker. All of them were very tolerant of my ideas about Near Eastern elements in Greek and Roman myth, at a time when this topic was still controversial. It seems somehow fitting that a project that began in graduate school has come to fruition at the end of my career, albeit in a very different form.

I owe a debt of gratitude to many people. I would like to thank Professor Athanassios Vergados of Newcastle University, who has provided support in many ways over the years, most importantly by being a good friend. My wife, Angela, generously gave me the time that I needed to focus on the final stages of this book, while James Lipka, my long-suffering guitar teacher, offered me a much needed distraction from it. Todd Green, Will Croft, Skyler van Valkenburgh, and Andrew Minton, the editorial team at Wiley, made the production of this book virtually painless, as did my copy-editor, Manuela Tecusan, and Surendar Adhavan, who oversaw the production process. Any infelicities in the text are due to my inveterate stubbornness. Franklin & Marshall College provided sabbatical funds that allowed me to spend a year in the excellent library of Ruprecht Karl University in Heidelberg.

If nothing else, I hope to have left behind something to remind my children, Caelan Alexander Patrick O'Bryhim, Brendan Augustus Conchobhor O'Bryhim, Aidan Constantine Conlan O'Bryhim, and Collin Arthur Declan O'Bryhim, that their father was not, in Milton's words, a burden to the earth.

Shawn O'Bryhim
Arcadia, Indiana

Preface

Of Ovid's many works, Book 10 of the *Metamorphoses* has had perhaps the greatest impact on western culture. Its tales of Orpheus and Eurydice, Pygmalion and his statue, and Venus and Adonis have inspired artists, poets, writers, and composers from the Middle Ages to the modern era. Because most commentaries on Ovid's *Metamorphoses* survey large portions of the epic, the attention that they are able devote to individual books is limited. Bömer's German commentary is a scholarly resource that provides a wealth of information on the individual myths that constitute Book 10, but offers little analysis of their significance to the book as a whole. Although the German commentary on the *Metamorphoses* by Haupt, Korn, Ewaldt, and von Albrecht is better for literary analysis, the space devoted to Book 10 is limited by the commentary's broad scope. The same can be said of Bosselaar's *Metamorphoseon* in Dutch and Galasso's *Le metamorfosi* in Italian. Although Anderson's commentary on Books 6–10 is very good, it rarely ventures beyond literary analysis, as does Hill's short commentary on Books 9–12, which is intended for students of literature. Reed's *Ovidio: Metamorfosi*, vol. 5, a volume devoted to Books 10–13, is excellent, but it is in Italian and is far too advanced for undergraduates. Fratantuono's stand-alone commentary on Book 10 offers some observations on Orphism, but otherwise is purely literary. This book deals not only with the literary, grammatical, and textual matters that are integral parts of any commentary on a classical text but also examines the religious, archaeological, and cultural background of the myths. For Book 10, this background is not only Greek and Roman but also Near Eastern. It is my hope that this multidisciplinary approach will facilitate a more holistic understanding of Book 10, especially at a time when a broader conception of classics is coming to the fore – a conception that encompasses the contribution of the Near East to the Greek and Roman world.

Preface

This commentary is intended primarily for undergraduate students of Latin who have completed at least two years of language instruction. It may also be of use to graduate students, and perhaps even to researchers who are unfamiliar with some of the nonliterary elements of Book 10. Its focus, however, is on its primary audience. Since these students will have already mastered the basics of Latin grammar, only its more uncommon aspects receive comment here. While literary interpretations of some of the myths of Book 10 abound, several are not mentioned in this commentary for a variety of reasons, but they can be introduced during class to promote discussion, if the instructor so chooses. The text follows that of Tarrant and Anderson, with the substitution of some readings from other editors and from the manuscripts.

Introduction

i. Ovid's Biography

Most of what we know about the Roman poet Publius Ovidius Naso comes from *Tristia*, a collection of autobiographical poems that he wrote after Augustus relegated him to the Black Sea. Because this information cannot be confirmed by independent sources, it must be used with caution, particularly when it comes to Ovid's complaints about his place of exile.

At *Tristia* 4.10, Ovid says that he was born into a respectable equestrian family of moderate means on March 20, 43 BC, in Sulmo (modern Sulmona), a small city about 100 miles to the east of Rome. Ovid's brother, who was born in the previous year, shared his birthday. Both were educated by the best local teachers. While Ovid's brother favored oratory, Ovid himself gravitated toward poetry. When his father attempted to dissuade him from focusing on verse because he thought that there was no money in it, Ovid tried to please him by writing prose. This ultimately failed: as the rhetorician Seneca the Elder (*Controversiae* 2.2.8) put it, he simply wrote verse in prose. When his brother died at the age of 20, Ovid embarked upon a political career. He was first elected to the board of the *tresviri capitales* (three officials who oversaw policing), and later to that of the *decemviri stlitibus iudicandis* (ten officials who judged lawsuits) (*Fasti* 4.383–384). The next logical step was a major political office. Politics, however, did not interest Ovid. Instead of continuing on this course, he returned to his first love: poetry.

Ovid went to Rome and began giving public recitations of his love poetry, much of which centered on his (possibly fictional) lover, "Corinna." His talent made him popular in literary circles and provided access to the most famous

A Student's Commentary on Ovid's Metamorphoses *Book 10,* First Edition. Shawn O'Bryhim.
© 2021 John Wiley & Sons, Inc. Published 2021 by John Wiley & Sons, Inc.

poets of the time: Macer, Propertius, Ponticus, Bassus, and Horace. After two divorces, he married a woman who gave him a daughter and stood by him even after Augustus relegated him in AD 7 to Tomis, a settlement on the west shore of the Black Sea (modern Constanța, Romania). This punishment was particularly irksome to Ovid, as the locals did not know Latin and therefore were unable to appreciate his talent.

Ovid maintains that he was not expelled from Rome because of a crime (*Tristia* 4.10.90), but because of "a poem and a mistake" (*carmen et error, Tristia* 2.207). He provides few specifics, since – he claims – the details are well known. Nevertheless, he does identify the poem as *Ars amatoria*, a didactic work on seduction (*Tristia* 2.8; 3.1–8; *Ex Ponto* 2.9.76). The dissemination of this poem is a classic example of bad timing, coming as it did on the heels of Augustus' moral legislation and the exile of his daughter, Julia, on the charge of adultery. While Ovid is open about the incriminating poem, he does not reveal the nature of his error, claiming that he does not want to reopen the wound that he inflicted upon Augustus. Nevertheless, he repeatedly avers that his offense was no crime (*Tristia* 2.208–210, 4.4.37–42, 5.4.18–22; cf. *Ex Ponto* 2.3); it was not rebellion (*Tristia* 2.51–56), murder, fraud, or the breaking of any law (*Ex Ponto* 2.9.63–75). Rather it was something that he witnessed (*Tristia* 2.103–104). Whatever this was, his failure to report it offended Augustus, who banished Ovid on his own authority instead of sending his case to the Senate or to a court (*Tristia* 2.131–138). It may be that he was privy to something embarrassing and that the emperor, not wanting to make this matter public, used the *Ars amatoria* as a pretext for Ovid's exile. Although he defends himself at length against the charge of teaching adultery through the *Ars* (*Tristia* 2.211–212, 2.237–572), he steadfastly refuses to reveal the reason for his exile, perhaps because he hoped to obtain a pardon or, at the very least, a transfer to a more genial location.

Ovid was never allowed to return to Rome. He was forced to remain in Tomis, over eight hundred miles from his home, writing poetry when he could, trying to learn the native language, and even strapping on armor to ward off the neighboring tribes (*Tristia* 5.10). He died in the ninth year of his exile, during the winter of AD 17/18, at the age of 60.

ii. Ovid's Works

Ovid describes **Amores** as a work of his youth (*Tristia* 4.10.57–58). It originally consisted of five books; a revision reduced it to three, which is the version that has survived. At *Amores* 1.1–4, Ovid says that he had intended to write an epic poem on a military topic. Indeed, the first line begins with the word *arma*, as does Vergil's *Aeneid*. Cupid, however, stole a foot from every other line, thereby transforming an epic poem in dactylic hexameter into a collection of love poems in elegiac couplets. When Ovid complains that he should not be writing love poetry because he has never been in love, Cupid responds by shooting him with an arrow, thereby transforming him into a lover. The object of his desire is a woman named Corinna, whose identity was not known to Ovid's contemporaries or to later writers (*Ars amatoria* 3.53–58; Apuleius, *Apologia* 10.2). This suggests either that "Corinna" is a pseudonym for an unidentified woman or that the character who bears this name is fictional (*Tristia* 4.10.59–60). Ovid's *Amores* takes a light-hearted look at the vicissitudes of love and contains many of the tropes and characters found both in previous love poets and in New Comedy.

Heroides consists of verse letters in elegiac couplets written by the heroines of myth to their husbands, lovers, and potential lovers. Focused on character exposition and persuasion, these poems owe much to Ovid's education in rhetoric, and particularly to the tradition of *suasoriae*, "speeches of persuasion" (Seneca, *Controversiae* 2.2.8). They also involve *prosopopoeia* or *ethopoeia* ("character drawing"), a rhetorical exercise in which speeches are composed that portray the characteristics of famous individuals (Quintilian 3.8.52). While Ovid claims that *Heroides* represents an entirely new genre (*Ars amatoria* 3.346), the pieces in this collection are reminiscent of speeches from Euripidean tragedy and may have been inspired by a fictional letter in Propertius 4.3. Poems 1–15 appear to be youthful compositions in the *personae* of individual female characters, while poems 16–21 – the "double *heroides*," in which letters from heroines are answered by their male addressees – come from a later period. These poems take possibilities left open by earlier authors as their jumping-off point (e.g. a letter that Penelope could have written after her interview with Odysseus in the guise of a beggar). Ovid's use of varied source material allows for new perspectives on familiar tales, while his refashioning of his sources into something unique foreshadows his compositional technique in *Metamorphoses*.

Ars amatoria is a didactic poem in three books. Here Ovid plays the role of "teacher of love" (*praeceptor amoris*). The first two books teach men how to find and obtain lovers; the third does the same for women. While previous didactic poems were written in dactylic hexameter, Ovid uses elegiac couplets, a meter that is more appropriate to his erotic theme in that it is traditionally associated with love poetry. His advice does not have romance as its primary objective, but is geared toward achieving intercourse through various methods of seduction. After careful study of this poem and the application of its advice, Ovid's readers, unlike the lovers depicted by previous elegiac poets, will be able to control love rather than allow it to control them. In spite of (disingenuous) disclaimers that this poem is not intended for respectable women (1.31–34, 2.599–600, 3.57–58, 3.483–484, 3.613–616), Augustus used it as a pretext for Ovid's exile. In **Remedia amoris**, Ovid plays the role of the "doctor of love" who cures his love-sick patients by teaching them how to overcome passion and thereby extricate themselves from romantic relationships.

A second didactic poem, **Medicamina faciei feminae**, is a fragment of a longer work that Ovid describes as *parvus* (*Ars amatoria* 3.206). The passage that survives, which justifies the use of makeup and provides recipes for it, originally stood at the beginning of the poem. It is unclear whether this was a serious guidebook to cosmetics, a parody of didactic works, or Ovid's attempt to demonstrate his virtuosity as a poet by taking on an unpromising topic.

Fasti is a didactic poem on the Roman calendar in elegiac couplets. It focuses on myths and festivals, but also includes information on astronomy and on Augustus and his family. The broad learning that it contains is reminiscent of the scholarship of the Hellenistic period, particularly Callimachus' *Aetia*. Six books (January through June) were completed before Ovid's exile and were subsequently revised. It appears that books on the remaining six months were not written.

Ovid continued to write even after his exile. **Tristia** and **Epistulae ex Ponto** are elegiac poems addressed primarily to his wife and to anonymous individuals in Rome. The poems addressed to Augustus are pleas for a commutation of his sentence. Others are bleak descriptions of his new home and sorrowful reflections on his past, present, and future.

Ibis, which was modeled on a poem of the same name by Callimachus, is an invective in elegiac couplets instead of the iambics traditionally associated with this genre. In it, Ovid rails against an anonymous enemy who is trying to damage his reputation in Rome during his exile. This poem is replete with references to punishments inflicted on mythic figures that Ovid wishes upon his adversary. Here the unwarlike poet of love transforms himself into a soldier who threatens violence against his enemy through verse. Because Ovid cannot carry out his vengeance from Tomis, *Ibis* expresses his frustration with the situation in which he finds himself: helpless, in the middle of nowhere. In the end, however, the extreme punishments that he conjures up for his enemy are so ridiculous that the poem devolves into humor.

There are references to other works that have not survived. Quintilian (10.1.98) holds up the tragedy **Medea** as an example of Ovid's unrealized potential. This is his only work that is not in elegiac couplets or in dactylic hexameter. There was also a translation of Aratus' *Phaenomena*, a poem on the stars. Ovid refers in *Ex Ponto* (1.2.131, 1.7.30, 3.4, 4.6.17, 4.9.131) to occasional poems that would have focused on particular events. One of these was in Gaetic, the language spoken in Tomis (4.13.19–36).

iii. *Metamorphoses*

With *Metamorphoses*, Ovid exchanges the elegiac couplets of his love poetry for the dactylic hexameter of epic. Superficially, this poem fits the broad definition of an epic: it is in the traditional meter of epic (dactylic hexameter), it is a long work (15 books), and its main characters are gods and heroes. But Ovid departs from this definition in fundamental ways. While *Metamorphoses* is a *carmen perpetuum* ("continuous poem," 1.4) that begins with the creation of the earth and ends in Ovid's time, it is not a long story on one topic, like the *Iliad* or the *Aeneid*. Instead, it is a collection of shorter stories, some of which occupy a fraction of a book, while others are so long that they are categorized as *epyllia* ("mini-epics"). These tales are bound together not so much by chronology as by devices such as family relationships or similarities between metamorphoses, and these provide a segue from one story to the next. Not all the myths are about heroes; the story of Arachne, for example, is about a talented woman of the lower class. Moreover, Ovid incorporates nearly every imaginable genre into this work: *epyllion*, tragedy, comedy, rhetoric, hymn, erotic poetry, pastoral poetry, historical myth, and philosophy (Lafaye 1904: 141–159). *Metamorphoses* may be an epic poem, but it does not fit the traditional definition of an epic.

Ovid's sources for the nearly two hundred and fifty stories that comprise his *Metamorphoses* span the history of Greek and Latin literature from Homer to his own time. Many date from the Hellenistic period, when mythological compendia such as Boios' poem on bird metamorphoses and Nicander's work on mythic transformations were popular. The poems of Callimachus provided inspiration as well. It is likely that Ovid used the lost work *About Cyprus*, by the geographer Philostephanus, for many of the myths in Book 10. He also used contemporary poems such as Vergil's *Aeneid* and Cinna's *Myrrha*, and perhaps two separate *Metamorphoses*, one by Parthenius and another by Theodorus. But Ovid was not a slavish copier of his sources. He created variants of myths that would allow his educated audience to make comparisons between traditional versions of these stories and his adaptations. Like Pygmalion, he fashioned raw material into something that was uniquely his.

Metamorphoses was completed shortly before Ovid's exile. Although he burned his copy of the manuscript before departing for Tomis, he says that several others survived. Indeed, there were so many of them that Ovid asked that a preface be added that begged his audience's pardon for the unpolished state of the poem (*Tristia* 1.7.13–40). The sheer number of times that *Metamorphoses* was copied in the Middle Ages and the Renaissance (nearly four hundred manuscripts survive today) testifies to its popularity throughout the ages.

iv. Summary of Book 10

Book 10 of Ovid's *Metamorphoses* tells the story of the mythic bard Orpheus, whose wife died just after their wedding from the bite of a snake. Thereupon he travels to the underworld to persuade its rulers to release her. Pluto agrees, on the condition that he not look back at her until he reaches the earth. When Orpheus violates this agreement at the last possible moment, she is forced to return to the underworld, and he is denied a second chance to rescue her. Because of this tragic experience, he renounces the love of women and devotes himself to a life of pederasty. Orpheus expresses his attitude toward sexuality in a song that recounts various stories about the love of the gods for boys and the punishment meted out to women who indulged their illicit lusts. This song consists of the myths of Ganymede, Hyacinthus, the Cerastae, the Propoetides, Pygmalion, Myrrha, Venus and Adonis, and Atalanta and Hippomenes. Book 10 ends with the conclusion of Orpheus' song; Book 11 begins with his death at the hands of the Thracian women and his subsequent reunion with Eurydice in the Elysian Fields.

v. Scansion

The meter of English poetry is determined by the arrangement of stressed and unstressed syllables:

> Ón the Moúntains óf the Praírie,
> Ón the greát Red Pípe-stone Quárry ...

The meter of Latin poetry, by contrast, is determined by the arrangement of long and short syllables.

1. A syllable can be *long by nature* or *long by position*:
   a. A syllable that is long by nature contains a long vowel (*lēgis*) or a diphthong (*arae*).
   b. A syllable that is long by position contains a short vowel followed by two consonants (such groups include the sounds rendered by the letters "x" and "z," namely "ks" and "ds"). These two consonants can occur in the same word (*āttrāctam*) or at the end of one word and the beginning of the next (*fortēm virum*). Note that "ch," "ph," and "th" do not count as two consonants because they represent the Greek letters χ, φ, and θ (*Pērsĕphŏnēn*). Moreover, an "h" at the beginning of the word does not make a vowel long by position (*dĕŭs horum*).

2. A short syllable contains a short vowel that has not been made long by position (e.g. tŏt aves).
3. A vowel followed by a consonant cluster consisting of a mute (b, c, d, f, g, p, t) and a liquid (l, r) can be counted either as a long or as a short syllable. For example, the word *volucris* appears twice at *Metamorphoses* 13.607. In the first instance, "u" is short; it is long in the second.

ēt prīmō sĭmĭlīs vŏlŭcrī, mōx vēră vŏlūcrīs.

Elision occurs when a word that ends in a vowel or in the case ending "-um," "-am," or "-em" is followed by a word that begins with a vowel or an "h." When this happens, the vowel or the "-um," "-am," or "-em" drops out (omn~~em~~ hominem).

The meter of Ovid's *Metamorphoses* is the meter of Greek and Latin epic: dactylic hexameter. It consists of six feet, which can contain dactyls (– ⌣⌣) or spondees (– –). A spondee may occur in any of the first four feet, the fifth foot is normally a dactyl, and the final foot is scanned as a spondee regardless of the quantity of the last syllable.

– ⌣⌣ | – ⌣⌣ | – ⌣⌣ | – ⌣⌣ | – ⌣⌣ | – –

īndĕ pĕr | īmmēn | sūm crŏcĕ | ō vē | lātŭs ă | mīctū. (*Met.* 10.1)

In contrast to Vergil, Ovid uses more dactyls than spondees (a ratio of 20 to 12), which allows his lines to move more rapidly than Vergil's, whose cadence is generally graver. This befits Ovid's tone, which is often playful and humorous. He also employs elision much less frequently than Vergil.

vi. Suggestions for Further Reading

Galinsky, G.K. 1975. *Ovid's* Metamorphoses*: An Introduction to the Basic Aspects*. University of California Press: Berkeley.
Green, P. 1989. *Classical Bearings*. University of California Press: Berkeley.
Halporn, J., M. Ostwald, and T. Rosenmeyer. 1963. *The Meters of Greek and Latin Poetry*. Hackett: Indianapolis, IN.
Hardie, P. 2002. *The Cambridge Companion to Ovid*. Cambridge University Press: Cambridge.
Knox, P. 2009. *A Companion to Ovid*. Wiley Blackwell: Oxford.
Solodow, J. 1988. *The World of Ovid's Metamorphoses*. University of North Carolina Press: Chapel Hill.
Weiden Boyd, B. 2002. *Brill's Companion to Ovid*. Brill: Leiden.

Glossary of Terms

Anaphora The repetition of a word at the beginning of successive lines or phrases. See lines 121–123.
Caesura A break between words within a foot. E.g. | īndĕ || pĕr |.
Chiasmus The repetition of a grammatical structure in reverse order. E.g. *nunc arbor, puer ante* (adverb–noun, noun–adverb).
Emphasis The use of a word that has both an obvious and an implicit meaning.
Enjambment The continuation of a sentence or clause into the next line, often for emphasis. E.g. *fessus in herbosa posuit sua corpora terra | cervus* (128–129).
Figura etymologica The use of two etymologically related words in close proximity to each other. E.g. *voce vocatur*.
Hapax legomenon A word that occurs only once in the extant records of a language.
Hyperbaton The separation of a noun from its adjective by several words.
Metonymy The substitution of an attribute or property for a related entity. E.g. the use of "crown" for "king."
Parataxis The avoidance of subordinate clauses in favor of coordinate clauses.
Pleonasm The use of more words than is necessary to convey an idea. E.g. *muta silentia*.
Proleptic A reference to something that has not yet occurred. E.g. Pygmalion is called "Paphian hero" before his daughter, Paphos, has been born.

Transferred epithet This occurs when an adjective that describes one noun is transferred to another. E.g. *copia digna procorum* instead of *copia dignorum procorum*.

Tricolon Three parallel words or phrases in immediate succession. E.g. *iam iuvenis, iam vir, iam se formosior ipso*.

Zeugma A rhetorical device in which a literal and a figurative meaning are linked. E.g. *hanc [feminam] simul et legem Rhodopeius accipit heros*.

Abbreviations

CAF	*Comicorum atticorum fragmenta*
CIL	*Corpus inscriptionum latinarum*
FGrHist	*Die Fragmente der griechischen Historiker*
FHG	*Fragmenta historicorum graecorum*
FRL	*Fragmentary Republican Latin*
KAI	*Kanaanäische und aramäisch Inschriften*
LIMC	*Lexicon iconographicum mythologiae classicae*
OLD	*Oxford Latin Dictionary*
RE	*Realencyclopädie des classischen Altertumswissenschaft*

Text of Book 10

inde per inmensum croceo velatus amictu
aethera digreditur Ciconumque Hymenaeus ad oras
tendit et Orphea nequiquam voce vocatur.
adfuit ille quidem, sed nec sollemnia verba
nec laetos vultus nec felix attulit omen. 5
fax quoque quam tenuit lacrimoso stridula fumo
usque fuit nullosque invenit motibus ignes.
exitus auspicio gravior. nam nupta per herbas
dum nova Naiadum turba comitata vagatur,
occidit in talum serpentis dente recepto. 10
quam satis ad superas postquam Rhodopeius auras
deflevit vates, ne non temptaret et umbras,
ad Styga Taenaria est ausus descendere porta
perque leves populos simulacraque functa sepulcro
Persephonen adiit inamoenaque regna tenentem 15
umbrarum dominum pulsisque ad carmina nervis
sic ait: 'o positi sub terra numina mundi,
in quem reccidimus, quicquid mortale creamur,
si licet et falsi positis ambagibus oris
vera loqui sinitis, non huc ut opaca viderem 20
Tartara descendi, nec uti villosa colubris
terna Medusaei vincirem guttura monstri.
causa viae est coniunx, in quam calcata venenum
vipera diffudit crescentesque abstulit annos.
posse pati volui nec me temptasse negabo: 25

vicit Amor. supera deus hic bene notus in ora est.
an sit et hic, dubito. sed et hic tamen auguror esse,
famaque si veteris non est mentita rapinae,
vos quoque iunxit Amor. per ego haec loca plena timoris,
per Chaos hoc ingens vastique silentia regni, 30
Eurydices, oro, properata retexite fata.
omnia debemur vobis, paulumque morati
serius aut citius sedem properamus ad unam.
tendimus huc omnes, haec est domus ultima, vosque
humani generis longissima regna tenetis. 35
haec quoque, cum iustos matura peregerit annos,
iuris erit vestri. pro munere poscimus usum;
quod si Fata negant veniam pro coniuge, certum est
nolle redire mihi. leto gaudete duorum.'
talia dicentem nervosque ad verba moventem 40
exsangues flebant animae. nec Tantalus undam
captavit refugam, stupuitque Ixionis orbis,
nec carpsere iecur volucres, urnisque vacarunt
Belides, inque tuo sedisti, Sisyphe, saxo.
tunc primum lacrimis victarum carmine fama est 45
Eumenidum maduisse genas. nec regia coniunx
sustinet oranti nec qui regit ima negare,
Eurydicenque vocant. umbras erat illa recentes
inter et incessit passu de vulnere tardo.
hanc simul et legem Rhodopeius accipit heros, 50
ne flectat retro sua lumina donec Avernas
exierit valles aut inrita dona futura.
carpitur adclivis per muta silentia trames,
arduus, obscurus, caligine densus opaca,
nec procul afuerunt telluris margine summae. 55
hic, ne deficeret metuens avidusque videndi,
flexit amans oculos. et protinus illa relapsa est,
bracchiaque intendens prendique et prendere certans
nil nisi cedentes infelix arripit auras.
iamque iterum moriens non est de coniuge quicquam 60
questa suo (quid enim nisi se quereretur amatam?)
supremumque 'vale,' quod iam vix auribus ille
acciperet, dixit revolutaque rursus eodem est.
non aliter stupuit gemina nece coniugis Orpheus
quam tria qui timidus, medio portante catenas, 65
colla canis vidit. quem non pavor ante reliquit,

quam natura prior saxo per corpus oborto.
quam qui in se crimen traxit voluitque videri
Olenos esse nocens, tuque, o confisa figurae,
infelix Lethaea, tuae, iunctissima quondam					70
pectora, nunc lapides, quos umida sustinet Ide.
orantem frustraque iterum transire volentem
portitor arcuerat. septem tamen ille diebus
squalidus in ripa Cereris sine munere sedit.
cura dolorque animi lacrimaeque alimenta fuere.			75
esse deos Erebi crudeles questus, in altam
se recipit Rhodopen pulsumque aquilonibus Haemum.
tertius aequoreis inclusum Piscibus annum
finierat Titan, omnemque refugerat Orpheus
femineam Venerem, seu quod male cesserat illi,			80
sive fidem dederat. multas tamen ardor habebat
iungere se vati, multae doluere repulsae.
ille etiam Thracum populis fuit auctor amorem
in teneros transferre mares citraque iuventam
aetatis breve ver et primos carpere flores.			85
collis erat collemque super planissima campi
area, quam viridem faciebant graminis herbae.
umbra loco deerat. qua postquam parte resedit
dis genitus vates et fila sonantia movit,
umbra loco venit. non Chaonis afuit arbor,			90
non nemus Heliadum, non frondibus aesculus altis,
nec tiliae molles, nec fagus et innuba laurus,
et coryli fragiles et fraxinus utilis hastis
enodisque abies curvataque glandibus ilex
et platanus genialis acerque coloribus inpar			95
amnicolaeque simul salices et aquatica lotos
perpetuoque virens buxum tenuesque myricae
et bicolor myrtus et bacis caerula tinus.
vos quoque, flexipedes hederae, venistis et una
pampineae vites et amictae vitibus ulmi			100
ornique et piceae pomoque onerata rubenti
arbutus et lentae, victoris praemia, palmae
et succincta comas hirsutaque vertice pinus,
grata deum matri, siquidem Cybeleius Attis
exuit hac hominem truncoque induruit illo.			105
adfuit huic turbae metas imitata cupressus,
nunc arbor, puer ante deo dilectus ab illo,

qui citharam nervis et nervis temperat arcum.
namque sacer nymphis Carthaea tenentibus arva
ingens cervus erat lateque patentibus altas   110
ipse suo capiti praebebat cornibus umbras.
cornua fulgebant auro demissaque in armos
pendebant tereti gemmata monilia collo.
bulla super frontem parvis argentea loris
vincta movebatur parilesque ex aere nitebant   115
auribus e geminis circum cava tempora bacae.
isque metu vacuus naturalique pavore
deposito celebrare domos mulcendaque colla
quamlibet ignotis manibus praebere solebat.
sed tamen ante alios, Ceae pulcherrime gentis,   120
gratus erat, Cyparisse, tibi. tu pabula cervum
ad nova, tu liquidi ducebas fontis ad undam,
tu modo texebas varios per cornua flores,
nunc eques in tergo residens huc laetus et illuc
mollia purpureis frenabas ora capistris.   125
aestus erat mediusque dies, solisque vapore
concava litorei fervebant bracchia Cancri.
fessus in herbosa posuit sua corpora terra
cervus et arborea frigus ducebat ab umbra.
hunc puer imprudens iaculo Cyparissus acuto   130
fixit et, ut saevo morientem vulnere vidit,
velle mori statuit. quae non solacia Phoebus
dixit et ut leviter pro materiaque doleret
admonuit. gemit ille tamen munusque supremum
hoc petit a superis, ut tempore lugeat omni.   135
iamque per immensos egesto sanguine fletus
in viridem verti coeperunt membra colorem.
et modo qui nivea pendebant fronte capilli
horrida caesaries fieri sumptoque rigore
sidereum gracili spectare cacumine caelum.   140
ingemuit tristisque deus 'lugebere nobis
lugebisque alios aderisque dolentibus' inquit.
tale nemus vates attraxerat inque ferarum
concilio, medius turbae, volucrumque sedebat.
ut satis inpulsas temptavit pollice chordas   145
et sensit varios, quamvis diversa sonarent,
concordare modos, hoc vocem carmine movit:
'ab Iove, Musa parens (cedunt Iovis omnia regno),

carmina nostra move. Iovis est mihi saepe potestas
dicta prius. cecini plectro graviore Gigantas 150
sparsaque Phlegraeis victricia fulmina campis.
nunc opus est leviore lyra. puerosque canamus
dilectos superis inconcessisque puellas
ignibus attonitas meruisse libidine poenam.
rex superum Phrygii quondam Ganymedis amore 155
arsit et inventum est aliquid quod Iuppiter esse,
quam quod erat, mallet. nulla tamen alite verti
dignatur nisi quae posset sua fulmina ferre.
nec mora, percusso mendacibus aere pennis
abripit Iliaden qui nunc quoque pocula miscet 160
invitaque Iovi nectar Iunone ministrat.
te quoque, Amyclide, posuisset in aethere Phoebus,
tristia si spatium ponendi fata dedissent.
qua licet, aeternus tamen es, quotiensque repellit
ver hiemem Piscique Aries succedit aquoso, 165
tu totiens oreris viridique in caespite flores.
te meus ante omnes genitor dilexit et orbe
in medio positi caruerunt praeside Delphi,
dum deus Eurotan inmunitamque frequentat
Sparten. nec citharae nec sunt in honore sagittae. 170
immemor ipse sui non retia ferre recusat,
non tenuisse canes, non per iuga montis iniqui
ire comes, longaque alit adsuetudine flammas.
iamque fere medius Titan venientis et actae
noctis erat spatioque pari distabat utrimque. 175
corpora veste levant et suco pinguis olivi
splendescunt latique ineunt certamina disci.
quem prius aerias libratum Phoebus in auras
misit et oppositas disiecit pondere nubes.
reccidit in solidam longo post tempore terram 180
pondus et exhibuit iunctam cum viribus artem.
protinus inprudens actusque cupidine lusus
tollere Taenarides orbem properabat. at illum
dura repercusso subiecit pondere tellus
in vultus, Hyacinthe, tuos. expalluit aeque 185
quam puer ipse deus conlapsosque excipit artus.
et modo te refovet, modo tristia vulnera siccat,
nunc animam admotis fugientem sustinet herbis.
nil prosunt artes. erat inmedicabile vulnus.

ut, siquis violas riguoque papavera in horto 190
liliaque infringat fulvis horrentia linguis,
marcida demittant subito caput illa gravatum
nec se sustineant spectentque cacumine terram,
sic vultus moriens iacet et defecta vigore
ipsa sibi est oneri cervix umeroque recumbit. 195
'laberis, Oebalide, prima fraudate iuventa,'
Phoebus ait 'videoque tuum, mea crimina, vulnus.
tu dolor es facinusque meum. mea dextera leto
inscribenda tuo est. ego sum tibi funeris auctor.
quae mea culpa tamen, nisi si lusisse vocari 200
culpa potest, nisi culpa potest et amasse vocari.
atque utinam pro te vitam tecumve liceret
reddere. quod quoniam fatali lege tenemur,
semper eris mecum memorique haerebis in ore.
te lyra pulsa manu, te carmina nostra sonabunt, 205
flosque novus scripto gemitus imitabere nostros.
tempus et illud erit, quo se fortissimus heros
addat in hunc florem folioque legatur eodem.'
talia dum vero memorantur Apollinis ore,
ecce cruor, qui fusus humo signaverat herbas, 210
desinit esse cruor, Tyrioque nitentior ostro
flos oritur formamque capit quam lilia, si non
purpureus color his, argenteus esset in illis.
non satis hoc Phoebo est (is enim fuit auctor honoris).
ipse suos gemitus foliis inscribit et AI AI 215
flos habet inscriptum funestaque littera ducta est.
nec genuisse pudet Sparten Hyacinthon honorque
durat in hoc aevi celebrandaque more priorum
annua praelata redeunt Hyacinthia pompa.
at si forte roges fecundam Amathunta metallis 220
an genuisse velit Propoetidas, abnuat aeque
atque illos, gemino quondam quibus aspera cornu
frons erat, unde etiam nomen traxere Cerastae.
ante fores horum stabat Iovis Hospitis ara.
ignarus sceleris quam si quis sanguine tinctam 225
advena vidisset, mactatos crederet illic
lactantes vitulos Amathusiacasque bidentes.
hospes erat caesus. sacris offensa nefandis
ipsa suas urbes Ophiusiaque arva parabat
deserere alma Venus. 'sed quid loca grata, quid urbes 230

peccavere meae? quod' dixit 'crimen in illis?
exilio poenam potius gens inpia pendat
vel nece vel si quid medium est mortisque fugaeque.
idque quid esse potest, nisi versae poena figurae?'
dum dubitat, quo mutet eos, ad cornua vultum   235
flexit et admonita est haec illis posse relinqui
grandiaque in torvos transformat membra iuvencos.
sunt tamen obscenae Venerem Propoetides ausae
esse negare deam. pro quo sua numinis ira
corpora cum fama primae vulgasse feruntur.   240
utque pudor cessit, sanguisque induruit oris,
in rigidum parvo silicem discrimine versae.
quas quia Pygmalion aevum per crimen agentis
viderat, offensus vitiis quae plurima menti
femineae natura dedit, sine coniuge caelebs   245
vivebat thalamique diu consorte carebat.
interea niveum mira feliciter arte
sculpsit ebur formamque dedit, qua femina nasci
nulla potest operisque sui concepit amorem.
virginis est verae facies quam vivere credas   250
et, si non obstet reverentia, velle moveri.
ars adeo latet arte sua. miratur et haurit
pectore Pygmalion simulati corporis ignes.
saepe manus operi temptantes admovet, an sit
corpus an illud ebur, nec adhuc ebur esse fatetur.   255
oscula dat reddique putat loquiturque tenetque
et credit tactis digitos insidere membris
et metuit pressos veniat ne livor in artus.
et modo blanditias adhibet, modo grata puellis
munera fert illi: conchas teretesque lapillos   260
et parvas volucres et flores mille colorum
liliaque pictasque pilas et ab arbore lapsas
Heliadum lacrimas. ornat quoque vestibus artus,
dat digitis gemmas, dat longa monilia collo,
aure leves bacae, redimicula pectore pendent.   265
cuncta decent. nec nuda minus formosa videtur.
conlocat hanc stratis concha Sidonide tinctis
adpellatque tori sociam adclinataque colla
mollibus in plumis tamquam sensura reponit.
festa dies Veneris tota celeberrima Cypro   270
venerat, et pandis inductae cornibus aurum

conciderant ictae nivea cervice iuvencae,
turaque fumabant, cum munere functus ad aras
constitit et timide 'si, di, dare cuncta potestis,
sit coniunx, opto,' non ausus 'eburnea virgo' 275
dicere, Pygmalion 'similis mea' dixit 'eburnae.'
sensit, ut ipsa suis aderat Venus aurea festis,
vota quid illa velint et, amici numinis omen,
flamma ter accensa est apicemque per aera duxit.
ut rediit, simulacra suae petit ille puellae 280
incumbensque toro dedit oscula. visa tepere est.
admovet os iterum, manibus quoque pectora temptat:
temptatum mollescit ebur positoque rigore
subsidit digitis ceditque, ut Hymettia sole
cera remollescit tractataque pollice multas 285
flectitur in facies ipsoque fit utilis usu.
dum stupet et dubie gaudet fallique veretur,
rursus amans rursusque manu sua vota retractat.
corpus erat. saliunt temptatae pollice venae.
tum vero Paphius plenissima concipit heros 290
verba, quibus Veneri grates agit, oraque tandem
ore suo non falsa premit dataque oscula virgo
sensit et erubuit timidumque ad lumina lumen
attollens pariter cum caelo vidit amantem.
coniugio, quod fecit, adest dea, iamque coactis 295
cornibus in plenum noviens lunaribus orbem
illa Paphon genuit, de qua tenet insula nomen.

editus hac ille est, qui si sine prole fuisset,
inter felices Cinyras potuisset haberi.
dira canam. procul hinc natae, procul este parentes. 300
aut, mea si vestras mulcebunt carmina mentes,
desit in hac mihi parte fides, nec credite factum,
vel, si credetis, facti quoque credite poenam.
si tamen admissum sinit hoc natura videri,
gentibus Ismariis et nostro gratulor orbi, 305
gratulor huic terrae, quod abest regionibus illis
quae tantum genuere nefas. sit dives amomo
cinnamaque costumque suum sudataque ligno
tura ferat floresque alios Panchaia tellus,
dum ferat et murram. tanti nova non fuit arbor. 310
ipse negat nocuisse tibi sua tela Cupido,
Myrrha, facesque suas a crimine vindicat isto.

stipite te Stygio tumidisque adflavit echidnis
e tribus una soror. scelus est odisse parentem.
hic amor est odio maius scelus. undique lecti   315
te cupiunt proceres, totoque oriente iuventus
ad thalami certamen adest. ex omnibus unum
elige, Myrrha, virum, dum ne sit in omnibus unus.
illa quidem sentit foedoque repugnat amori
et secum 'quo mente feror? quid molior?' inquit   320
'di, precor, et pietas sacrataque iura parentum,
hoc prohibete nefas scelerique resistite nostro,
si tamen hoc scelus est. sed enim damnare negatur
hanc Venerem pietas. coeunt animalia nullo
cetera dilectu, nec habetur turpe iuvencae   325
ferre patrem tergo. fit equo sua filia coniunx,
quasque creavit init pecudes caper, ipsaque, cuius
semine concepta est, ex illo concipit ales.
felices quibus ista licent. humana malignas
cura dedit leges, et quod natura remittit,   330
invida iura negant. gentes tamen esse feruntur,
in quibus et nato genetrix et nata parenti
iungitur, ut pietas geminato crescat amore.
me miseram, quod non nasci mihi contigit illic
fortunaque loci laedor. quid in ista revolvor?   335
spes interdictae, discedite. dignus amari
ille, sed ut pater, est. ergo, si filia magni
non essem Cinyrae, Cinyrae concumbere possem.
nunc, quia iam meus est, non est meus, ipsaque damno
est mihi proximitas. aliena potentior essem.   340
ire libet procul hinc patriaeque relinquere fines,
dum scelus effugiam. retinet malus ardor amantem,
ut praesens spectem Cinyran tangamque loquarque
osculaque admoveam, si nil conceditur ultra.
ultra autem spectare aliquid potes, inpia virgo,   345
et quot confundas et iura et nomina sentis?
tune eris et matris paelex et adultera patris?
tune soror nati genetrixque vocabere fratris?
nec metues atro crinitas angue sorores,
quas facibus saevis oculos atque ora petentes   350
noxia corda vident? at tu, dum corpore non es
passa nefas, animo ne concipe neve potentis
concubitu vetito naturae pollue foedus.

velle puta. res ipsa vetat. pius ille memorque est
moris. et o vellem similis furor esset in illo!'   355
dixerat. at Cinyras, quem copia digna procorum,
quid faciat dubitare facit, scitatur ab ipsa,
nominibus dictis, cuius velit esse mariti.
illa silet primo patriisque in vultibus haerens
aestuat et tepido suffundit lumina rore.   360
virginei Cinyras haec credens esse timoris,
flere vetat siccatque genas atque oscula iungit.
Myrrha datis nimium gaudet consultaque qualem
optet habere virum, 'similem tibi' dixit. at ille
non intellectam vocem conlaudat et 'esto   365
tam pia semper' ait. pietatis nomine dicto
demisit vultus sceleris sibi conscia virgo.
noctis erat medium, curasque et corpora somnus
solverat. at virgo Cinyreia pervigil igni
carpitur indomito furiosaque vota retractat.   370
et modo desperat, modo vult temptare, pudetque
et cupit, et quid agat non invenit. utque securi
saucia trabs ingens, ubi plaga novissima restat,
quo cadat in dubio est omnique a parte timetur,
sic animus vario labefactus vulnere nutat   375
huc levis atque illuc momentaque sumit utroque.
nec modus et requies, nisi mors, reperitur amoris.
mors placet. erigitur laqueoque innectere fauces
destinat et zona summo de poste revincta
'care vale Cinyra. causamque intellege mortis!'   380
dixit et aptabat pallenti vincula collo.
murmura verborum fidas nutricis ad aures
pervenisse ferunt limen servantis alumnae.
surgit anus reseratque fores mortisque paratae
instrumenta videns spatio conclamat eodem   385
seque ferit scinditque sinus ereptaque collo
vincula dilaniat. tum denique flere vacavit,
tum dare conplexus laqueique requirere causam.
muta silet virgo terramque immota tuetur
et deprensa dolet tardae conamina mortis.   390
instat anus canosque suos et inania nudans
ubera per cunas alimentaque prima precatur,
ut sibi committat quidquid dolet. illa rogantem
aversata gemit. certa est exquirere nutrix

nec solam spondere fidem. 'dic' inquit 'opemque   395
me sine ferre tibi. non est mea pigra senectus.
seu furor est, habeo, quae carmine sanet et herbis.
sive aliquis nocuit, magico lustrabere ritu.
ira deum sive est, sacris placabilis ira.
quid rear ulterius? certe fortuna domusque   400
sospes et in cursu est. vivunt genetrixque paterque.'
Myrrha patre audito suspiria duxit ab imo
pectore. nec nutrix etiamnum concipit ullum
mente nefas aliquemque tamen praesentit amorem.
propositique tenax quodcumque est orat ut ipsi   405
indicet, et gremio lacrimantem tollit anili
atque ita conplectens infirmis membra lacertis
'sensimus,' inquit 'amas. sed et hic mea (pone timorem)
sedulitas erit apta tibi, nec sentiet umquam
hoc pater.' exiluit gremio furibunda torumque   410
ore premens 'discede, precor, miseroque pudori
parce' ait. instanti 'discede aut desine' dixit
'quaerere quid doleam. scelus est quod scire laboras.'
horret anus tremulasque manus annisque metuque
tendit et ante pedes supplex procumbit alumnae.   415
et modo blanditur, modo, si non conscia fiat,
terret et indicium laquei coeptaeque minatur
mortis et officium commisso spondet amori.
extulit illa caput lacrimisque implevit obortis
pectora nutricis conataque saepe fateri   420
saepe tenet vocem pudibundaque vestibus ora
texit et 'o' dixit 'felicem coniuge matrem.'
hactenus, et gemuit. gelidus nutricis in artus
ossaque (sensit enim) penetrat tremor, albaque toto
vertice canities rigidis stetit hirta capillis.   425
multaque ut excuteret diros, si posset, amores,
addidit. at virgo scit se non falsa moneri.
certa mori tamen est, si non potiatur amore.
'vive,' ait haec, 'potiere tuo' – et, non ausa 'parente'
dicere, conticuit promissaque numine firmat.   430
festa piae Cereris celebrabant annua matres
illa, quibus nivea velatae corpora veste
primitias frugum dant spicea serta suarum
perque novem noctes Venerem tactusque viriles
in vetitis numerant: turba Cenchreis in illa   435

regis adest coniunx arcanaque sacra frequentat.
ergo legitima vacuus dum coniuge lectus,
nacta gravem vino Cinyran male sedula nutrix
nomine mentito veros exponit amores
et faciem laudat. quaesitis virginis annis   440
'par ait 'est Myrrhae.' quam postquam adducere iussa est
utque domum rediit, 'gaude, mea' dixit 'alumna.
vicimus.' infelix non toto pectore sentit
laetitiam virgo, praesagaque pectora maerent,
sed tamen et gaudet. tanta est discordia mentis.   445
tempus erat quo cuncta silent interque Triones
flexerat obliquo plaustrum temone Bootes.
ad facinus venit illa suum. fugit aurea caelo
luna, tegunt nigrae latitantia sidera nubes.
nox caret igne suo. primus tegis, Icare, vultus,   450
Erigoneque pio sacrata parentis amore.
ter pedis offensi signo est revocata, ter omen
funereus bubo letali carmine fecit.
it tamen, et tenebrae minuunt noxque atra pudorem,
nutricisque manum laeva tenet, altera motu   455
caecum iter explorat. thalami iam limina tangit,
iamque fores aperit, iam ducitur intus. at illi
poplite succiduo genua intremuere fugitque
et color et sanguis, animusque relinquit euntem.
quoque suo propior sceleri est, magis horret et ausi   460
paenitet et vellet non cognita posse reverti.
cunctantem longaeva manu deducit et alto
admotam lecto cum traderet 'accipe' dixit,
'ista tua est, Cinyra' devotaque corpora iunxit.
accipit obsceno genitor sua viscera lecto   465
virgineosque metus levat hortaturque timentem.
forsitan aetatis quoque nomine 'filia' dixit,
dixit et illa 'pater' sceleri ne nomina desint.
plena patris thalamis excedit et inpia diro
semina fert utero conceptaque crimina portat.   470
postera nox facinus geminat, nec finis in illa est,
cum tandem Cinyras, avidus cognoscere amantem
post tot concubitus, inlato lumine vidit
et scelus et natam verbisque dolore retentis
pendenti nitidum vagina deripit ensem.   475
Myrrha fugit: tenebrisque et caecae munere noctis

intercepta neci est latosque vagata per agros
palmiferos Arabas Panchaeaque rura relinquit.
perque novem erravit redeuntis cornua lunae,
cum tandem terra requievit fessa Sabaea. 480
vixque uteri portabat onus. tum nescia voti
atque inter mortisque metus et taedia vitae
est tales conplexa preces: 'o si qua patetis
numina confessis, merui nec triste recuso
supplicium. sed ne violem vivosque superstes 485
mortuaque exstinctos, ambobus pellite regnis
mutataeque mihi vitamque necemque negate.'
numen confessis aliquod patet. ultima certe
vota suos habuere deos. nam crura loquentis
terra supervenit, ruptosque obliqua per ungues 490
porrigitur radix, longi firmamina trunci,
ossaque robur agunt, mediaque manente medulla
sanguis it in sucos, in magnos bracchia ramos,
in parvos digiti, duratur cortice pellis.
iamque gravem crescens uterum perstrinxerat arbor 495
pectoraque obruerat collumque operire parabat.
non tulit illa moram venientique obvia ligno
subsedit mersitque suos in cortice vultus.
quae quamquam amisit veteres cum corpore sensus,
flet tamen et tepidae manant ex arbore guttae. 500
est honor et lacrimis stillataque cortice murra
nomen erile tenet nulloque tacebitur aevo.
at male conceptus sub robore creverat infans
quaerebatque viam qua se genetrice relicta
exsereret. media gravidus tumet arbore venter. 505
tendit onus matrem neque habent sua verba dolores
nec Lucina potest parientis voce vocari.
nitenti tamen est similis curvataque crebros
dat gemitus arbor lacrimisque cadentibus umet.
constitit ad ramos mitis Lucina dolentes 510
admovitque manus et verba puerpera dixit.
arbor agit rimas et fissa cortice vivum
reddit onus, vagitque puer quem mollibus herbis
Naides inpositum lacrimis unxere parentis.
laudaret faciem Livor quoque. qualia namque 515
corpora nudorum tabula pinguntur Amorum,
talis erat. sed, ne faciat discrimina cultus,

aut huic adde leves aut illi deme pharetras.
labitur occulte fallitque volatilis aetas,
et nihil est annis velocius. ille sorore   520
natus avoque suo, qui conditus arbore nuper,
nuper erat genitus, modo formosissimus infans,
iam iuvenis, iam vir, iam se formosior ipso est,
iam placet et Veneri matrisque ulciscitur ignes.
namque pharetratus dum dat puer oscula matri,   525
inscius exstanti destrinxit harundine pectus.
laesa manu natum dea reppulit. altius actum
vulnus erat specie primoque fefellerat ipsam.
capta viri forma non iam Cythereia curat
litora, non alto repetit Paphon aequore cinctam   530
piscosamque Cnidon gravidamque Amathunta metallis.
abstinet et caelo. caelo praefertur Adonis.
hunc tenet, huic comes est adsuetaque semper in umbra
indulgere sibi formamque augere colendo
per iuga, per silvas dumosaque saxa vagatur   535
fine genus vestem ritu succincta Dianae
hortaturque canes tutaeque animalia praedae,
aut pronos lepores aut celsum in cornua cervum
aut agitat dammas. a fortibus abstinet apris
raptoresque lupos armatosque unguibus ursos   540
vitat et armenti saturatos caede leones.
te quoque ut hos timeas, si quid prodesse monendo
possit, Adoni, monet, 'fortis' que 'fugacibus esto'
inquit. 'in audaces non est audacia tuta.
parce meo, iuvenis, temerarius esse periclo,   545
neve feras quibus arma dedit natura lacesse,
stet mihi ne magno tua gloria. non movet aetas
nec facies nec quae Venerem movere leones
saetigerosque sues oculosque animosque ferarum.
fulmen habent acres in aduncis dentibus apri,   550
impetus est fulvis et vasta leonibus ira,
invisumque mihi genus est.' quae causa roganti
'dicam,' ait 'et veteris monstrum mirabere culpae.
sed labor insolitus iam me lassavit et ecce
opportuna sua blanditur populus umbra   555
datque torum caespes. libet hac requiescere tecum'
(et requievit) 'humo' pressitque et gramen et ipsum
inque sinu iuvenis posita cervice reclinis

sic ait ac mediis interserit oscula verbis:
'forsitan audieris aliquam certamine cursus   560
veloces superasse viros. non fabula rumor
ille fuit (superabat enim). nec dicere posses
laude pedum formaene bono praestantior esset.
scitanti deus huic de coniuge 'coniuge' dixit
'nil opus est, Atalanta, tibi. fuge coniugis usum.   565
nec tamen effugies teque ipsa viva carebis.'
territa sorte dei per opacas innuba silvas
vivit et instantem turbam violenta procorum
condicione fugat 'nec sum potienda nisi' inquit
'victa prius cursu. pedibus contendite mecum.   570
praemia veloci coniunx thalamique dabuntur,
mors pretium tardis. ea lex certaminis esto.'
illa quidem inmitis sed (tanta potentia formae est)
venit ad hanc legem temeraria turba procorum.
sederat Hippomenes cursus spectator iniqui   575
et 'petitur cuiquam per tanta pericula coniunx?'
dixerat ac nimios iuvenum damnarat amores.
ut faciem et posito corpus velamine vidit
(quale meum, vel quale tuum, si femina fias),
obstipuit tollensque manus 'ignoscite' dixit   580
'quos modo culpavi. nondum mihi praemia nota,
quae peteretis, erant.' laudando concipit ignes
et ne quis iuvenum currat velocius optat
insidiasque timet. 'sed cur certaminis huius
intemptata mihi fortuna relinquitur?' inquit   585
'audentes deus ipse iuvat.' dum talia secum
exigit Hippomenes, passu volat alite virgo.
quae quamquam Scythica non setius ire sagitta
Aonio visa est iuveni, tamen ille decorem
miratur magis. et cursus facit ipse decorem.   590
aura refert ablata citis talaria plantis,
tergaque iactantur crines per eburnea, quaeque
poplitibus suberant picto genualia limbo.
inque puellari corpus candore ruborem
traxerat, haud aliter quam cum super atria velum   595
candida purpureum simulatas inficit umbras.
dum notat haec hospes, decursa novissima meta est
et tegitur festa victrix Atalanta corona.
dant gemitum victi penduntque ex foedere poenas.

non tamen eventu iuvenis deterritus horum 600
constitit in medio vultuque in virgine fixo
'quid facilem titulum superando quaeris inertes?
mecum confer' ait. 'seu me fortuna potentem
fecerit, a tanto non indignabere vinci.
namque mihi genitor Megareus Onchestius, illi 605
est Neptunus avus, pronepos ego regis aquarum,
nec virtus citra genus est. seu vincar, habebis
Hippomene victo magnum et memorabile nomen.'
talia dicentem molli Schoeneia vultu
aspicit et dubitat, superari an vincere malit. 610
atque ita 'quis deus hunc formosis' inquit 'iniquus
perdere vult caraeque iubet discrimine vitae
coniugium petere hoc? non sum, me iudice, tanti.
nec forma tangor (poteram tamen hac quoque tangi)
sed quod adhuc puer est. non me movet ipse, sed aetas. 615
quid quod inest virtus et mens interrita leti?
quid quod ab aequorea numeratur origine quartus?
quid quod amat tantique putat conubia nostra
ut pereat, si me fors illi dura negarit?
dum licet, hospes, abi thalamosque relinque cruentos. 620
coniugium crudele meum est. tibi nubere nulla
nolet, et optari potes a sapiente puella.
cur tamen est mihi cura tui tot iam ante peremptis?
viderit. intereat, quoniam tot caede procorum
admonitus non est agiturque in taedia vitae. 625
occidet hic igitur, voluit quia vivere mecum,
indignamque necem pretium patietur amoris?
non erit invidiae victoria nostra ferendae.
sed non culpa mea est. utinam desistere velles,
aut, quoniam es demens, utinam velocior esses. 630
at quam virgineus puerili vultus in ore est.
a, miser Hippomene, nollem tibi visa fuissem.
vivere dignus eras. quod si felicior essem,
nec mihi coniugium fata importuna negarent,
unus eras cum quo sociare cubilia vellem.' 635
dixerat, utque rudis primoque cupidine tacta,
quid facit ignorans amat et non sentit amorem.
iam solitos poscunt cursus populusque paterque,
cum me sollicita proles Neptunia voce
invocat Hippomenes 'Cytherea' que 'conprecor, ausis 640

adsit' ait 'nostris et quos dedit adiuvet ignes.'
detulit aura preces ad me non invida blandas.
motaque sum, fateor, nec opis mora longa dabatur.
est ager, indigenae Tamasenum nomine dicunt,
telluris Cypriae pars optima, quem mihi prisci   645
sacravere senes templisque accedere dotem
hanc iussere meis. medio nitet arbor in arvo,
fulva comas, fulvo ramis crepitantibus auro.
hinc tria forte mea veniens decerpta ferebam
aurea poma manu nullique videnda nisi ipsi   650
Hippomenen adii docuique quis usus in illis.
signa tubae dederant, cum carcere pronus uterque
emicat et summam celeri pede libat harenam.
posse putes illos sicco freta radere passu
et segetis canae stantes percurrere aristas.   655
adiciunt animos iuveni clamorque favorque
verbaque dicentum 'nunc, nunc incumbere tempus.'
Hippomene, propera. nunc viribus utere totis.
pelle moram. vinces.' dubium, Megareius heros
gaudeat an virgo magis his Schoeneia dictis.   660
o quotiens, cum iam posset transire, morata est
spectatosque diu vultus invita reliquit.
aridus e lasso veniebat anhelitus ore
metaque erat longe. tum denique de tribus unum
fetibus arboreis proles Neptunia misit.   665
obstipuit virgo nitidique cupidine pomi
declinat cursus aurumque volubile tollit.
praeterit Hippomenes. resonant spectacula plausu.
illa moram celeri cessataque tempora cursu
corrigit atque iterum iuvenem post terga relinquit.   670
et rursus pomi iactu remorata secundi
consequitur transitque virum. pars ultima cursus
restabat. nunc' inquit 'ades, dea muneris auctor.'
inque latus campi, quo tardius illa rediret,
iecit ab obliquo nitidum iuvenaliter aurum.   675
an peteret, virgo visa est dubitare. coegi
tollere et adieci sublato pondera malo
impediique oneris pariter gravitate moraque.
neve meus sermo cursu sit tardior ipso,
praeterita est virgo. duxit sua praemia victor.   680
dignane, cui grates ageret, cui turis honorem

ferret, Adoni, fui? nec grates inmemor egit
nec mihi tura dedit. subitam convertor in iram,
contemptuque dolens ne sim spernenda futuris
exemplo caveo meque ipsa exhortor in ambos. 685
templa, deum Matri quae quondam clarus Echion
fecerat ex voto, nemorosis abdita silvis,
transibant et iter longum requiescere suasit.
illic concubitus intempestiva cupido
occupat Hippomenen a numine concita nostro. 690
luminis exigui fuerat prope templa recessus,
speluncae similis, nativo pumice tectus,
religione sacer prisca, quo multa sacerdos
lignea contulerat veterum simulacra deorum.
hunc init et vetito temerat sacraria probro. 695
sacra retorserunt oculos, turritaque Mater
an Stygia sontes dubitavit mergeret unda.
poena levis visa est. ergo modo levia fulvae
colla iubae velant, digiti curvantur in ungues,
ex umeris armi fiunt, in pectora totum 700
pondus abit, summae cauda verruntur harenae.
iram vultus habet, pro verbis murmura reddunt,
pro thalamis celebrant silvas aliisque timendi
dente premunt domito Cybeleia frena leones.
hos tu, care mihi, cumque his genus omne ferarum 705
quod non terga fugae, sed pugnae pectora praebet
effuge ne virtus tua sit damnosa duobus.'
illa quidem monuit iunctisque per aera cycnis
carpit iter. sed stat monitis contraria virtus.
forte suem latebris, vestigia certa secuti, 710
excivere canes silvisque exire parantem
fixerat obliquo iuvenis Cinyreius ictu.
protinus excussit pando venabula rostro
sanguine tincta suo trepidumque et tuta petentem
trux aper insequitur totosque sub inguine dentes 715
abdidit et fulva moribundum stravit harena.
vecta levi curru medias Cytherea per auras
Cypron olorinis nondum pervenerat alis.
agnovit longe gemitum morientis et albas
flexit aves illuc, utque aethere vidit ab alto 720
exanimem inque suo iactantem sanguine corpus,
desiluit pariterque sinum pariterque capillos

rupit et indignis percussit pectora palmis.
questaque cum fatis 'at non tamen omnia vestri
iuris erunt' dixit. 'luctus monimenta manebunt 725
semper, Adoni, mei, repetitaque mortis imago
annua plangoris peraget simulamina nostri.
at cruor in florem mutabitur. an tibi quondam
femineos artus in olentes vertere mentas,
Persephone, licuit. nobis Cinyreius heros 730
invidiae mutatus erit?' sic fata cruorem
nectare odorato sparsit, qui tactus ab illo
intumuit sic, ut fulvo perlucida caeno
surgere bulla solet. nec plena longior hora
facta mora est, cum flos de sanguine concolor ortus, 735
qualem, quae lento celant sub cortice granum,
punica ferre solent. brevis est tamen usus in illo.
namque male haerentem et nimia levitate caducum
excutiunt idem, qui praestant nomina, venti.

Commentary

Book 10 begins with the story of Orpheus, who was believed to have lived before Homer and Hesiod, the earliest known Greek poets. His lineage is disputed. While many sources make him the offspring of a Muse and a Thracian king named Oegreus, Ovid says that he was the son of Calliope (the Muse of epic poetry) and Apollo, a pedigree that made him such a talented singer that animals, rocks, and trees were attracted to his music. As one of the Argonauts who accompanied the hero Jason on his journey to retrieve the Golden Fleece, he once saved his comrades by singing a song that surpassed that of the Sirens – creatures who would also endanger Odysseus and his men with their alluring song. He also established the Orphic Mysteries, a cult that promised its initiates a pleasurable afterlife in the Elysian Fields.

While the story of Orpheus and his wife Eurydice can be traced as far back as the early fifth century BC, Vergil and Ovid provide the fullest versions of this tale. Sometime after his adventure with the Argonauts, Orpheus married Eurydice, who died from the bite of a viper immediately after their wedding. Thereupon Orpheus descended to the underworld and begged its rulers to send her back with him. His song so charmed Pluto and Proserpina that they agreed to return Eurydice to Orpheus, but on one condition: he could not look at her until he reached the earth. Unable to restrain himself, he glanced back just before they arrived, thereby forcing Eurydice to return to Hades. Overcome by sorrow, Orpheus foreswore all sexual involvement with women. In its place, he invented pederasty. This enraged the Thracian maenads, whose romantic overtures he had rejected. While he was singing a song in the mountains, they tore him limb from limb. His head floated down the Hebrus River, still singing. Thereupon his soul descended to the underworld, where Orpheus spent an idyllic afterlife with Eurydice in the Elysian Fields.

A Student's Commentary on Ovid's Metamorphoses *Book 10,* First Edition. Shawn O'Bryhim.
© 2021 John Wiley & Sons, Inc. Published 2021 by John Wiley & Sons, Inc.

From the sixth century BC through the imperial period, several anonymous authors wrote poems in dactylic hexameter, primarily hymns and theogonies, that they attributed to Orpheus. These may have played a role in various mystery cults, especially in the Dionysiac and the Eleusinian Mysteries (West 1983: 15–29). Orpheus, however, is most closely associated with the Orphic Mysteries. According to the Orphic *Argonautica* (40–43; Diodorus Siculus 1.92.3), he based these rites on what he saw in the underworld while on his way to retrieve Eurydice. Inscribed gold sheets found in graves in Greece, Crete, Italy, and southern Russia suggest that the object of the ritual was to grant initiates a pleasurable afterlife in the Elysian Fields (Graf and Johnston 2007: 165–184), which both Orpheus and Eurydice enjoy in Ovid's account at the beginning of Book 11.

1–5   The first two lines, dominated by dactyls, skip along joyfully until line 3, where the mood turns more solemn with the addition of spondees.

1   ***inde***: Ovid uses the adverb *inde* to shift from the joyful wedding of Iphis and Ianthe on Crete, at the end of Book 9, to the disastrous wedding of Orpheus and Eurydice in Thrace. The concatenation of these stories changes the tone of the narrative. Although born a girl, Iphis is raised as a boy by her mother. When she reaches adulthood, Iphis' father, who thinks that she is male, betrothes her to a woman named Ianthe. Although she loves Ianthe, Iphis recognizes that such a marriage is impossible (9.724–763). In the end, Isis changes Iphis into a man, thereby facilitating the marriage. The presence of Juno, Venus, and Hymenaeus at the wedding augurs well for a happy life together. Conversely, Orpheus marries Eurydice in spite of numerous bad omens, and she soon dies from the bite of a serpent. He turns to pederasty after her death, a choice that ultimately leads to his demise. Thus Iphis moves from homoerotic to heterosexual love and happiness, while Opheus moves from heterosexuality to homoeroticism and death. For Ovid's view of Orpheus' sexuality, see Makowski 1996: 29–32.

croceo velatus amictu: the word order paints a picture of Hymenaeus enveloped by his clothing. For Ovid's arrangement of words to reflect what he is describing, see Lateiner 1990. This Roman god of marriage is traditionally dressed in the attire of a bride, which included a saffron-colored *palla*; see Catullus 61.6–10. Although his name is not mentioned until line 2, the Romans would have recognized Hymenaeus by his characteristic dress and the masculine *velatus*.

1–2   ***per immensum ... aethera***: the separation of the adjective from the noun it modifies (hyperbaton) reflects the distance that Hymenaeus had to cover. He traveled all the way from the island of Crete to Thrace, which lies to the Northeast of Greece.

2   ***aethera***: Greek accusative.
Ciconumque: Thracians.
Hymenaeus: this god of marriage figures prominently in Catullus' wedding hymns (61 and 62). For his role in the wedding ceremony, see Hersch 2010: 236–261.

3   ***Orphea***: adjective derived from "Orpheus."
Orphea nequiquam voce vocatur: this does not mean that Orpheus' invitation went unanswered, but rather that the presence of Hymenaeus did not guarantee that the marriage would be a happy one, as subsequent omens indicate (4–7). Cf. Seneca, *Medea* 67–70, where Hymenaeus is called upon to attend the ill-fated wedding of Jason and Creusa. Juno and Venus also played an important role in the Roman wedding. Their absence here presages failure for the union of Orpheus and Eurydice. See Hersch 2010: 168–169, 262–266.
voce vocatur: a figura etymologica, in which two etymologically related words stand near each other.

4   ***adfuit ille***: Ovid employs this phrase to indicate that a deity is present at a wedding (6.429, 10.295). Cf. Catullus 62.5 (*Hymen ades o Hymenaee*).
sollemnia verba: perhaps Hymenaeus did not inspire the guests to raise the wedding cry (*Hymen Hymenaee!*).

5   ***nec laetos vultus***: a sullen expression at a wedding would have been a bad omen. For a happy and therefore propitious Hymenaeus, see Catullus 61.8 (*flammeum cape laetus*).
nec felix ... omen: signs of a prosperous union were sought during the wedding ceremony, particularly at the bride's home, where the auspices were taken; see Hersch 2010: 115–119. The omens listed at 6–7 are bad for Orpheus and Eurydice. Cf. the wedding of Procne and Tereus (6.429–432), where Juno Pronuba and Hymenaeus are absent and the ceremony is accompanied by evil omens. Many of the same omens appear at Apuleius, *Metamorphoses* 4.33.

6   ***fax ... lacrimoso stridula fumo | usque fuit***: "the torch was screeching continually with tear-producing smoke." For Hymenaeus and the wedding torch, see Hersch 2010: 164–175. This torch was carried during the procession to the groom's house; see Catullus 61.114–115. Anderson 1972: 476 suggests that the smoke from the sputtering torch brought tears to the eyes of the wedding guests – a bad omen that foreshadows Orpheus' mourning after the death of Eurydice (11–12). These smoke-induced tears would also account for the unhappy visages of the guests (*nec laetos vultus*, 5). Note that torches were also associated with funerals, which, again, foreshadows the death of Eurydice. Cf. Ovid, *Heroides* 2.20.

7   ***nullosque invenit motibus ignes***: one can rekindle failing torches by shaking them; cf. 4.758–759; *Amores* 1.2.11. For Hymenaeus shaking a wedding torch, see Catullus 61.14–15.

8–10 Anderson 1972: 476 identifies this as a stock theme: a young woman becomes the victim of violence while she wanders with female companions in a natural setting. Cf. the stories of Europa (2.844–845) and Persephone (5.391–397), who are kidnapped by gods while in a rural environment. In Vergil's version of the Orpheus story (*Georgics* 4.457–459), Eurydice was almost raped by Aristaeus, the son of Apollo and the nymph Cyrene, in the deep grass on the banks of a river. Ovid's audience, who knew Vergil's version, may have expected Aristaeus to make an appearance, but Ovid cuts him out of the story as he adapts the work of his predecessor.

9 Naiadum: Eurydice's relationship with the Naiads, nymphs associated with fresh water, suggests that she herself may have been one of them. Vergil (*Georgics* 4.460) makes her one of the dryads, nymphs associated with oaks. Neither naiads nor dryads are immortal.

nova ... nupta: perhaps the marriage had just taken place but had not yet been consummated.

10 occidit in talum serpentis dente recepto: cf. Vergil, *Georgics* 4.457–459, where Eurydice stepped on the serpent while fleeing from Aristaeus, who was trying to rape her. Ovid also employs this motif in the story of Aesacus and Hesperia (11.773–777).

11–12 quam satis ad superas postquam Rhodopeius auras | deflevit vates: although Ovid does not specify the duration of Orpheus' mourning, lines 48–49 imply that it was not lengthy: *umbras erat illa recentes | inter*. The Romans believed that excessive mourning was effeminate; see Hope 2009: 122–129; Williams 2010: 151. Vergil (*Georgics* 4.465–466) has Orpheus call upon Eurydice three times, which reflects the Roman practice of calling the name of the deceased over the corpse to ensure that the person is dead. Cf. Catullus 101.10; Propertius 2.13.27.

11 satis: "sufficiently." *OLD* s.v. *satis* 8. Cf. 145, where Orpheus tunes the lyre *satis*. For the Romans, the mourning period ended nine days after burial. See Servius, *ad Aeneadem* 5.64; Pomponius Porphyrion, *Commentarii in Q. Horatium Flaccum, Epod.* 17.48; Erker 2011. Perhaps Orpheus did not go beyond his ritual duty because he planned to regain Eurydice as soon as possible by beseeching the gods for her return (11–12).

quam: the relative pronoun refers to Eurydice, who has yet to be named.

Rhodopeius: *Rhŏdŏpēĭŭs*. Rhodope is mountain in southern Thrace. For the adjective, see Vergil, *Georgics* 4.461.

vates: Ovid describes Orpheus as a *vates* at 10.12. 82, 89, 143; 11.2, 19, 27, 38, 68. A *vates* is a prophet or poet who claims divine inspiration. At this point, Orpheus is a poet/singer. Later he will become the *vates* of the mystic rites of Bacchus (11.68, 92–93; Horace, *Ars poetica* 391–392: *interpretes deorum*). Tradition held that even his severed head prophesized. See Faraone 2004.

ad superas ... auras: *superas auras* refers to the sky (i.e. the Olympian gods) as opposed to *umbras* (12), which refers to the underworld. Vergil uses this phrase in connection with the return of Eurydice (*Georgics* 4.486) and Aeneas (*Aeneid* 6.128–129) from Hades.

12   ***deflevit vates ne non temptaret et umbras***: note the lugubrious spondees. *umbras* stands in contrast to *auras* (11), both of which occur at the end of their respective lines to form an end rhyme, which is unusual in classical Latin.

et: apparently Orpheus had tried to persuade (*OLD* s.v. *tempto* 6) the Olympian gods to return Eurydice from the dead, probably through mournful prayer. Since he was unsuccessful, he will now try his luck in the underworld (*umbras*).

deflevit: "to weep bitterly" (*OLD* s.v. *defleo* 3).

ne non: *ne* introduces the negative purpose clause, while *non* negates *temptaret* ("lest he not try the shades, too"). Cf. *ne non* in the speeches of forbidden love delivered by Byblis (9.589) and Iphis (9.735).

Orpheus in the Underworld

While Greek sources beginning in the fifth century BC mention Orpheus' descent to the underworld to retrieve Eurydice, the only extensive accounts of his journey are in Vergil and Ovid. Vergil's account appears in *Georgics* 4, where it is embedded in the myth of Aristaeus, which is itself embedded in a guide to beekeeping. After a lengthy account of the behavior of bees, Vergil discusses what to do when a hive fails: a new one must be produced from the carcass of a dead bull, through a process of spontaneous generation known as *bugonia*. Vergil attributes the institution of this practice to the mythic character Aristaeus. When his bees died, Aristaeus sought an explanation from his mother, the nymph Cyrene. She advised him to ask the shape-shifting sea god Proteus, who attributed their death to the anger of Orpheus. Aristaeus had chased Orpheus' bride along a river with the intent of raping her, when she accidentally stepped on a poisonous snake. After her death, Orpheus tried to console himself by singing about her day and night, and then traveled to the underworld to plead for her return. All its inhabitants listened in awe to his song, even Cerberus and the Eumenides. In the end, Persephone allowed him to return with Eurydice on one condition – that he not look back at her until they reached the earth. Overcome by madness, Orpheus looked back at the last minute, and Eurydice returned to the underworld. For seven days he mourned for his wife in song and rejected the love of the Thracian women, who tore him limb from limb. His head floated down the Hebrus River, still calling out "Eurydice."

Vergil's Orpheus is a counterpart to his Aristaeus, whose attempt to rape Eurydice has caused suffering for them both: Aristaeus lost his bees, while

Orpheus lost his wife. Both take the loss very hard: Aristaeus mourns for his bees to such an extent that he gives up on life, while Orpheus mourns for Eurydice until he is killed by the Thracian women. Aristaeus descends beneath the water to find out how to restore his hive, while Orpheus descends to the underworld to regain his wife. Finally, Aristaeus recognizes his responsibility for the loss of his bees and takes steps to atone for his guilt by following Proteus' advice and sacrificing to Orpheus and Eurydice. In contrast, Orpheus loses Eurydice a second time as a result of his inability to carry out the orders of the gods. Thus the proper role model is not Orpheus, the self-indulgent singer, but Aristaeus, the man who does what he must to succeed (Anderson 1982: 33–36).

One of the most notable differences between the accounts of Vergil and Ovid is that Ovid alone records the song that Orpheus sings in the underworld. Many scholars are critical of its artistic value. Anderson 1982: 36, for example, believes that Ovid turned Vergil's Orpheus into "a shallow, egoistic poet of overblown rhetoric and shallow self-indulgent sentimentality." There is no disputing that Orpheus' song has much in common with a *suasoria*, a "speech of persuasion" of a kind that was used as a rhetorical exercise to train budding Roman orators. Even though it is full of commonplaces and concentrates primarily on flattering its audience, Orpheus' piece succeeds nonetheless. It may be that "his audience of dead souls was not the most sophisticated" (Anderson 1989: 3), so that they were swayed more easily by Orpheus' rhetoric. Johnson 2008: 208, 108, however, rightly notes that this is the only successful performance of an artist in the *Metamorphoses*. Perhaps Orpheus's success is due to the fact that he knows his audience. And, like any good orator, he plays to it. First he must reassure Pluto that he has not come to the underworld to abduct one of his subjects. Second, he has to flatter the king of the underworld. Third, he has to make Pluto empathize with him, which means bringing up the potentially toxic subject of the abduction of Persephone. Clearly Orpheus knows how to speak before an audience of his superiors. Indeed, his technique mirrors the formal petitions found in the letters of Pliny the Younger to the emperor Trajan (e.g. 10.26). Even though a different type of speech may have been more artistically satisfying to a modern audience, Orpheus constructs a speech that is effective in this situation (Pagan 2004).

13–14   the dactyls in these lines that describe Orpheus' journey to the underworld are reminiscent of lines 1–2, where Hymenaeus travels to Thrace. Both characters hurry toward a goal that will ultimately fail.

13 **Styga**: Greek accusative. Styx, Lethe, Acheron, Phlegethon, and Cocytus were the rivers of the underworld. Styx formed its boundary. Charon, the ferryman of the dead, transported souls across the Styx into Hades.

Taenaria ... porta: this entrance to the underworld is a cave located in the extreme southern part of the Peloponnesus; cf. 2.247. There were other gates to the underworld at the Acherusian Chersonese (Xenophon, *Anabasis* 6.2.2), at Troezene (Pausanias 2.31.2; Apollodorus 2.15.2), in Boeotia (Pausanias 9.34.5), and in Argos (Pausanias 2.35.10). Although any of these locations would have been more convenient for the descent of Thracian Orpheus, the more distant Taenarian gate is the one mentioned in Vergil's account (*Georgics* 4.467) and in the *Orphic Argonautica* (41). It is no accident that this gate was also associated with the myth of Hercules, who succeeded in capturing Cerberus and in bringing him from the underworld to Mycenae (Apollodorus 2.5.12), an event to which Ovid alludes in lines 64–66. The hero Orpheus will bring back his wife through the same gate.

ausus: the journey to the underworld was fraught with peril and was rarely attempted. When Theseus and Perithous went to the underworld to kidnap Persephone, they found themselves stuck there, chained to chairs; see Apollodorus, 2.5.12 and epitome 1.23–24. Hermesianax (fr. 7.7–8 Powell) and Diodorus Siculus (4.25) both remark on Orpheus' daring in this respect.

14 **leves**: "insubstantial" or "incorporeal." *OLD* s.v. *levis* 7. Vergil (*Georgics* 4.472) calls them *tenues*.

simulacraque functa sepulcro: "ghosts who had experienced burial." Only those who were buried could cross the Styx. Cf. 4.435: *simulacraque functa sepulcris*.

simulacraque: "ghosts" or "images." Cf. 280, where this word is used of Pygmalion's statue.

15 **Persephonen**: Greek accusative. Her Latin name is "Proserpina." Cf. 5.554.

inamoena: this is the first known occurrence of *inamoena* in Latin literature. Statius (*Thebaid* 1.89) and Claudian (5.467) also use this adjective to describe the underworld.

15–16 **regna tenentem | dominum umbrarum**: Pluto. The ancients avoided saying his name. They preferred to use euphemisms instead.

18–39 Orpheus' song is a *suasoria* – a speech of persuasion (Otis 1966: 186; VerSteeg and Barclay 2003). It follows the tradition according to which Orpheus' song *persuaded* the gods of the underworld to release Eurydice (Hermesianax, fr. 7.13; Diodorus Siculus 4.25.4; Apollodorus 1.3.2). Johnson 2008: 106–107 describes it as "a self-consciously encomiastic appeal by an obsequious applicant for the mercy of the court." As a speech before a judge who will adjudicate property rights, it follows an orderly sequence and makes points that will appeal to Pluto:

1. All mortals must eventually come to the underworld.
2. I have not come here to steal from you, as others have.
3. I have come for my wife, who died before her time.
4. I was forced to come to the underworld by love, just as love brought you to the earth.
5. After Eurydice has lived out her allotted years, she will return to you.
6. She is yours by law, but I want to borrow her for a short time.
7. If you will not let her come with me, I will stay here with her.

The poetic merits of this song are debatable, but its rhetorical effectiveness vis-à-vis the gods of the underworld is beyond doubt. Orpheus is speaking like a Roman advocate in a legal proceeding, who succeeds because he knows his audience. For a rhetorical analysis of Orpheus' song, see von Albrecht 2014: 129–134.

17 *numina*: Pluto and Persephone.

mundi: a large tract of earth, sometimes used to refer to the underworld. *OLD* s.v. *mundus*³ b; cf. 5.507.

18 **in quem reccidimus quidquid mortale creamur**: this commonplace is traditionally employed to comfort the living when they are confronted by death; cf. Catullus 3.11–12; Horace, *Odes* 2.3.25–28.

reccidimus: variant of *recidimus*. Cf. 180.

quidquid mortale creamur: "in as much we are made mortal."

19–20 **falsi positis ambagibus oris | vera loqui sinitis**: by assuring Pluto of his sincerity, Orpheus tries to put his mind at ease with regard to his intentions and thereby make him more receptive to his request. Cf. 15.879: *si quid habent veri vatum praesagia*. Orpheus asks for the gods to grant him true words at *Orphic Argonautica* 4. Smith 1987: 152–153 traces the idea of the poet's veracity back to Hesiod, *Theogony* 22–28.

ambagibus: "obfuscations." *OLD* s.v. *ambages* 2.

20–22 In light of his previous experiences with visitors to the underworld, Pluto has good reason to be suspicious. Orpheus attempts to allay his suspicions at the very beginning of his song. He assures the gods of the underworld that he has not come as a tourist. Compare Aeneas, who came to obtain information about the future from his deceased father and, in the process, saw many of the inhabitants of Hades (Vergil, *Aeneid* 6.554–572). Nor has he come to disrupt Pluto's kingdom by stealing one of its inhabitants. Compare Hercules, who led away Cerberus (7.408–414); Dionysus, who retrieved Semele (Aristophanes, *Frogs* 330; Diodorus Siculus 4.25.4); and Theseus and Perithous, who tried to kidnap Persephone (Apollodorus 2.5.12). For Pluto's aversion to being deprived of his subjects, see Aeschylus, *Persae* 688–690; Diodorus Siculus 4.71.2; Statius, *Thebaid* 8.48–98.

21 ***Tartara***: neuter plural variant of *Tartarus*, a place of punishment for those who have committed particularly heinous crimes, such as the wrongdoers mentioned in lines 40–45.

22 ***Medusaei ... monstri***: this refers to Cerberus, the guardian of the underworld. Both Cerberus and Medusa had snaky hair (*villosa colubris*) and were able to turn humans into stone; cf. 4.449, 10.65–66; Vergil, *Aeneid* 6.417.

23 ***causa viae est coniunx***: after telling Pluto why he has not come to Hades, Orpheus now reveals his reason for making the journey.

in quam calcata venenum | vipera diffudit: at Vergil, *Georgics* 4.57–59, Eurydice stepped on the snake while running from Aristaeus, who was trying to rape her. Here Eurydice's death occurred while she was walking through the grass with the Naiads (8–10). Orpheus has no one but the Fates to blame for this devastating accident (38).

24 ***crescentesque abstulit annos***: "it stole her youth." Cf. *Ars amatoria* 1.61: *primis et adhuc crescentibus annis*. Orpheus speaks as though Eurydice has been robbed of her allotted fate, which was a longer life. This sets up his argument that her death was unjust and that her proper fate should be reinstated (31, 36).

25–26 ***posse pati volui nec me temptasse negabo; | vicit Amor***: in spite of what he says, Orpheus does not appear to have tried very hard to reconcile himself to Eurydice's death. His period of lamentation was not long (11) and he finds his wife among the recently deceased (48). He shifts the blame for his lack of self-control to Amor. Orpheus claims that he would have come to terms with Eurydice's death, but the god forced him to take this drastic action. Thus he absolves himself of responsibility for trespassing into Pluto's domain and introduces the theme of the power of Amor, to whom even Pluto was subject.

26 ***vicit Amor***: cf. Vergil, *Eclogues* 10.69: *omnia vincit Amor*.

26–29 These lines are replete with dactyls, which mark the transition from the mournful fate of Eurydice to the elegiac theme of love. They contain a reference to the kidnapping of Persephone, a potential minefield that Orpheus is wise to move past quickly with swift dactyls.

27 ***auguror***: here "surmise," but with close connections to augury and prophesy. *OLD s.v. auguro* 4. As a *vates*, Orpheus had the power of prophecy, which included the ability to see the past.

et hic: "even here," among the bloodless ghosts.

28–29 *famaque si veteris non est mentita rapinae,* | *vos quoque iunxit Amor*: Orpheus refers to the story of Pluto's kidnapping of Persephone, which Ovid recounted at 5.362–409. This could have been a serious *faux pas*. Persephone did not come willingly to the underworld and returned to her mother for an extended period every year. Orpheus takes this risk to create empathy by equating his love for Eurydice to Pluto's love for Persephone. Love drove both of them to extreme measures: Hades ascended to the earth to capture his wife and Orpheus descended to the underworld to retrieve his wife. Both left their proper spheres for love. Note that the story of the kidnapping of Persephone appears in Orphic poetry (fr. 379–402 Bernabé).

29–30 *per ego haec loca plena timoris,* | *per Chaos hoc ingens vastique silentia regni*: tricolon, which is common in oratory.

30 *Chaos*: the underworld.

31 *Eurydices*: Greek genitive. This is the first occurrence of Eurydice's name in Book 10. Moschus, *Idyll* 3 (second century BC) is the first to identify her by this name. Hermesianax (fr. 7 Powell, third century BC) calls her Agriope. For the history of her name, see Bremmer 1991: 13–17.

properata retexite fata: "reweave," but in the sense of "reverse" or "restore." *OLD* s.v. *retexo* 2. Cf. 15.249: *idemque retexitur ordo*. The Fates are three sisters who spin destinies, which resemble threads incorporated into the great tapestry of history. Orpheus argues that Eurydice's death came too quickly (24) and that the gods should allow her to live out her *iustos ... annos* (36). The Fates must now reweave Eurydice's fate in order to correct their mistake. Cf. Petronius 111.11: *quid proderit ... si antequam fata poscant indemnatum spiritum effuderis?*

32–37 Orpheus employs these commonplaces to reassure Pluto that he will not be robbed of a subject (cf. 20–22). Eurydice will return to Hades as soon as she has completed the number of years that the Fates have allotted to her. For parallels, see Bömer 1980: 23–24.

32 *serius aut citius sedem properamus ad unam*: another commonplace. Cf. Propertius 2.28.59: *longius aut propius mors sua quamque manet*. For further examples, see Courtney 2001: 169–170.

omnia: adverbial, "in all respects."

33 *sedem*: "abode."

35 *humani generis*: genitive of governed. *OLD* s.v. *regnum* 4b.

36 *cum iustos matura peregerit annos*: Orpheus once again suggests that Eurydice's death ran contrary to fate (cf. 24: *crescentesque abstulit annos*).

iustos: this is the first in a group of forensic terms. Orpheus' song now turns to questions of legal possession.

37   *iuris erit vestri*: "she will be subject to your authority," predicate genitive.

pro munere poscimus usum: "I am asking for a loan instead of a gift." Orpheus is making a contractual agreement with the gods of the underworld. He does not ask for a gift based on a just request (*munus*). What he wants is usufruct (*usus*), the temporary right to use another's property; see Dörrie 1974: 20–25. This distinction is intended to lessen Pluto's anxiety over losing one of his subjects.

38   *quod si Fata negant veniam pro coniuge*: Orpheus attributes any potential denial of his request not to Pluto and Persephone but to the Fates, thereby suggesting that they are the only ones who are hard-hearted enough to do such a thing.

38-39   *certum est | nolle redire mihi. leto gaudete duorum*: this rhetorical flourish concludes Orpheus' song. In Plato (*Symposium* 179d), Phaedrus says that Orpheus was too cowardly to kill himself in order to be with his wife. Consequently the gods gave him a phantom instead of his real wife and ordained that he be killed by women. Cf. Pausanias 9.30.6, where Orpheus commits suicide when Eurydice returns to Hades. There is no indication in Ovid that Orpheus seriously considers killing himself. Rather, if Eurydice is not returned, he will stay with her in the underworld, thereby giving its rulers two subjects for the price of one.

41-44   Several individuals who were tortured in Tartarus for their crimes get a respite from their punishments during Orpheus' performance. Apparently the Furies are neglecting their duties as taskmasters as they listen to Orpheus' song (45–46; Vergil, *Aeneid* 6.554–572; Hyginus, *Fabulae* 79). The same catalogue of wrongdoers also appears at 4.457–463 (but in a different order) and at Seneca, *Hercules Oetaeus* 942–948. Variants on this list occur in other authors. Homer has Tityos, Tantalus, and Sisyphus; Horace (*Odes* 3.11.21–24) has Ixion, Tityos, and the Danaids; Vergil has Tityos, Ixion, Tantalus, and Sisyphus at *Aeneid* 6.595–617, but only Ixion and Tantalus at *Georgics* 3.37–38, and Ixion alone at *Georgics* 4.484; Propertius (4.11.23–28) has Sisyphus, Ixion, Tantalus, and the Danaids.

41   *exsangues flebant animae*: even though the ghosts were drained of one bodily fluid (blood), they still had tears. The imperfect indicates that this was not a mere sniffle, but sustained weeping. Alternatively, the imperfect may be conative: "the bloodless spirits tried to weep."

Tantalus: Tantalus attempted to feed the flesh of his son, Pelops, to the gods. His punishment was to be tied to a tree in a pool of water. When he tried to eat its fruit, the branch moved away. When he tried to drink, the water receded. Pindar (*Olympian* 1.59–64) says that Tantalus became immortal by eating nectar and ambrosia at the table of the gods. He stole some of this food and gave it to his friends, who presumably became immortal as well.

42 **captavit**: frequentative. His task was neverending.

stupuit: personification. The song of Orpheus enchanted even inanimate objects, such as the trees in lines 90–106. This verb also occurs at 64 and 287.

Ixionis orbis: Ixion was a Lapith who tried to rape Juno. His punishment was to be tied to a flaming wheel that turned forever.

Ixionis: Ĭxĭŏnĭs.

43 **nec carpere iecur volucres**: this is a reference to Tityos, who tried to rape Leto. He was tied to the ground in Tartarus so that birds could tear out his liver.

44 **Belides**: the descendants of Belus, who were also called "Danaids." These 50 daughters of Danaus were to be wed to their cousins, the sons of Aegyptus. On their wedding night, 49 of them killed their husbands. Their punishment in the underworld was to fill a vessel that constantly leaked.

inque tuo sedisti, Sisyphe, saxo: note the alliteration, which is reminiscent of archaic Latin. Cf. Ennius, fr. 104 Skutch: *O Tite tute Tati tibi tanta tyranne tulisti*.

Sisyphe: Sisyphus committed a variety of offenses. He drew the ire of Jupiter by identifying him as the kidnapper of Aegina, the daughter of Asopus. When Death (or Hades himself) came to kill him, Sisyphus imprisoned the god. As a result, no one died during his captivity (scholiast on Homer, *Iliad* 6.153; Pherecydes, *FHG* i 91, fr. 98). When Sisyphus discovered that he was to be taken to the underworld by force, he instructed his wife not to bury his body so that his soul could not cross the river Styx. He then complained to Persephone that his wife was dishonoring him by refusing to bury his body. Once the goddess allowed him to return to the earth to rebuke her, he refused to return to the underworld (Theognis 1.701–712). His punishment was to roll a boulder up a hill. Just as it reached the top, it would roll back down again (Apollodorus 1.9.3).

It is possible that Ovid lists all these characters simply to fill a gap left by Vergil, who mentions Ixion alone in his account of Orpheus' descent to the underworld. But he may also have chosen them because they have some relevance to the story of Orpheus. Tantalus tried to overcome death, as did Orpheus. Ixion and Tityos tried to rape a goddess, just as Aristaeus tried to rape Eurydice in Vergil's account. The Belides' collective murders of their husbands recall the death of Orpheus' spouse. Sisyphus persuaded Persephone to allow his soul to return to earth from the underworld, just as Orpheus persuaded Pluto to release Eurydice. Thus the theme of overcoming death opens and closes the catalogue, while the middle contains the most important events in Eurydice's story.

45–57   Reed 1997: 174 observes that the Eumenides respond to Orpheus' *carmen*, while Pluto and Persephone are overpowered by his *oratio*. This suggests that his primary goal was to construct a rhetorical argument that the rulers of the underworld would find persuasive; the poetic aspect was secondary.

46   **Eumenidum**: the Furies punished mortals who committed crimes against family members. They became "eumenides," placated spirits, in Aeschylus' play of the same name. The appellations "Furies" and "Eumenides" are used interchangeably in the *Metamorphoses*.

nec regia coniunx | sustinet oranti nec qui regia ima negare: Johnson 2008: 107–108 argues that Orpheus' song succeeded because these "denizens of an Olympian backwater" did not have high standards. Be this as it may, the inhabitants of Hades were not accustomed to hearing this type of music. As Plutarch (*Moralia* 394b) says, the only song that Hades ever hears is lamentation, which is not sung to the accompaniment of the lyre, as is the song of Orpheus (16). According to Conon (*FGrHist* 26 F 1 45.20), Orpheus got Eurydice back with a magical song (ᾠδαῖς γοητεύσας). This recalls Orpheus' reputation as a γόης, a sorcerer who establishes a connection between the living and the dead, especially in the context of mystery religions (Graf and Johnston 2007, 170–171). His song not only persuaded but also charmed the residents of the underworld, which made it impossible for them to refuse his request.

48   **Eurydicen**: Greek accusative.

recentes: Eurydice died a short time before Orpheus' descent to the underworld (11–12).

umbras erat illa recentes | inter: Eurydice (*illa*) is both physically and verbally surrounded by a crowd of ghosts (*umbras ... illa recentes*). Reed 1997: 176–177 observes that Eurydice's physical status is problematic. If she is now a spirit, how can she possibly return to earth and function as a living being? Cf. Vergil, *Georgics* 4.501, where Eurydice vanishes like smoke when she returns to the underworld. Reed suggests that her soul would have been reunited with her body on earth. Perhaps this is why Orpheus descended to the underworld so quickly after her death: Eurydice's soul had to return to her body before the flesh became corrupt. The same idea is at work in the myth of Sisyphus, who ordered his wife to leave his corpse unburied (see the note to line 44). Aside from providing a pretext for his soul's return from the underworld, he may have also intended for it to reenter his body. Otherwise there would be no point in having his soul return to the earth. Similarly, the soul of Alcestis must have reentered her body after Heracles freed it from the underworld (Euripides, *Alcestis* 8460). For the belief that souls can return to corpses and reanimate them, see Clearchus of Soli, fr. 7–8 Wehrli; Heliodorus 6.12–15; Lucan 6.588–831; Maximus of Tyre 10.2; Philostratus, *Vita Apollonii* 4.45.

49 ***incessit passu de vulnere tardo***: cf. Vergil's description of Dido in the underworld at *Aeneid* 6.450: *inter quas Phoenissa recens a vulnere Dido.*

50 ***hanc simul et legem Rhodopeius accipit heros***: zeugma, a rhetorical device in which a literal and a figurative meaning are linked: Orpheus received Eurydice (literally) and a condition (figuratively). According to Vergil (*Georgics* 4.487), Persephone imposed the restriction.

   legem: Pluto's pronouncements are described in legal language. Note that the subjunctive *flectat* (51) in the indirect command represents an imperative in direct speech.

   Rhodopeius ... heros: cf. 290, where Pygmalion is called *Paphius ... heros*. According to the Orphic texts, heroes are those who are able to navigate Hades and arrive at the Elysian Fields (Bernabé and San Cristóbal 2008: 20), which Orpheus does at 11.61–63. Several manuscripts have *Orpheus* instead of *heros*.

51–52 ***Avernas | exierit valles***: this refers to the underworld in general, not to Lake Avernus in Italy (14.105), which happens to be another gate to the underworld. Cf. 6.662: *Stygia de valle*. See *OLD* s.v. *exeo* 13 for the accusative.

52 ***aut inrita dona futura***: Ovid uses *inrita* in its legal sense: "null and void." *OLD* s.v. *irritus* 1. This fits with his depiction of Pluto as a ruler (*qui regit ima*, 47) who makes laws (*legem*, 50). Cf. Vergil, *Georgics* 4.519–520: *inrita Ditis | dona querens*.

   futura: *futura esse* in indirect speech.

53 ***per muta silentia***: pleonasm. Cf. *vastique silentia regni*, 30.

   trames: a footpath instead of a road, perhaps because those who ascend from the underworld are few.

54 ***arduus, obscurus, caligine densus opaca***: tricolon. Cf. Vergil, *Aeneid* 6.126–129: *facilis descensus Averno: | noctes atque dies patet atri ianua Ditis; | sed revocare gradum superasque evadere ad auras, | hoc opus, hic labor est.*

55 ***telluris margine summae***: the border between the upper and lower worlds. Ovid creates suspense by placing the loss of Eurydice at the very moment when the two were about to return to the earth.

56–57 ***deficeret***: "fail."

   metuens avidusque videndi: Orpheus cannot control his feelings of trepidation and love. According to Vergil (*Georgics* 4.488–489), a sudden madness took control of the careless lover that he deems "forgivable" (*ignoscenda*).

57–59 ***flexit amans oculos***: because Orpheus has violated the conditions of Eurydice's release, she must return to the underworld immediately. This may explain why she says no more than *vale*. Cf. the story of Lot's wife at Genesis 19.17–26. The angel tells her not to look back at the destruction of Sodom as she walks behind Lot. When she disobeys, she turns into a pillar of salt. Phlegon of Tralles (*Mirabilia* 1) says that the ghost of a young woman visited a young man for two nights. On the third, her parents saw her and she was forced to return to "her appointed place." See also Proclus, *In Platonis Rem publicam* 2.116 Kroll.

58-59   **bracchiaque intendens prendique et prendere certans | nil nisi cedentes infelix adripit auras**: Orpheus is trying to grasp the insubstantial soul of Eurydice. Cf. Vergil, *Georgics* 4.498-502, where Eurydice stretches out her hands and vanishes like smoke as Orpheus tries to grasp her. At Vergil, *Aeneid* 700-702, Aeneas tries in vain to embrace the soul of his father.

60-62   **iterum moriens ... vale**: Ovid's Eurydice utters no complaint against her husband because she knows that he loves her (61). Cf. Vergil's Eurydice, who is none too happy about Orpheus' mistake, which she attributes to *furor*. She complains for five lines at *Georgics* 4.494-498, but Ovid gives her just one word. Note that the word *vale* is also employed by participants in Roman funerals (*Fasti* 3.563-564).

61   **quid enim nisi se quereretur amatam?**: *quid enim quereretur nisi se amatam* [*esse*]?

62   **quod**: refers to *vale*.

63   **revolutaque**: "to return" or, in legal language, "to revert." Cf. *OLD* s.v. *revolvo* 4d. Because Orpheus did not hold up his part of the contract, possession of Eurydice reverted to Pluto.

64-67   This is probably an allusion to the story of Hercules taking Cerberus from the underworld. Earlier on, at 21-22, Orpheus tells Pluto and Persephone that he has not come to the underworld to see Cerberus, but now he is paralyzed like the man who saw this monster. The sight of Eurydice falling back into the underworld is just as horrifying as the sight of the infernal hound. Heath 1996 argues that Ovid includes this myth in order to make Orpheus a failed Hercules.

64   **stupuit**: for the use of *stupere* to describe petrification in Ovid, cf. 3.418-419, 5.205-206, 5.509-510.

   gemina nece coniugis: cf. *iterum moriens* at 10.60.

68   **quam qui**: this is the reading of M. The other manuscripts have *quique*. Anderson 1972: 480 argues that *quam qui* is the better reading because it echoes the construction found in line 65 and avoids confusion with *quem* in line 66.

68-71   **Olenos**: Greek nominative singular. This story appears only in Ovid. Olenus' wife, Lethaea, was proud of her beauty. She must have offended a goddess and was on the verge of being punished, when her husband tried to rescue her by taking the blame for her error. They were both transformed into stones. Similarly, Orpheus wants to share Eurydice's fate by returning to the underworld, presumably to live with her there (cf. 38–39). Heath 1996 believes that this myth denigrates Orpheus by emphasizing his unwillingness to die in order to be with his wife.

70–71   ***iunctissima quondam pectora***: "once closest in love." Their emotional closeness is reflected in the physical closeness of the rocks that they became.

71   ***umida ... Ide***: given that Ovid describes Mount Ida as *umida*, he is probably referring to the mountain near Troy, as opposed to the Cretan Ida. Homer (*Iliad* 12.19–22) says that eight rivers water the Trojan Ida.

Ide: Greek nominative.

72–73   ***orantem frustraque iterum transire volentem | portitor arcuerat***: Orpheus tries to return to the underworld, but Charon will not allow it. Since Vergil (*Georgics* 4.505) says that Orpheus had no material for a second song, he is probably not returning to argue for a second chance to retrieve his wife. Rather he wants to remain with Eurydice in the underworld without having to die in order to do so, a possibility that he mentioned at 38–39. Plato (*Symposium* 179d) calls Orpheus a coward for trying to be with his wife without dying. See Heath 1994: 264–267.

72   ***orantem***: "begging" or "pleading his case"; cf. 10.47. *OLD* s.v. *oro* 2a–b. Once again, Orpheus is making a rhetorical argument.

73   ***portitor***: Charon, the ferryman of the dead, who transported souls across the river Styx. For his refusal to transport Orpheus a second time, see Vergil, *Georgics* 4.502–503.

73–75   After losing Eurydice again, Orpheus sits in squalor on the shores of the Styx and fasts for seven days. A squalid condition, fasting, and isolation from society are important elements in mourning rites. Orpheus appears to have already completed the rites of the *novemdialis*, which imposes nine days of lamentation after a death (11). Perhaps he believes that this second death requires some type of mourning (60, 64). Cf. Vergil (*Georgics* 4.507), who says that Orpheus mourned for seven months after his return from the underworld. Note that an Orphic tablet from Thurii (L 12.6) speaks of a seven-day fast.

74   ***squalidus in ripa Cereris sine munere sedit***: compare Clytië, who mourns for nine days without food (4.260–264); Ceres' behavior during her search for Persephone (5.446–447); and Apollo's mourning after the death of Phaëthon (2.381–382).

Cereris sine munere: the gift of Ceres, the goddess of agricultural fertility, is bread.

76   ***esse deos Erebi crudeles questus***: instead of taking responsibility for the loss of Eurydice, Orpheus shifts the blame onto Pluto and Persephone.

Erebi: the land of the dead; cf. Homer, *Odyssey* 10.528.

77 **Rhodopen ... Haemum**: These siblings, who dared to call themselves Jupiter and Juno, were turned into Thracian mountains; see 6.87–89; Pseudo-Plutarch, *De fluviis* 11.3. Cf. Oleanus and Lethaea (69–71), who were also transformed into stones on a mountain.

Rhodopen: Greek accusative.

Aquilonibus: the north wind, which is particularly forceful.

78 ***tertius ... Titan***: Hyperion the Titan was associated with the sun. This is a poetic way of marking the passage of time. Because the Romans counted inclusively, Orpheus sings his second song two years after Eurydice's death.

Titan: Greek nominative.

Piscibus: the constellation Pisces, which places the second song of Orpheus in March. Orpheus has ended his period of mourning and is now engaging in intercourse with boys. Note the mention of a metaphorical spring in Ovid's description of Orpheus' pederasty: *citraque iuventam | aetatis breve ver et primos carpere flores* (84–85).

79–81 Orpheus decided to shun women either because he was traumatized by the loss of Eurydice or because he took an oath to remain celibate. Presumably this oath required him to avoid intercourse with women, but not with boys. Similarly, Admetus promised not to remarry after Alcestis died in his place (Euripides, *Alcestis* 299–374). Cf. Vergil (*Georgics* 4.516), who says that neither intercourse nor marriage interested Orpheus.

80 ***femineam Venerem***: metonymy for "the love of women."

82 ***iungere***: "to marry" or "to have intercourse with." See Adams 1990: 179–180.

doluere: "resented."

83 ***auctor***: "the first"; cf. Phanocles (fr. 1.9–10 Powell) on Orpheus as the inventor of pederasty. He says that Orpheus was in love with just one boy, Calais. For Ovid's use of Phanocles as a source for the myth of Orpheus, see Gärtner 2008: 31–43. Apollodorus (1.3.3) says that the first pederast was Thamyris, the teacher of Orpheus; cf. Diodorus Siculus 3.67.

84 ***citraque iuventam***: "before they reached manhood."

The Catalogue of Trees

88–105 Orpheus' second song attracted to it a wide variety of trees, which Ovid records in a catalogue. Such catalogues are as old as Homer (*Iliad* 2.484–759) and were a favorite of Hellenistic poets and the Roman neoterics

(Curtius 1954: 201; Bömer 1980: 38–39). According to Pöschl 1960, the catalogue of trees can be divided into three groups: stately trees (with the exception of the hazel) associated with epic (90–94); water-loving trees associated with bucolic poetry (95–98); and plants associated with love and lyric poetry (99–105). These generic themes also appear in Orpheus' story: he makes a heroic journey to the underworld, he creates a pastoral landscape on Mt. Rhodope, and he sings about love.

While most of the trees in this catalogue are deciduous, the last four are evergreen. The deciduous trees "die" every year, but the evergreens are eternal. The last of the trees, the cypress, shares characteristics of both groups: it is an evergreen that is associated with funerals. The cypress holds special significance for Orphics because it stands in the underworld by the waters of Lethe, which the initiate must avoid (Graf and Johnson 2007: 108–109). Plutarch (*Alexander* 14) mentions a statue of Orpheus made of cypress wood.

89   dis genitus vates: Ovid makes Orpheus the son of Calliope (145) and Apollo (157); cf. Pindar, *Pythian* 4.177–178 and Apollodorus 1.3.2.

88–90   *umbra loco deerat* (88) is answered by *umbra loco venit* (90). Phanocles (fr. 1.3 Powell) says that Orpheus sat in a grove and sang about his lover, a boy named Calais.

90   non Chaonis afuit arbor: oak; cf. 7.623. Servius (*ad Aeneadem* 3.297, 334) says that the Trojan seer Helenus accidentally killed his brother Chaon during a hunt in Epirus and named the region "Chaonia" after him. This probably refers to the oracular oak of Zeus at Dodona, which may have been located in Chaonia.

Chaonis: Chāŏnĭs.

91   nemus Heliadum: poplars. The Heliades were the sisters of Phaethon. They mourned their brother after he crashed the chariot of the sun, then they turned into poplars; cf. 2.340–366.

non frondibus aesculus altis: durmast (or sessile) oak; cf. Vergil, *Georgics* 2.16.

92   tiliae molles: linden.

fagus: beech.

innuba laurus: laurel. Cf. 1.452–567, where the nymph Daphne preserved her virginity by turning into laurel and thereby thwarted Apollo's advances. Thus she merits the epithet *innuba*, which she shares with Atalanta at line 567.

93   coryli fragiles: hazels.

fraxinus utilis hastis: ash; cf. 5.142, 12.122; Pliny, *Natural History* 16.228.1–2.

94   ***enodisque abies***: silver fir. Its smooth bark accounts for the adjective *enodis*.

curvataque glandibus ilex: holm oak, which bears acorns. Cf. *Ars amatoria* 3.149: *sed neque ramosa numerabis ilice glandes*.

95   ***platanus genialis***: the plane tree, which is *genialis* because its spreading canopy creates shade.

acerque coloribus inpar: maple.

96   ***amnicolaeque simul salices***: willow, which grows near fresh water.

aquatica lotos: lotus. At 9.340–345, Dryope changes into the lotus after unwittingly plucking a flower from this tree.

97   ***perpetuoque virens buxum***: boxwood, which is an evergreen.

tenuesque myricae: tamarisk.

98   ***bicolor myrtus***: myrtle, which can bear black or white berries; cf. 11.234; Cato, *De agricultura* 8.2 and 133.2.

bacis caerula tinus: virbinum, a small tree that produces clusters of blue berries.

99   ***hederae***: ivy.

100   ***amictae vitibus ulmi***: elm. Anderson 1972: 483 notes that elms were used to support grape vines. Cf. Catullus 62.49–55.

101   ***ornique***: mountain ash.

piceae: spruce.

101–102   ***pomoque onerata rubenti | arbutus***: arbutus, which produces red berries.

102   ***lentae, victoris praemia, palmae***: palm. Livy (10.47.3) records its use as an award for victors in athletic contests at Rome. Note the insertion of the appositive between the adjective and noun.

103   ***succincta comas hirsutaque vertice pinus***: the Italian pine, sometimes called umbrella pine, has all of its foliage gathered at the top, much like the hairdo of a Roman woman. Makowski 1996: 34 suggests that, like Attis, "the pine tree is really a foppishly coiffed eunuch."

104   ***deum matri***: one of the names by which the Romans knew Cybele.

Cybeleius: *Cўbĕlēĭŭs*.

deum: genitive plural.

Attis: the mortal lover of the goddess Cybele, who tried to escape from her. In the process he castrated himself (Catullus 63; Lucretius 2.598–643; Vergil, *Aeneid* 6.784–787).

105   ***exuit hac hominem truncoque induruit illo***: the metamorphosis of Attis into a tree is not known outside Ovid. According to Arnobius (*Adversus*

nationes 5.7) and Servius Danielis (*ad Aeneadem* 9.115), Attis died under a pine tree. Anderson 1972: 484 suggests that *exuit hac hominem* may be an allusion to his castration.

Cyparissus

The final entry in the catalogue of trees is the cypress. Ovid recounts its origin at great length, thereby emphasizing its importance to the upcoming myth. He says that Apollo loved a boy named Cyparissus, who had formed a strong emotional attachment to a tame stag that was sacred to the local nymphs. While hunting on a hot day, he accidentally killed the animal as it was relaxing in the shade. His mourning knew no bounds; even Apollo could not assuage it. After Cyparissus asked the gods to allow him to mourn forever, he turned into a cypress, a tree associated with mourning.

Ovid uses this story to comment on the extreme grief of Orpheus who, like Cyparissus, did not mourn for the stag in an appropriate way. The boy's grief was unmeasured, and he turned into the tree of mourning. Similarly, Orpheus mourns for Eurydice for two years (78–79), rejecting the Thracian women, who could have been his mates, and singing of the superiority of pederasty. This ultimately leads to his death and to the transformation of his head into a stone, which sings as it floats down a river. Just as Cyparissus became mourning, Orpheus became song.

Several versions of this myth are extant. While in most sources Cyparissus is a Greek, some make him a Cretan (Servius Danielis, *ad Aeneadem* 3.680) or an Assyrian (Nonnus 11.363–365). He is the lover of Apollo, Zephyrus, or Silvanus (Servius Danielis, *ad Aeneadem* 3.680). The scholiast on Statius (*Thebaid* 4.460) says that Apollo gave him the stag as a love gift. Most sources say that Cyparissus killed the stag, but Servius (*ad Georgicon* 1.20) makes Silvanus responsible for its death. While it is generally agreed that the boy's transformation is linked to his mourning for the stag, Servius Danielis (*ad Aeneadem* 3.680) tells us that he fled to the Levant in an effort to remain chaste and changed into a cypress there.

106 **adfuit huic turbae ... cupressus**: the mention of the cypress at the end of the catalogue and the length of its myth of origin are indicative of its significance. For the cypress in Latin poetry, see Connors 1992: 1–17.

metas: the *metae* were the turning posts of the circus; they stood at either end of the *spina*, the central divider. They resemble the cypress on account of their conical shape; cf. 597, 664.

cupressus: note the alternative spelling *cyparissus*. *OLD* s.v. *cupressus*.

107 **nunc arbor, puer ante**: chiasmus.

deo dilectus ab illo: the story of Apollo's love for Cyparissus foreshadows the pederastic myths of Orpheus' upcoming song: *puerosque canamus | dilectos superis* (152–153).

108 **citharam nervis et nervis temperat arcum**: *nervi* refers to the strings of the cithara and to the bowstring. Both the cithara and the bow fall under the purview of Apollo.

citharam nervis et nervis ... arcum: chiasmus.

temperat: "to control." *OLD* s.v. *tempero* 8. This word is used in connection with the lyre at Propertius 2.34.79–80 and Horace, *Carmina* 4.3.18.

109 **namque**: "well then," signaling the beginning of the story. *OLD* s.v. *namque* 4.

Carthaea: a town on the island of Ceos, where Apollo had an important sanctuary. See Antoninus Liberalis 1.1; Strabo 10.5.6; Athenaeus 10.456f.

110–111 **patentibus altas | ipse suo capiti praebebat cornibus umbras**: the hyperbaton, which extends from *patentibus* to *cornibus* and from *altas* to *umbras*, reflects the stag's widely spreading horns. Like the branches of a tree, they provide shade for his head (*capiti*), which stands in the middle of this phrase. Cf. the description of Silvia's stag at Vergil, *Aeneid* 1.190: *cornibus arboreis*.

110 **cervus**: according to the scholiast on Statius' *Thebaid* 4.460, Cyparissus received the stag as a gift from Apollo. For tame deer in Rome, see Martial 13.96; Justinian, *Institutiones* 2.1.15; Starr 1992.

ingens: Vergil uses this adjective to describe stags at *Aeneid* 1.192–193 and 7.483.

112 **cornua fulgebant auro**: the gilded horns mark the stag as sacred. Compare the Ceryneian Hind (Apollodorus 2.81) and the deer that pulled the chariot of Artemis (Callimachus, *Hymns* 3.102). Note that the Romans gilded the horns of victims before sacrifice. This foreshadows the death of the stag; cf. 7.161–162, 10.271.

112–113 **demissaque in armos | pendebant tereti gemmata monilia collo**: although Latinus' horses also wore *monilia* (Vergil, *Aeneid* 7.278), the excessive adornment of the stag feminizes it. Cf. the jewelry that Pygmalion places on his statue at 264–265; Attis' jewelry at 5.53 (*ornabant aurata monilia collum*); Hercules with Omphale at *Fasti* 2.317 (*in Herculeo suspensa monilia collo*).

114 **bulla**: some *bullae* were amulets that boys from aristocratic families wore as necklaces until they adopted the *toga virilis*: Propertius 4.1.131–132; Persius 5.30–31. According to Plutarch (*Moralia* 288a), it marked a boy as

freeborn and therefore off limits for pederastic relationships. It also contained a substance that protected him from *invidia* (Macrobius 1.6.8). Cucchiarelli 2002: 620–622 interprets the presence of *bullae* on Pallas' baldric as an allusion to his youth (Vergil, *Aeneid* 12.942). Other *bullae* were jewelry for women or animals (Palmer 1989: 1–69). The *bulla* worn by Cyparissus' stag hangs from its horns onto its forehead, much like the *bulla* found strapped to a horse's head in an Etruscan burial (Warden 1983: 70).

115   ***parilique aetate***: cf. 8.618. This phrase describes the pearls, which were of equal age, and therefore of equal size. Bömer 1980: 55–56, however, believes that it refers to the *bulla*, which would have been the same age as the stag if it were given to him at birth, when *bullae* were usually given to baby boys.

118   ***celebrare domos***: the stag crosses a boundary by leaving its natural environment and entering houses. This behavior, along with its adornment, humanizes the animal.

120   **Ceae**: *Cēae*.

121–125   The stag has become so tame that it seems to have lost the ability to forage for itself. Cyparissus leads it to food and water, decorates it with flowers, puts a harness on it, and rides it. The animal is no longer wild; it has become his pet. Cf. Vergil, *Aeneid* 7.487–492, where Silvia places garlands on the stag's antlers, grooms it, bathes it, and feeds it. For similarities to Silvia's stag, see Connors 1992: 7–12, who postulates a Hellenistic source used by both authors.

121–123   ***tu ... tu ... tu***: tricolon.

125   ***purpureis ... capistris***: for purple reins placed on pet goats, see *Anthologia palatina* 6.312.1.

126   ***aestus erat mediusque dies solisque vapore | concava litorei fervebant bracchia Cancri***: cf. *Amores* 1.5: *aestus erat mediamque dies exegerat horam*. The mention of heat at midday often precedes a description of the *locus amoenus*, a deceptively pleasant location that will soon be the site of violence, often of a sexual nature. See Segal 1969; and cf. 3.144–145; 10.174–175; 11.353–354.

Cancri: Ovid's mention of the constellation Cancer dates this event to late June or July.

128–129   ***fessus in herbosa posuit sua corpora terra | cervus***: the reader expects Cyparissus to be the subject. Enjambment creates a surprise – it is the stag. *sua corpora* is surrounded by *herbosa terra*. This reflects the body of the stag when it sinks into the grass.

129   ***arborea ... umbra***: the stag now enjoys the shade of trees instead of that provided by his own horns (110–111). Thus he has become more like a human who finds repose in a *locus amoenus*.

130 ***imprudens***: although Ovid absolves Cyparissus from any guilt for killing the stag, there is a suggestion of carelessness. *OLD* s.v. *imprudens* 4. Cf. 182: [*Hyacinthus*] *imprudens actusque cupidine lusus*.

133 ***ut leviter pro materiaque doleret***: "moderately and in proportion to its significance." Cf. 3.334: *nec pro materia fertur doluisse*. The Greeks and the Romans thought that excessive mourning displayed by males was dishonorable and womanly. See Hope 2009: 122–129. According to Plutarch (*Solon* 7.3), immoderate mourning for a pet was shameful. See the story of Lucius Crassus (Aelian, *De natura animalium* 8.4), who adorned an eel "with earrings and jeweled necklaces as though it were a beautiful girl ... Crassus mourned for it when it died, as I hear it, and he buried it. And once when Domitius said to him, 'Fool, you've mourned for a dead eel,' he said, 'But you have buried three wives and have not mourned.'"

pro materiaque: Connors 1992: 10–11 detects an allusion to genre. Cyparissus should mourn in a manner befitting *epyllion*, not epic.

136–137 ***per inmensos egesto sanguine fletus | in viridem verti coeperunt membra colorem***: the green color of Cyparissus' limbs anticipates his metamorphosis into a tree. Apparently, excessive crying has diluted his blood. According to Hippocrates (*Epidemics* 2.2.12), loss of blood can cause the skin to take on a green pallor.

138 ***nivea***: for this adjective in erotic poetry, see *Amores* 1.16.29; Tibullus 1.4.12; Propertius 2.13.53. Cf. the *niveum ebur* of Pygmalion's statue (247–248).

140 ***sidereum gracili spectare cacumine caelum***: the Mediterranean cypress is a tall and slender tree.

141 ***gemuit***: Apollo groans for Cyparissus' fate just as Cyparissus groaned (*gemit*, 131) for the stag's fate. See Miller 1999: 416–417.

141–142 ***lugebere nobis | lugebisque alio aderisque dolentibus***: Apollo also mourns for Hyacinthus (203–204) just as Venus mourns for Adonis at the end of Orpheus' song (725–726).

142 ***aderisque dolentibus***: the cypress was a tree of mourning that was often found in cemeteries. On its role in Roman funerary ritual, see Servius, *ad Aeneadem* 3.64; Piacente 1978; Bömer 1958: 50–51; Connors 1992; Reed 1997: 190. It also played an important role in Orphic doctrine. The cypress stood next to the waters of Lethe. If the initiates recognized this tree and did not drink the water of forgetfulness, they could remember the words that would allow them to enter the Elysian Fields. See Graf and Johnson 2007: 108–114.

143–144 Up to this point, Ovid has spoken of the trees that were drawn to Orpheus' song. Now he adds animals and birds to the list; cf. 11.20–21. Orpheus' ability to attract both animate and inanimate objects with his song is part of the tradition surrounding the bard; cf. Simonides, fr. 62/567 Page (birds and fish), Aeschylus, *Agamemnon* 1630 (everything), Apollonius Rhodius 1.26–31 (rocks, rivers, trees), Conon, *FGrHist* 26 F45.3 (animals, birds, trees, and rocks), Horace, *Carmina* 3.11.13 (beasts, forests, and rivers), Ovid, *Amores* 3.9.21 (beasts), *Ars amatoria* 3.321 (rocks and beasts), and *Tristia* 4.1.17 (forests and rocks), and Tzetzes, *Chiliades* 1.12 (men). For a Roman performance that reinacted Orpheus' summoning of beasts, see Varro, *De re rustica* 3.13.3.

143   ***attraxerat***: this verb implies compulsion. *OLD* s.v. *attraho* 1 and 2; cf. 3.563, 7.313. Since *carmen* can mean "spell," the song may have acted as an incantation that forced trees, animals, and birds to come. Cf. 46 for Orpheus as a sorcerer.

143–144   ***ferarum | concilio medius turba volucrumque***: Orpheus sits in the midst of these beasts both verbally and physically as he begins his song. This recalls how Roman authors gave public readings of their works.

144   ***concilio ... turba***: Reed 1997: 195 notes that both words can refer to the plebs. Orpheus is like a charismatic political leader who is speaking to an assembly of the common people.

145   ***satis***: "as much as required" to tune them. Cf. 11, where Orpheus mourned Eurydice *satis*.

   pollice: the bard tunes the strings with his thumb, which produces a purer tone than the *plectrum*. Cf. 5.339: *Calliope querulas praetemptat pollice chordas*. For the tuning of lyres, see Maas and Snyder 1989: 64, 93–94.

   chordas: Vergil (*Aeneid* 6.645) says that Orpheus' lyre had seven strings.

147   ***concordare modos***: "that the notes were in tune." *OLD* s.v. *modus* 8. This phrase may be a translation of Plato, *Symposium* 187a5.

148–154   This is the proem to Orpheus' second song, which consists of his theme and an invocation; cf. 1.1–4, 15.622; Vergil, *Aeneid* 7.641, 10.163.

148   ***ab Iove***: although Orpheus will sing of sexual desire, he begins with an invocation that is appropriate to a weightier theme; cf. Aratus, *Phaenomena* 1; Theocritus 17.1; Vergil, *Eclogues* 3.60; Ovid, *Fasti* 5.111. The mention of Jupiter three times in two successive lines gives the proem a hymnic tone. Orpheus' motive, however, may have been similar to Strato's (*Anthologia palatina* 12.1), who begins with Zeus because he wants to speak of pederasty, which is alien to the Muses. For the use of this phrase in Orphic sources, see Fantuzzi 1985: 163–172.

   Musa parens: Orpheus was the son of Calliope, the Muse of epic poetry. He asks her for inspiration, an appropriate request for the epic topic that he mentions in 148–151. But in 153–154 he chooses an elegiac theme, which is usually under the purview of his father, Apollo (167).

149-150 *Iovis est mihi saepe potestas | dicta prius*: Orpheus was famous for his cosmogonies and theogonies, in which Jupiter would have played an important role. Cf. Apollonius Rhodius 1.496–511; West 1983; Gee 2013: 13; Reed 1997: 197.

150 *plectro grauiore*: i.e. "in epic mode." Cf. Horace, *Carmina* 4.2.33; Statius, *Silvae* 1.5.1. At Vergil, *Aeneid* 6.647, Orpheus sometimes uses his thumb to pluck the strings, sometimes a plectrum. According to Roberts 1980: 43–77, the plectrum was used for musical interludes, but never to accompany vocals. Asconius, *In Verrem* 2.1.53 specifies when to use the fingers (*intus canere*) and when to use the plectrum (*foris canere*).

Gigantas: the Giants and the Olympians engaged in a battle for divine supremacy, which Ovid records at 1.151–162 and at *Fasti* 5.35–42. Janan 1988: 114 discusses Orpheus' role as a foil to Ovid, who once failed to write a Gigantomachy because his lover distracted him (*Amores* 2.1.11–22). For the rejection of the Gigantomachy as a theme in Augustan poetry, see Knox 1986: 50–51. There appears to be a reference to an Orphic Gigantomachy at *Orphic Argonautica* 17–20.

151 *Phlegraeis ... campis*: the Phlegraean Fields are on the slopes of Mount Vesuvius. These volcanic vents were thought to have been created by Jupiter's thunderbolts during the Gigantomachy. For their association with epic, see Propertius 2.1.39–40; 3.9.46–47.

152-153 Orpheus begins with Jupiter and his love for Ganymede in order to provide divine justification for his adoption of pederasty. Cf. Theognis (1345–1350), who also traces the origin of pederasty to Zeus.

152 *leviore lyra*: cf. Horace, *Carmina* 2.1.40: *leviore plectro*. The cithara was a heavy lyre used by professional rhapsodes in concert performances. The chelys lyra was a lighter lyre used at weddings, symposia, and on other festive occasions. Of the two, it was the only one that could be played while seated (*sedebat*, 144); see Maas and Snyder 1989: 49–112. Amatory poetry was also described as "lighter"; see Horace, *Carmina* 2.1.40; Propertius 2.12.22; Ovid, *Amores* 1.1.19. Note the lighter rhythm of the dactyls in 152 and 154.

152-154 Note the change of construction, from *canamus* with a direct object (*puerosque dilectos superis*) to indirect speech (*inconcessisque puellas ignibus attonitas meruisse libidine poenam*). The first is a topic, the second is a statement of fact: "Let us sing of boys loved by the gods and that girls, out of their minds with illicit love, deserved the penalty for their lust." For *canere* with the infinitive, cf. Vergil, *Aeneid* 8.655–656: *anser | porticibus Gallos in limine adesse canebat*; see Reed 1997: 200. Since Myrrha is the only woman who truly fits this description in the song of Orpheus, the plural must refer to all women who fall into this category. Perhaps it is a veiled allusion to the Thracian women, who are infatuated with Orpheus and may threaten his resolve not to engage in heterosexual intercourse. Just as the myth of Ganymede justifies his introduction of pederasty, the myths of female lust justify his rejection of women. For Ovid's debt to Phanocles (fr. 1.9–10 Powell), see Barchiesi 2001: 56–57.

153 **superis**: common gender. Thus it may also refer the myth of Venus and Adonis, which is not pederastic.

inconcessisque: cf. 9.454: *Byblis in exemplo est ut ament concessa puellae.*

Ganymede

Orpheus tells the story of Ganymede in just seven lines. Jupiter lusts after this handsome Trojan boy, transforms himself into an eagle, and carries him off to Olympus, where Ganymede serves as Jupiter's cupbearer in spite of Juno's objections. There are variants in which mortal men kidnapped Ganymede, but with dire consequences for the boy. Mnaseas (*FHG* 3.154 F 30), Phanocles (fr. 4 Powell), and Eustathius (*ad Iliadem* 20.219) report that he was kidnapped by Tantalus, died during a hunt, and was buried on Mysian Olympus. Eustathius (*ad Iliadem* 20.219) and the Suda (s.v. Μίνως) say that he committed suicide after Minos carried him off from Troy while he was hunting. Obviously these versions of the story would not have been suitable to begin a song that glorified pederasty.

Details from various sources reveal that Ganymede, the first story in Orpheus' song, has much in common with Adonis, his last story. Ganymede was an avid hunter (Vergil, *Aeneid* 5.252–257). After he was killed by wild animals during a hunt (*scholia vetera* to *Iliad* 20.243), Aphrodite gave him immortality (Pindar, *Olympian* 10.104–106). The same happens in the myth of Adonis. And, just as Jupiter kidnapped Ganymede, Dionysus kidnapped Adonis (Plato Comicus in Athenaeus 10.456a–b; cf. Phanocles, fr. 3 Powell). The pairing of Ganymede and Adonis also occurs in art. Plautus' *Menaechmi* (143–144) contains a reference to "a picture painted on a wall in which an eagle carries off Ganymede and Venus carries off Adonis." Theocritus (*Idyll* 15.24) says that the marriage bed of Aphrodite and Adonis displayed at the Alexandrian Adonia festival was decorated with a carving of an eagle carrying off Ganymede. Reliefs from the sanctuary of Venus–Astarte at Baalbek depict a male being carried off by an eagle and a male hunting a boar (Ragette 1980: 85, 112). Given the similarities between these two characters, it can be no coincidence that Ovid chose to begin and end the song of Orpheus with their stories.

Orpheus wants the story of Ganymede to represent the joys of pederasty, but he undercuts this message with the words *invitaque Iunone* (161). Several authors describe Juno's anger at the presence of Jupiter's catamite at the banquets of the gods. According to Nonnus (25.445-450; 31.251-254), she claims that Ganymede has insulted Hebe by usurping her role as cupbearer. Statius (*Silvae* 3.4.13) says that she glares at the boy and refuses to take the cup from his hands. Vergil (*Aeneid* 1.26-28) attributes Juno's hatred for the Trojans to the judgment of Paris and to the honor that Jupiter paid to Ganymede. Their relationship brought suffering to the Trojans, who were the ancestors of Ovid's Roman audience.

155 **rex superum**: cf. 153. Plato (*Laws* 1, 636c-d) says that the Cretans created the story of Ganymede in order to trace their predilection for pederasty back to Zeus. Indeed, some of its plot elements reflect a historical Cretan practice recorded by Strabo (10.483-484) that may have originated with the Minoans (Willets 116-117; Koehl 1986: 105-107). Here a man kidnaps a handsome boy, gives him presents, and hunts and feasts with him for two months. After being presented with military equipment, an ox, a drinking cup, and other expensive items, the boy sacrifices the ox to Zeus and makes public the details of his experience during a feast. The boy continues to receive honors such as a privileged place at dances and races, and special clothing designed to mark his elevated status.

Phrygii: Phyrgia was a region in northwestern Turkey. For the use of Phrygia for Troy, see 11.203; 12.38, 70, 140, 612.

157 **quod ... mallet**: relative clause of characteristic.

nulla ... alite: the ablative specifies the object into which Jupiter transformed himself; cf. Horace, *Carmina* 1.35.4; *Ars poetica* 226.

alite: the eagle carried the thunderbolts of Jupiter (Vergil, *Aeneid* 5.254; Horace, *Carmina* 4.5.1). Like this bird of prey, Jupiter snatches whatever he desires. The earliest version of this myth places the responsibility for Ganymede's abduction on all the gods (Homer, *Iliad* 20.230-237). In other versions, Jupiter dispatched his eagle to fetch the boy (Vergil, *Aeneid* 5.255) or sent a whirlwind to bring him to Olympus (*Homeric Hymn to Aphrodite* 202-217). Many variants are depicted in art; see Sichtermann 1956; *LIMC* IV.1 154-170 and IV.2 75-97; Gantz 1996: 559-560.

verti: passive in a middle sense "to change into." *OLD* s.v. *verto* 23b.

158 **posset**: this verb is in the imperfect because Ovid considers the action to have occurred in the past despite the present tense of *dignatur*.

159 **percusso mendacibus aera pennis**: the word order reflects the air split by the beating of the eagle's wings.

mendacibus: the wings do not belong to a real eagle, but to Jupiter.

160 ***Iliaden***: Greek accusative. This is not a patronymic, but indicates the place of origin. Cf. 10.162: *Amyclide*.

nunc quoque: "even now." *OLD* s.v. *quoque* 4c. Ganymede still pours wine for the gods even in Orpheus' time.

pocula miscet: just as the Greeks and the Romans diluted their wine with water, Ganymede mixes the nectar with water before dispensing it to the gods at their banquets; cf. *Priapeia* 3.5-6. For the connection between this myth and homoeroticism in the symposium, see Barringer 2001: 119-123.

161 ***invitaque ... Iunone***: concessive. The happy tone of this myth ends with this ominous phrase. Ovid's audience would have recalled that one of Juno's reasons for opposing Aeneas was *rapti Ganymedis honores*, which caused much suffering for the Romans (Vergil, *Aeneid* 1.25-28; Ovid, *Fasti* 6.43; Statius, *Silvae* 3.4.13; Nonnus, *Dionysiaca* 25.429-448, 31.251-256). A similar situation is occurring in Thrace, where Orpheus' pederasty enrages the local women (79-85).

Hyacinthus

Apollo leaves Delphi to hunt with his young lover, essentially acting as Hyacinthus' assistant in this activity (171-173). After the boy is killed while retrieving an errant discus, Apollo changes his blood into a flower.

It is notable that Ovid's version of this myth is the only one to include a hunt. This addition to the story allows the god to carry on a pederastic relationship according to Greek norms: Apollo subordinates himself to his lover, just as a Greek *erastēs* subordinates himself to his *erōmenos*. Moreover, their exercise with the discus reflects the homoerotic relationship that sometimes developed between a trainer and a young athlete; see Hubbard 2013: 137-171. The link to Greek pederastic practices explains the order of the first two stories in the song of Orpheus. The myth of Ganymede provides the divine charter for pederasty, while the myth of Hyacinthus sets out its mechanics, thereby offering a model for Orpheus, the men of Thrace, and the Greeks in general to follow.

In order to use the myth of Hyacinthus so as to elevate pederasty over heterosexuality, Ovid must ignore the boy's sexual history, which is well documented in other sources. According to Apollodorus (1.3.3), his first lover was the bard Thamyris, a son of Calliope who introduced pederasty to Thrace. Next came Zephyrus, the west wind; vase paintings show the two engaged in intercourse (*LIMC* 5.2 379). Apollo and Zephyrus vied for the boy's affections (Pausanias 3.19.4-5; Lucian, *Dialogi deorum* 16.2; Philostratus the Elder, *Imagines* 1.24;

[Palaephatus] 46; Nonnus 10.253-255). When Hyacinthus chose Apollo, Zephyrus became so jealous that he blew the discus into the boy's face, thus causing his death. In order to make pederasty appear to be superior to heterosexuality, Ovid had to suppress Zephyrus' role in this myth. Without him, there is no lethal jealousy in this relationship, and the death of Hyacinthus becomes an unfortunate accident. In this way Ovid is able to contrast Apollo's homoerotic love for Hyacinthus with the heterosexual jealousy of Juno (161) and of the Thracian women (81-82). Moreover, both Ganymede and Hyacinthus gain immortality from their pederastic relationships, albeit in different ways. Ganymede receives eternal youth from his divine lover, while Apollo honors the dying Hyacinthus with a different kind of immortality: he turns him into a hyacinth and prophesies his role in the annual Hyacinthia festival at Amyclae.

The myth of Hyacinthus looks forward to the story of Adonis. Both are lovers of humanized gods, participate in the hunt, meet an accidental death, and are turned into flowers by their lovers. It also looks backward to the myth of Orpheus and Eurydice. After the accidental deaths of their lovers (10, 183-185), Orpheus and Apollo unsuccessfully attempt to revive the victims (57, 186-189). They are exculpated of any wrongdoing (60-61, 200-201) and state their desire to remain with their lovers in death (39, 202-203).

162   *Amyclide*: Greek vocative. This could be a patronymic (Apollodorus 3.10.3; Pausanias 3.1.3) or could indicate the place of origin; cf. Ganymede, who is referred to as *Iliaden* in line 160. Amyclae, which lies three miles (five kilometers) southeast of Sparta, was famous as the center of a cult of Apollo Amyclaeus. See Euripides, *Helen* 1468-1475; Herodotus 9.7.11; Xenophon, *Hellenica* 4.5.11.

164   *qua licet aeternus tamen es*: Apollo was not able to give Hyacinthus the same type of immortality that Jupiter gave Ganymede. Nevertheless, Hyacinthus is reborn every year as a flower.

165   *ver hiemem Piscique Aries succedit aquoso*: the name of the constellation Pisces is in the singular here, perhaps to parallel the singular Aries. Pisces (February 18-March 20) is the last sign of the zodiac; Aries (March 21-April 19) is the first. The timing of the myth is apt: the hyacinth will grow at the end of winter as a harbinger of spring. Note the chiastic word order: spring (*ver*)/winter (*hiemem*), then winter (*Piscique*)/spring (*Aries*).

166   *oreris*: this verb follows the pattern of the third conjugation in the present tense.

flores: from *florēre*.

167   *meus ... genitor*: Apollo. Not content with attributing pederasty to Jupiter, Orpheus makes it a family tradition.

ante omnes: cf. Vergil, *Aeneid* 12.391: *Phoebo ante alios delectus Iapyx*.

167-168 ***orbe | in medio positi caruerunt praeside Delphi***: for Delphi as the midpoint of the world, see Pindar, *Pythian* 4.74; Euripides, *Ion* 461-462; Strabo 9.3.6. Delphi was one of Apollo's most important sanctuaries; see 15.630-631; *Homeric Hymn to Apollo* 475-519.

169 ***Eurotan***: Greek accusative. Sparta lies on the west bank of the Eurotas River.

169-170 ***immunitamque ... Sparten***: Sparta had no walls until 317 BC. See Plato, *Laws* 778d; Livy 39.37.1-5; Plutarch, *Moralia* 217e and 228e, *Lycurgus* 19.52b.

Sparten: Greek accusative.

170-171 Ovid lists three of Apollo's provinces (prophecy, music, and the bow), all of which he has forgotten because he is consumed by love for Hyacinthus. According to Philostratus the Younger (*Imagines* 14), Apollo offered to teach Hyacinthus how to use the bow, play music, prophesy, and engage in athletic contests, if the boy agreed to become his lover. Cf. *POxy* 3723 9, where Apollo places an object at Hyacinthus' feet, which may be a love gift. This recalls the Athenian *erastēs/erōmenos* relationship, which involves both education and pederasty.

171-173 For role reversal in pederastic relationships, see Theognis 1345-1350; Plato, *Phaedrus* 240c-d, *Symposium* 184c. This type of behavior is acceptable in the hunt so long as the *erastēs* is not controlled by Eros; see Barringer 2001: 70-171. But clearly this has happened to Apollo, who has forgotten himself and his duties. He was also derelict while in the service of Admetus (Tibullus 2.3.11-38). Compare the fact that Venus deserts her cities when she falls in love with Adonis (529).

173 ***adsuetudine***: Apollo is following the advice that Ovid gives at *Ars amatoria* 2.345-346: *fac tibi consuescat: nil adsuetudine maius: | quam tu dum capias, taedia nulla fuge*. Apparently he is still trying to seduce Hyacinthus. By contrast, Jupiter simply transforms himself into an eagle and takes Ganymede to Olympus. While Jupiter behaves like a god, Apollo plays the part of a human *erastēs*.

174-175 ***iamque ... utrimque***: it was noon. See lines 446-447 for this method of indicating time.

174 ***medius***: cf. Cyparissus, who hunts at midday (*mediusque dies*, 126).

Titan: Greek nominative singular masculine. Helios, the sun, was one of the Titans. The sun's heat presages danger, often of a sexual nature. See Parry 1967: 277; Segal 1969.

176   ***corpora veste levant***: disrobing often occurs in the *locus amoenus* and is generally followed by intercourse, a metamorphosis, or both; cf. 2.417, 3.407, 5.586–641, 7.808–823; and see Segal 1969: 4–19. Ovid subverts his audience's expectations by substituting athletic exercises. For the connection between Greek athletics and pederasty, see Scanlon 2002: 64–97, 211–219, 236–249; Hubbard 2013: 137–171; Lear 2013: 246–257.

176–177   ***et suco pinguis olivi | splendescunt***: while public oiling (and public nudity) were commonplace in Greek culture, the Romans disapproved of it because they thought that this practice – along with pederasty – had weakened Greek men. See Cicero, *Tusculan Disputations* 4.70 (quoting Ennius); Plutarch, *Roman Questions* 40.274d.

177   ***splendescunt***: inchoative, "they begin to shine."

   latique ineunt certamina disci: Romans believed that such athletic competitions led the Greeks to stray from military exercises and made them effeminate; cf. Seneca, *Epistulae* 88.18–19; Tacitus, *Annales* 14.20; Plutarch, *Roman Questions* 40.274d; Edwards 1993: 1–33, 98–172; Kyle 2007: 274; Newby 2005: 38–44. See also the exercises of Romulus and Remus at Ovid, *Fasti* 2.365–368.

178   ***libratum ... misit***: this reflects a preference for avoiding coordinate clauses in Latin (*libravit et misit*). On Apollo's form as he throws the discus, cf. Philostratus the Younger, *Imagines* 1.24 and Myron's *Dyscobolos*.

   prius: Apollo makes the first throw, but Hyacinthus does not get his turn.

   aerias ... auras: this may be a subtle allusion to Zephyrus, who was the lover of Hyacinthus in other versions of the myth and was responsible for blowing the discus into his face. See Reed 1997: 208.

179   ***oppositas disiecit pondere nubes***: the discus (*pondere*) separates the clouds and the phrase.

180   ***reccidit***: variant of *recidit*; cf. 18.

181   ***pondus***: enjambment. Ovid may have delayed the subject until this line in order to make it reflect the length of time (*longo post tempore*, 180) that it took for the discus to fall.

   iunctam cum viribus artem: the same phrase is used with reference to the throw of a spear at 8.29.

182   ***imprudens***: cf. *puer imprudens ... Cyparissus*, 130.

183   ***Taenarides***: "Spartan." Taenarus is a promontory in southern Laconia where Orpheus descended to the underworld (13). The mention of Taenarus here foreshadows the upcoming death of Hyacinthus.

184   ***repercusso ... pondere***: "the discus having rebounded." It bounces because the ground is rocky (*solidam*, 180; *dura*, 184).

pondere: this is Koch's emendation for the manuscript reading *in aere* or *in aera*, which would result in an unacceptable repetition of the preposition: *in vultus tellus | in aere*. See Anderson 1972: 490.

185   ***in vultus, Hyacinthe, tuos***: the word *Hyacinthe* splits the noun from its adjective just as the discus splits the boy's face. Compare the somewhat similar Ennius, fr. 609 V (Spuria 5 S): *saxo cere comminuit brum*.

   vultus ... tuos: poetic plural for singular.

185–186   ***expalluit aeque | quam puer ipse deus***: the concatenation of *puer ipse deus* emphasizes the paleness of both Hyacinthus and Apollo, which is reinforced by *aeque*.

188   ***nunc animam admotis fugientem sustinet herbis***: cf. Bion, fr. 1, where Apollo applies nectar and ambrosia to Hyacinthus' wound.

189   ***nil prosunt artes. erat immedicabile vulnus***: cf. Bion, fr. 1.2–4. Apollo, who is *immemor sui* (171) and has turned his back on his divine gifts in order to follow Hyacinthus, now fails as a doctor. This is not a question of whether a god should bring the dead back to life (*quoniam fatali lege tenemur*, 203). Hyacinthus is still alive (*vultus moriens iacet*, 194), but Apollo is unable to heal him. Cf. 1.523–524, where Apollo cannot cure himself of love, and 2.617–618, where he cannot cure the dead Coronis.

190–195   See Reed 1997: 210 for the long history of this simile. Note especially *Aeneid* 9.434–437, where the head of the dying Nisus is compared to a drooping poppy. The simile is also used in connection with defloration. See Hardie 1994: 150; Forbes Irving 1990: 134–135.

190   ***ut si***: introduces a conditional clause of comparison.

   riguo: Roman gardens had sophisticated irrigation systems. See Jashemski 1993: 41, 62, 68, 71, 76; Stackelberg 2009: 38–40. The flowers listed in 190–191, including the hyacinth, appear in Columella's (10.97–104) list of the flowers that would be found in a Roman garden.

190–191   ***violas ... papavera ... | lilia***: these flowers reflect elements of Hyacinthus' story: the purple violets recall the blood that colored the purple hyacinth (210–211); the poppy and the lily are associated with death (Vergil, *Georgics* 4.545; *Aeneid* 6.883; Hardie 2004: 98–100); the lily reflects Hyacinthus' paleness following the death blow (185–186). The opiate derived from the poppy was used by physicians to deaden pain. See Reed 1997: 211, 360.

192   ***marcida demittant subito caput illa gravatum***: "those drooping (flowers) quickly bow their heavy heads."

193   ***nec se sustineant spectentque cacumine terram***: compare the cypress, which is able *spectare cacumine caelum* (140).

Commentary

195 ***ipsa sibi est oneri cervix umeroque recumbit***: double dative. Cf. Vergil, *Aeneid* 9.434: *inque umeros cervix conlapsa recumbit*.

196 ***Oebalide***: Greek vocative. Oebalus was a legendary king of Sparta. For Hyacinthus as the son of Oebalus, see Hyginus, *Fabulae* 271.1; Lucian, *Dialogi deorum* 16; Philostratus the Younger 14.

fraudate: this is the first of several legal terms in this passage that make Apollo's lament sound like a defence speech at a trial for murder; see *crimina* (197), *facinus* (198), and *culpa* (200). It also foreshadows the punishment for theft in lines 198–199.

prima ... iuventa: this indicates that Hyacinthus was near the age of puberty. Cf. Orpheus' lovers, who are *citraque iuventam* (84).

198 ***tu dolor es facinusque meum***: Apollo is the grieving lover of a murder victim and the murderer himself.

198–199 ***mea dextera leto | inscribenda tuo est***: Anderson 1972: 491 believes that this as a reference to branding, which was a punishment for thieves, fugitive slaves, and convicts destined for the arena. Jones 1987: 139–155 discusses tattooing for such offenses. According to Phanocles (fr. 1 Powell), the Thracian men tattooed the killers of Orpheus so that they would not forget their crime. Instead of placing the mark upon himself (*mea dextera ... inscribenda*, 198–199), Apollo transfers it to the hyacinth (*foliis inscribit*, 215).

199 ***ego sum tibi funeris auctor***: cf. Vergil, *Aeneid* 6.458: *funeris heu tibi causa fui?* Apollo will be *auctor honoris* (214) when he turns Hyacinthus into a flower. Through his use of the emphatic *ego*, Ovid signals that he is rejecting the version in which Zephyr blows the discus into Hyacinthus' face, which would have exonerated Apollo. Athenian law held that anyone who killed a person accidentally during the course of an athletic contest was not liable; cf. Plato, *Laws* 9, 873e; Demosthenes 23.53.

200–201 ***amasse vocari | ... ludisse vocari***: note the parallel line endings.

200 ***quae mea culpa tamen? ... nisi culpa potest et amasse vocari***: after claiming responsibility for the death of Hyacinthus, Apollo now tries to lessen his own guilt.

nisi si: "unless." *OLD* s.v. *nisi* 7.

lusisse: subject of *potest*.

201 *amasse*: syncopated form of *amavisse* and subject of *potest*.

202–203 ***utinam pro te vitam tecumve liceret | reddere***: compare Orpheus' offer to the gods of the underworld: *leto gaudete duorum* (39). As a mortal, Orpheus could have killed himself in order to be with Eurydice, but the immortal Apollo could not die to be with Hyacinthus; cf. 1.661–663; see Reed 1997: 213.

204 ***memorique haerebis in ore***: the phrase *ore haeret* usually indicates that a person cannot speak (Vergil, *Aeneid* 2.774, 3.48; Seneca, *Oedipus* 1009; Statius, *Thebaid* 10.688). Here Apollo means that the name of Hyacinthus will not be forgotten.

205–209 With the death of Hyacinthus, Apollo recovers his musical and prophetic abilities (*vero ore*, 209). Tarrant 2004 deletes lines 205–208, which Hill 1992: 173 describes as "the work of a crude interpolator." Anderson 1972: 492, however, detects a cross-reference to 13.396. And, as Reed 1997: 214 notes, *vero ore* implies that Apollo is prophesying at 209. Therefore the allusion to the future fate of Ajax must stand.

206 ***flosque novus scripto gemitus imitabere nostros***: "and as a new flower, you will imitate our groans in writing." Cf. Ovid, *Fasti* 5.224: *manet in folio scripta querela suo*. The flower becomes more of a memorial to Apollo's grief than to Hyacinthus' death; see von Glinski 2012: 26–33. The floral metamorphosis in the story of Hyacinthus does not occur until the Hellenistic period. See Reed 1997: 204.

207–208 ***fortissimus heros | addat in hunc florem***: Apollo is referring to Ajax, whose story is recounted at 13.394–398. After Ajax commits suicide at Troy, the hyacinth will carry his name, which Sophocles (*Ajax* 430–431) equates with the mourning cry αἰαῖ. Cf. 215: *gemitus foliis inscribit et AI AI*.

207 ***quo***: i.e. *quo tempore*.

208 ***hunc florem***: Lindsell 1937: 82–83 identifies the flower as *Delphinium ajacis*, which Theocritus (*Idylls* 10.28) calls γραπτὰ ὑάκινθος, "hyacinth marked with letters."

209 ***vero ... ore***: Apollo foretells the honors that will be granted to Hyacinthus. For the association of this phrase with prophecy, see Tibullus 3.4.49–50. For similar phrases, see *Fasti* 6.425–426; Lucretius 6.6.

211 ***Tyrioque ... ostro***: Phoenician Tyre was famous for its purple dye. See Pliny, *Naturalis historia* 5.17, 9.61–64.

212 ***formamque capit quam lilia, si non | pupureus color his, argenteus esset in illis***: "(the hyacinth) takes the form that lilies would take, if the former (hyacinths) did not have a purple color, and if the latter (lilies) did not have a silver color."

214 ***auctor honoris***: Apollo is responsible for Hyacinthus' death (*funeris auctor*, 199) and for this honor. Cf. Orpheus as the *auctor* of pederasty (83).

215 ***AI AI***: a Greek cry of lamentation.

216 **littera:** "inscription." *OLD* s.v. *littera* 6b. Instead of a funerary inscription on a tombstone, this one is written on a petal.

ducta est: "drawn." *OLD* s.v. *duco* 12.

217 **nec genuisse pudet Sparten Hyacinthon:** cf. the shame that Cyprus feels on account of the Propoetides and the Cerastae (220–223), whose stories come next.

Sparten: Greek accusative.

Hyacinthon: Greek accusative.

217–219 *honorque | durat in hoc aevi celebrandaque more priorum*: the Hyacinthia, one of the most important Peloponnesian festivals, took place in the summer month of Hyacinthios. See Pettersson 1992: 9–41. Little is known about it beyond what is related by the grammarian Athenaeus (4.139c-f) and the geographer Pausanias (3.1.3, 18.6–19.5). On the first day of this three-day festival, worshipers lament the death of Hyacinthus and offer a funerary sacrifice at his tomb in the monumental base of a statue of Apollo Amyclaeus. On the second and third days, they hold a joyous celebration in honor of the god. In his description of the sanctuary at Amyclae, Pausanias (3.19.4–5) says that the poets' stories about the death of Hyacinthus are erroneous and incomplete. The true myth is illustrated on a relief in the sanctuary that depicts the apotheosis of an adult, bearded Hyacinthus along with his sister, Polyboea. Cf. Nonnus 19.101.

217 **in hoc aevi:** partitive genitive.

218 **more priorum:** the continuation of the Hyacinthia without modification stands in stark contrast to the alteration of the rites of the Cerastae (221–237).

219 **praelata ... pompa:** the funerary procession preceeds the rites. *OLD* s.v. *praefero* 2; *pompa* 1b.

The Amathusian Myths

Orpheus now moves from Troy and Greece to Cyprus in order to recount a series of myths located at Amathus, a city heavily influenced by the Phoenicians, who had established trading colonies throughout the Mediterranean. A Levantine presence can be detected as early as the eighth century BC at Amathus – the location of Ovid's myths of the Cerastae, the Propoetides, and Pygmalion (Hermary 1987). The influence of the Phoenicians was especially strong in the religious life of the city. Excavations have yielded numerous dedications to

Astarte, the Near Eastern Venus, whose temple stood on the acropolis of Amathus (Hermary and Tatton-Brown 1981: 74–83). An Assyrian inscription that identifies Mukul as "the god of the Amathusians" warrants the inclusion of Reshef Mekal, the Levantine Apollo, among the deities worshiped there (Power 1929). Hesychius (s.v. Μάλικα) says that the Amathusians called Heracles "Malika"; this name recalls the Levantine god "Melkart," who shares traits of both Heracles and Jupiter. Considering the importance of Levantine religion at Amathus, it is prudent to consider the possibility that the cult practices reflected in Ovid's Amathusian myths are Levantine in origin, especially since Venus, Jupiter, and Apollo – the deities who play prominent roles in the song of Orpheus – are Roman equivalents of the Levantine gods who were worshiped by the Amathusians.

Cerastae

Having concluded his tales of pederasty, Orpheus now embarks upon his second theme – women punished for their illicit lust. He begins with the Propoetides, a group of Cypriot women from the city of Amathus whom Venus transformed into the first prostitutes. Orpheus interrupts their story to recount the tale of the Cerastae, a brotherhood of horned priests from Amathus who sacrificed strangers on the altar of Jupiter Hospes until Venus turned them into bulls.

Although Ovid gives the fullest account of these priests, they are also mentioned by a number of other authors. Philostephanus of Cyrene, a Greek geographer of the third century BC, says that Cyprus was called "Cerastia" (Κεραστία) on account of its horned men (*FHG* 3.30). This suggests that the Cerastae were not confined to Amathus but were dispersed throughout the island. "Lactantius Placidus," the name given to a summarizer of Ovid's *Metamorphoses* from late antiquity, locates a group of them in the Cypriot city of Salamis (*argumentum* 10, *fabula* 6), where they sacrificed human victims to Zeus (Lactantius Firmianus, *Divinae institutiones* 1.21.1). The hagiographer Polybius of Rhinocoluros (*Life of Saint Epiphanus* 53, Migne 41, cols. 89c–91a) says that anyone who approached a sanctuary called "the safety of Zeus" (Διὸς Ἀσφάλεια) in this same city was killed. Since safety is exactly what a stranger would expect from Jupiter Hospes, the Salaminian and Amathusian gods were most likely identical.

Some elements of this story are based on a ritual that had actually been performed on Cyprus (O'Bryhim 1999). Horned bull skulls that had been modified for use as ritual masks have been found in the sanctuaries of Kition and

Enkomi, two Bronze Age cities located in the eastern part of Cyprus. After an earthquake destroyed Enkomi, its inhabitants founded Salamis, where "Lactantius Placidus" locates a band of Cerastae. Terracotta dedicatory figurines depicting men who wear bull masks have been uncovered at several sanctuaries on Cyprus, which confirms that the Cerastae performed their rites throughout the island (see Figure 1). This includes Amathus, where excavators found a mask depicting a man with bull horns (GR 1894.1101.202 British Museum) that fits Ovid's description of the Cerastae as men "whose foreheads bristled with twin horns" (222–223).

The rites of the Cerastae probably originated in the Near East, where archaeologists have found bull masks and terracotta figurines that are nearly

Figure 1 Terracotta figurine from Amathus that depicts a man wearing a bull mask. *Source:* Published by permission of the Director of Antiquities and the Cyprus Museum.

identical to their Cypriot analogues. In Phoenicia and its colonies, human sacrifices were part of the worship of Baal, a bull-horned god associated with rainfall. Victims were cremated and their ashes were buried in a sacred area called a "tophet." These burial areas have been discovered in Phoenician cities throughout the Mediterranean and on Cyprus at Idalion, Paphos, and Amathus, all of which have strong ties to the Phoenicians (Cross 1994: 93–107; Karageorghis 1982; Agelarakis 1998). When the Greeks began to gain power on the island, they attempted to suppress the practice of human sacrifice. This process is reflected in the philosopher Porphyry's account (*De abstinentia* 2.55) of a king named Diphilos who replaced the human victims of this rite with animals. The myth of the Cerastae, in which priests were turned into bulls, may have been created to provide divine support for the Greek alteration of this long-standing Phoenician rite.

Although a myth about human sacrifice seems out of place in a song about sexuality, Orpheus uses it to comment on the behavior of the Propoetides. These women, who became the first prostitutes, shame Cyprus through their licentious behavior, just as the Cerastae shame Cyprus through their impious behavior. By equating the two groups (*abnuat aeque*, 221), Orpheus implies that the sexual excesses of women are just as offensive to Venus as human sacrifice.

220   *at*: this word is employed to draw a strong contrast with the preceding story. The Spartans were proud to have produced Hyacinthus, but Cyprus was ashamed of the Propoetides.

roges: generalizing second-person singular of the potential subjunctive. The second-person singular suggests that Orpheus has a human audience in mind instead of the trees, beasts, and birds that surround him (133–134). The Byzantine poet Tzetzes (*Chiliades* 1.12) said that men were drawn to Orpheus' song, while vases depict Orpheus singing before Thracian men. See Mannack 2001: 91.

fecundam ... metallis: Cyprus was rich in copper (*cyprum*). It was mixed with tin to make bronze, which was exported from Cyprus in the form of oxhide ingots: large, flat pieces of copper shaped like a cow pelt. Since *fecundam* is commonly associated with pregnancy, this adjective personifies the island and makes copper its offspring; see also *genuisse* (221) and *gravidamque Amathunta metallis* (531). Fertile Amathus has produced beings that are at odds with fertility: the Cerastae kill strangers and the Propoetides refuse to have intercourse. Because they offend Venus, the goddess of fertility, they must be punished.

Amathunta: Greek accusative singular. Amathus was a city on the southern coast of Cyprus. Tacitus (*Annales* 3.62) says that, after Paphos, it had the island's oldest temple of Venus. Excavations at the site have uncovered a temple to Venus and Adonis that is mentioned by Pausanias (9.41.2). For a description of the site, see Maier and Karagheorghis 1984.

221 **an genuisse velit Propoetidas**: cf. 217: *nec genuisse pudet Sparten Hyacinthon. velit*, like *fecundam* at 220, personifies the island.

221–222 **aeque | atque**: "equally as," "the same as."

222 **quondam**: this implies that the situation will change and looks forward to Venus' transformation of the Cerastae into bulls. *OLD* s.v. *quondam* 1.

223 **Cerastae**: masculine of the first declension.

224 **ante fores horum stabat Iovis Hospitis ara**: this seems to indicate that the living quarters of the Cerastae adjoined the sanctuary.

Iovis Hospitis: *Iupiter Hospes* is a translation of Zeus Xenios, the name of the Greek god who protected strangers; see Farnell, vol. 1: 737–4. For Jupiter Hospitalis, see Cicero, *Ad Quintum* 2.10.3 and *Pro rege Deiotaro* 18. For Jupiter as the god of hospitality, see Ovid's stories of Lycaon (1.163–243) and Baucis and Philemon (8.613–724).

225–226 **ignarus sceleris quam si quis sanguine tinctam | advena vidisset**: *quam [aram] si quis aduena, ignarus sceleris, sanguine tinctam uidisset*. The various readings contained in the manuscripts for the first two words do not fit the meter. *ignarus sceleris* is Madvig's emendation (see Madvig 1873). This makes perfect sense, because no stranger would approach this temple unless he or she were ignorant of the type of sacrifice that was offered there.

227 **bidentes**: this technical term refers to sheep that are destined for sacrifice. *OLD* s.v. *bidens*² 1. A "two-tooth" sheep has its first set of adult incisors when it is approximately one year old.

228 **hospes erat caesus**: compare the myth of Busiris, where strangers were sacrificed on an altar of Jupiter. Hercules killed the king and put an end to the practice; see 9.182–183 and *Ars amatoria* 1.647–652. According to Apollodorus (2.5.11), the seer who advised Busiris to sacrifice humans was from Cyprus.

sacris offensa nefandis: *nefas* indicates that the sacrifice of humans should have been offensive to the gods in general, including Jupiter. It is noteworthy that the god does not stop this practice, even though it takes place at his temple. Most likely, Orpheus has Venus punish the Cerastae because she is the tutelary deity of Cyprus and the heroine of his song.

229–230 **ipsa suas urbes Ophiusiaque arva parabat | deserere alma Venus**: compare the goddesses who flee from human corruption at Hesiod, *Works and Days* 197–201. Venus temporarily abandons her cities, including Amathus and Paphos, when she falls in love with Adonis (529–532).

229 **suas urbes**: for Venus' Cypriot cities, see Vergil, *Aeneid* 10.51–52: *est Amathus, est celsa mihi Paphus atque Cythera | Idaliaeque domus.*

Ophiusiaque: Ovid alone applies to Cyprus this epithet, which may mean "infested with snakes." St. Helena reportedly brought cats to Cyprus to control the snake infestation at the monastery of St. George, which arose because of a long drought. See Arbel 2012: 339–341.

230   **alma Venus**: *alma* is a common epithet for Venus; see Carter 1902: 100. She will demonstrate her beneficence toward the island by ridding it of the Cerastae.

230–231   *"sed quid loca grata, quid urbes | peccavere meae? quod"* dixit *"crimen in illis?"*: the cities of Cyprus are personified; cf. 220.

232   **gens**: not the entire population of Cyprus, but the Cerastae as a group. *OLD* s.v. *gens* 4b.

233   *quid medium est mortisque fugaeque*: cf. the punishment of Myrrha at 487: *mutataeque mihi vitamque necemque negate*.

235–236   **ad cornua vultum | flexit et admonita est haec illis posse relinqui**: the Cerastae retain their horns when they are transformed into bulls. Compare the hardness of the Propoetides, which remains after they turn into stone (241–242).

235   **quo**: *in quam formam*. See *OLD* s.v. *muto* 12b for the ablative.

237   **grandiaque in torvos transformat membra iuvencos**: poetic justice because the sacrificers have become sacrificial victims. This marks a transitional phase in the cult, in which animals replace human victims.

grandiaque ... membra: their limbs are full-grown because these adult priests become bulls instead of *lactantes vitulos* (227). *OLD* s.v. *grandis* 1.

torvos: they retain their fierce nature.

transformat: *transformo* is a Latin translation of μεταμορφόω. Cf. Vergil, *Georgics* 4.441: *omnia transformat sese in miracula rerum*.

iuvencos: in Roman cult, the bull is the sacrifice par excellence for Jupiter. The myth of the Cerastae is etiological in that it accounts for how bull sacrifice was established in the Amathusian cult of Jupiter. This may explain the absence of bulls in line 227, where only calves and sheep are mentioned as possible sacrifices at Jupiter's temple.

Propoetides

The Propoetides, a group of women from Amathus, denied the divinity of Venus, who transformed them into the first prostitutes. When they grew so shameless that they were no longer able to blush, they turned into stone. Orpheus' attempt to make them the epitome of female lustfulness fails for one simple reason: these women were not inherently lustful. On the contrary, they denied the divinity of Venus, which implies that they wanted to remain celibate. The goddess transformed them into prostitutes because they were chaste, not because they were licentious. Their spontaneous metamorphosis into stone reflects the hard-hearted shamelessness that Venus forced upon them.

Forbes Irving 1990: 298 posits a connection between Ovid's myth and stories associated with the daughters of Cinyras, a Cypriot king and priest of Venus. According to Apollodorus (3.14.3), three daughters of Cinyras had intercourse with foreigners and moved to Egypt because Aphrodite was angry with them. Ovid tells a different story (6.99–100): they were transformed into the steps of a temple, a punishment that "Lactantius Placidus" attributes to their arrogance. Another potential source appears in Plutarch's *Moralia* (777d), according to which Aphrodite was not angry with the daughters of the πρόπολος ("priest") because they were the first to hate young men. This appears to be a correction of an earlier version of the myth, which asserted that the goddess was angered by the celibacy of the Propoetides. In any case, this priest may be Cinyras, whose daughters (like the Propoetides) drew the wrath of the goddess by choosing to remain celibate.

The myth of the Propoetides has been linked to a practice known as "sacred prostitution," whereby women have intercourse with male worshippers at the temple of a fertility goddess as part of her cult. While its existence has been hotly disputed (Beard and Henderson 1998: 56–79; Kurke 1996: 49–75; Budin 2008; Lightfoot 2003: 323–325), ancient sources contain references to different types of institutionalized prostitution on Cyprus. Herodotus (1.199) says that the women of Babylon had to offer themselves for sexual intercourse with foreigners at the temple of a goddess once before marriage, most likely for ritual defloration. The Cypriots, he adds, have a similar custom (cf. Apollodorus 3.14.3). The behavior of the Propoetides, however, is not consonant with Herodotus' description. Whereas Herodotus specifies an obligation that was limited to a single act, the Propoetides prostituted themselves for so long that they became shameless and turned into stone. Justin (18.5.3–7) describes how the Cypriots sent their daughters to the seashore a few days before their marriage to earn a dowry through prostitution. This custom, too, is confined to a brief period before marriage. There is a reference to the sanctuary of Amathusian Venus in *The Acts of Barnabas* (20): "from there we came to Amathus and saw on the sacred hill a large number of indecent Greek women and men pouring libations." It is difficult to discern what is happening here because this practice may have been distorted by the Christian author. At the very least, the story of the Propoetides is an etiological myth that was created to explain the genesis of prostitution (sacred or otherwise) at Amathus, which agrees with Ennius' assertion, at *Euhemerus* 134–136 Warmington (10 *FRL*), that Venus introduced prostitution to Cyprus.

The myth of the Propoetides may also provide an etiology for a group of statues. The word *silex*, which describes the ultimate form of the Propoetides (242), appears in myths about individuals who have been turned into statues. For example, twice during the story of Perseus, both men and animals are turned into *silices* by the Gorgon's head. By describing them as *simulacra* (4.781) and noting *mansit imago* (5.199), Ovid leaves us in no doubt that they retain their former shape. When king Polydectes suffers the same fate, Ovid uses the word *silex* to describe his altered state. There can be no doubt that he, too, becomes a statue, because all the others who are changed into *silices* by the Gorgon's head retain their human form. Therefore the hard-hearted Propoetides, who were turned into *rigidum silicem*, may have become anthropomorphic statues.

Support for this comes from the story of Anaxarete (14.693–764), in which a man of humble birth named Iphis falls in love with Anaxarete, a princess of Cypriot Salamis. Even though he tries everything to win this woman's heart, Anaxarete, who is "harder than rock" (*durior ... saxo*), robs Iphis of any hope of success by acting cruelly and arrogantly toward him. Unable to live with this rejection, Iphis hangs himself from the lintel of the palace's doorway to demonstrate the magnitude of his love for the princess. This proves futile, because servants remove his body and return it to his mother before Anaxarete discovers what had happened. As Iphis' funeral procession passes by the palace, Anaxarete looks out of the window and catches sight of his corpse. Her body turns into stone to match her character (*quod fuit in duro iam pridem pectore, saxum*, 14.758). Even though the word *silex* does not appear here, Ovid says that "Salamis still preserves a statue in the shape of the princess and also has a temple under the name of Venus Prospiciens" (14.759–761). Anaxarete's pose at the moment of her metamorphosis reveals that she is the "woman at the window" (see Figure 2), a representation of a fertility goddess that appears throughout the Near East and on Cyprus (Cazeaux 1980: 237–247).

Any sculptural group associated with the Propoetides must have possessed some quality that led a viewer to identify the statues as prostitutes. One characteristic that both Greek and Roman authors consistently associate with harlots is their willingness to engage in public displays of nudity. Athenaeus (13.568c–e and 13.569b–c) mentions this when he discusses the depiction of prostitutes in Greek New Comedy; Catullus (55.11–12) recalls a prostitute who bares her breasts in response to his question about the whereabouts of a friend; Ovid speaks of how respectable matrons could see the nude bodies of harlots in public (*Tristia* 2.309–312); and Dio Cassius (80.13.3) says that Elagabalus "always stood naked in front of his doorway like the whores" when he played the prostitute. Nudity is also the distinguishing characteristic of a type of Near Eastern statue known as "Astarte holding her breasts," which originated in

Figure 2 Phoenician woman at the window, 9th–8th century BC. Found at Nimrud, Iraq. British Museum, ME 118159.

Mesopotamia during the second millennium BC and spread westward to Cyprus, where it became a popular dedication to Venus. Although most are small terracotta figurines, life-sized versions such as the ones found at Idalion (Ohnefalsch-Richter 1893, vol. 1: 399–402; vol. 2, pl. 56) may have provided the inspiration for the myth of the Propoetides (see Figure 3).

238   **tamen**: "in spite of this." The Propoetides have learned nothing about the power of Venus from the fate of the Cerastae.

obscenae: both "disgusting" and "lewd." *OLD* s.v. *obscenus* 2 and 3. This powerful word highlights the repulsion that Orpheus feels toward the Propoetides and their behavior. Compare his description of the consummation of the "wedding" of Cinyras and his daughter (465): *accipit obsceno genitor sua uiscera lecto.*

238–239   **Venerem Propoetides ausae | esse negare deam**: i.e. the Propoetides remain chaste in an attempt to demonstrate that Venus is not a goddess and therefore has no power over them. Orpheus does not specify that sexual abstinence was the cause of their punishment, because this would have undercut one of the themes of his song: the unbridled lust of women. So he leaves the precise nature of their offense unclear and focuses more generally

Figure 3 Statues from Idalion. Ohnefalsch-Richter 1893, vol. 2, pl. 56. Public Domain
Source: Ohnefalsch-Richter, M. 1893. Kypros, the Bible, and Homer. Asher: London.

on their refusal to honor Venus. Cf. 4.2–3: *Bacchum | progeniem negat esse Iovis.* For the punishment of the Propoetides, see also Liveley 1999: 200–204.

Propoetides: this may be a "speaking name" that describes the distinguishing characteristic of these women. If the word is scanned Prŏpŏētĭdĕs, πρό may mean "publicly" (*LSJ* s.v. πρό D III 2b), while the suffix -ιδες may be an agentive ending meaning "those who do something." The base is derived from ποιεῖν, which appears as ποη- in words like ποητής. Since ποιεῖν is slang for "to copulate" (Henderson 1991: 158; cf. Adams 1990: 143 for *facere*), Propoetides can mean "women who copulate publicly," a fitting appellation for the first prostitutes. Bauer 1962: 14, note 13 rejects an attempt to alter Plutarch's προπόλου to Πρωποίτου "solely in order to comply with Ovid" and thereby to create an imaginary ancestor, Propoetus, for the Propoetides.

239 **pro quo**: "as punishment for this." *OLD* s.v. *pro* 10. Because the Propoetides refuse to have intercourse, by turning them into prostitutes Venus forces them to worship her with a vengeance.

240 ***corpora cum fama primae vulgasse feruntur***: "they are said to have been the first women to make their bodies public domain along with their reputations." Most manuscripts have *fama*, while some from the thirteenth century have *forma. fama* indicates that the Propoetides gained a reputation for their sexual behavior; *corpora cum forma* is a tautology. As Hollis 1970: xxvii says, when deciding upon the best reading, "our touchstone must be the excellence of individual readings – neither the number nor the prejudged value of their manuscript sponsors."

vulgasse: syncopated form of *vulgavisse*.

241 ***utque pudor cessit sanguisque induruit oris***: cf. 14.757–758: *paulatimque occupat artus, | quod fuit in duro iam pridem pectore, saxum*. The Propoetides lose their sense of shame and, with it, the ability to blush. This is what leads to their spontaneous transformation into stone, not the anger of the goddess. Their hard-heartedness is reflected in the stone into which they transform.

242 ***silicem***: Ovid often uses this word when describing a metamorphosis into a statue; cf. 4.799–781, 5.198–199, 9.219–227.

parvo ... discrimine: there was little difference between the hard (shameless) women that the Propoetides were and the hard stone that they became. *OLD* s.v. *durus* 4c. This may also indicate that there was little difference between their human form and the statues that they became.

uersae: "turned into." *OLD* s.v. *verto* 22.

Pygmalion

Ovid's probable source for the myth of Pygmalion is the treatise *About Cyprus* by Philostephanus (*FHG* III 31 fr. 13), a Greek monographer of the third century BC. Although this work is lost, two church fathers summarize his version. Clement of Alexandria (*Protrepticus* 4.57.3) says: "that famous Cypriot Pygmalion loved an ivory statue. It was a statue of Aphrodite and it was nude. The Cypriot Pygmalion is overcome by its figure and has intercourse with it." Arnobius (*Adversus nationes* 6.22) provides a more detailed summary:

> Philostephanus says that Pygmalion, the king of Cyprus, conceived a passion for a statue of Aphrodite that was sacrosanct to the Cypriots and had long been an object of reverence. He says that Pygmalion loved it as though it were a woman – his mind, soul, power of reasoning, and judgment blinded – and that the madman was accustomed to lift the deity onto a bed as if he were married to it and to be united with it through embraces and kisses and, because of his delusion, to perform other acts of empty lust that could not be carried to completion.

Philostephanus' account contains several elements that are not immediately recognizable in Ovid's version: Pygmalion's royal status, his copulation with an inanimate statue, and the identification of this statue as a preexisting cult image of Venus. These discrepancies led Dörrie 1974: 26 to conclude that Ovid borrowed little of importance from Philostephanus, beyond the fact that the statue was made of ivory. Given that Ovid often made a tale more intriguing by insinuating what he could have said openly, it is not surprising to find these elements lurking beneath the surface of his version.

First, Pygmalion's social status. At the end of the story, Orpheus says that the union between Pygmalion and the statue produced a daughter named Paphos (297). She in turn gave birth to Cinyras, a mythical king of Cyprus. Since kings do not spring from humble stock in Greek myth, Cinyras' grandfather must have been a ruler of Cyprus. Therefore Ovid's Pygmalion was not a sculptor by trade, but a king with an artistic bent.

Second, the identity of the statue. Orpheus' assertion that Pygmalion's statue possessed a beauty "with which no woman can be born" (248–249) implies that it did not represent a mortal woman, but a goddess (Miller 1988: 206; Sharrock 1991: 171; Elsner 1991: 158–159). This is reinforced by his description of its physical features: the statue was made of ivory and it was nude (247, 267). The word *simulacrum* is commonly used to refer to cult statues (Knox 1986: 52–53), and the only large-scale statues that were made of ivory were images of the gods (Caubet 1989: 247–254). Since all nude female cult statues represented Aphrodite (Clement of Alexandria, *Protrepticus* 4.50), Pygmalion's creation must have depicted Venus. Therefore, when Ovid says that Venus "was present at the marriage that she made" (295), he does not mean that she was there simply as one of the deities associated with marriage. Ovid's Pygmalion is joining with her cult statue, as he did in Philostephanus' version (Hardie 2002: 190).

Finally, the point at which Pygmalion has intercourse with the statue. At several junctures, Ovid hints that Pygmalion was having intercourse with the statue before its metamorphosis. Soon after he finishes the statue, Pygmalion begins to behave like a lover: he kisses it, flatters it, fondles it, and gives it gifts (256–269). Then he undresses the statue, puts it on a bed, calls it his wife, and imagines that it can feel what he is doing. The audience waits for the expected climax, but Ovid abruptly shifts the scene to the temple of Venus. Pygmalion needed her approval to marry the statue, but was afraid to make such a request in public. Instead of asking Venus to have the ivory statue of a woman as his wife, he asks instead for a woman who is *like* ivory. When he returns home, he does not expect to find any change in the statue because he did not ask the goddess to transform it into a living woman. He immediately begins to kiss it and fondle it while lying with it on a bed (281), just as he did before he left for the temple. And, once again, the anticipated climax is interrupted, this time by the transformation of the statue into a living being. Pygmalion is struck dumb because he did not expect the statue to come to life. Instead, he wanted Venus to allow him to continue his previous conduct with the inanimate statue. When he recovers from the shock, Pygmalion renews the foreplay that had been interrupted by the metamorphosis, and the climax is interrupted yet again. Instead of telling his audience that intercourse occurred after the statue became flesh, Orpheus says "and soon, when the horns of the moon had been formed into a full circle nine times, she gave birth to Paphos, from whom the island derives its name" (295–297). Thus Pygmalion appears to have had intercourse with the statue both before and after its metamorphosis, even though Ovid never explicitly says that intercourse occurred at any time.

Thus all the elements that Ovid found in Philostephanus appear just beneath the surface of his version. Ovid's originality lies not in how he changed the information he found in his source, but in the unique way in which he related it, which would have delighted those who were familiar with the earlier version of the myth.

The myth of Pygmalion has much in common with a ritual called "the sacred marriage rite" (Lapinkivi 2004: 241–252), an annual ceremony in which the king married the goddess of fertility, who was represented by a statue or by a human substitute. The purpose of this ritual was to ensure the prosperity of the ruler's domain for the coming year. A myth preserved in a papyrus fragment from Oxyrhynchus in Egypt (*POxy* XXXIV 2688) suggests that the descendants of Cinyras, the high priests of Venus, performed the sacred marriage rite at Paphos. It asks: "Why in the temple of the Paphian Aphrodite ... and ... [with] garlands of roses?" The response attributes to Cinyras the custom of dedicating garlands of roses to the goddess: "Because [Cinyras?], son of Paphos the citizen of the metropolis, stealing [the image] of the Cyprian Aphrodite, took it away to his house. [The goddess coming?] and seeing the young man holding it in his hand approached him for the purpose of sexual relations. He [was deceived and?] had intercourse with her as if she were a mortal woman and ... [with] garlands of roses." The similarities between the myths of Pygmalion and Cinyras make sense if Cinyras, the grandson of Pygmalion (298–299), is carrying out his inherited role as priest-king of Aphrodite, which included the performance of the sacred marriage rite and somehow involved the cult statue of the goddess.

Orpheus incorporates the myth of Pygmalion into his song as a tale of wish fulfillment: both Orpheus and Pygmalion reject the women around them and resort to stopgap measures to satisfy their sexual needs until they can have what they truly desire. Orpheus spends his lust on infertile sexual relationships with boys until he can be reunited with Eurydice, his perfect woman. Pygmalion resorts to a lifeless statue of the perfect woman, which he intends to use as a sexual surrogate until he finds a pure woman. Unlike the other characters in Orpheus' song, Pygmalion achieves long-term happiness in his relationship, which is what Orpheus so desperately desires.

243 **Pygmalion**: Greek nominative singular. This name came to Cyprus from the Levant (Müller 1988: 192–205). Hesychius of Alexandria (s.v. Πυγμαίων), a Greek grammarian, identifies it as a form of "Pygmaion," which was a name for Adonis on Cyprus. Pygmalion is linked with Astarte, the Phoenician Venus, in an inscription on a medallion from the Cypriot city of Kition (*CIS* I 6057 = *KAI* 73). A king of Cyprus was named Pygmalion (Diodorus Siculus 19.79.4), as was the Tyrian king who was the brother of Dido (Vergil, *Aeneid* 4.325; Josephus, *Against Apion* 1.18.2).

aevum ... agentes: *OLD* s.v. *aevum* 5b: "to live one's life (in a specified condition)."

per crimen: "reprehensibly." The Propoetides did not become prostitutes of their own free will. Venus forced this behavior on them because they wanted to remain celibate.

244–245 **offensus vitiis quae plurima menti | femineae natura dedit**: cf. 153–154: *inconcessisque puellas | ignibus attonitas*. This is an editorial comment on the part of Orpheus, who equates the Propoetides with the Thracian women who want to have intercourse with him. Orpheus views female licentiousness as an inherent vice. Pygmalion is able to eliminate this flaw in his perfect woman, upon whom he projects his own view of feminine morality.

245–246 **sine coniuge caelebs | vivebat thalamique diu consorte carebat**: Pygmalion honors Venus by spurning the women who offended her and by creating a statue that allows him to remain sexually active. Similarly, Orpheus abstains from intercourse with women, but resorts to pederasty. Although neither relationship was fertile (at least not until the vivification of Pygmalion's statue), any sexual act would have been pleasing to the goddess. For Aphrodite and homoeroticism, see Asclepiades, fr. 1 GP; Meleager, fr. 119 GP; Sappho, fr. 1; Theognis 1305–1310.

caelebs: while *caelebs* means that a man is not married, it does not mean that he abstains from intercourse; see *OLD* s.v. *caelebs* 1.

coniuge caelebs ... consorte carebat: the same type of alliteration ends both lines.

246 **thalami** "marriage chamber." *OLD* s.v. *thalamus* 2.

diu: this implies that Pygmalion will eventually marry.

247 **interea**: the statue is intended as a stopgap measure, to tide Pygmalion over until he finds a suitable woman. Intercourse with it allows him to continue to worship Venus and thereby avoid the crime of the celibate Propoetides.

feliciter: "with good results, successfully." *OLD* s.v. *feliciter* 2. Cf. Pliny's comment on Praxiteles at *Naturalis historia* 34.69: *qui marmore feliciter fecit ... pulcherrima opera*. Praxiteles' most famous statue, the Aphrodite of Cnidus, was said to have had its own suitors. See O'Bryhim 2015: 419.

248 ***sculpsit***: Hellanicus (*FGrHist* 4 F 57), Asclepiades of Cyprus (*FGrHist* 752 F 1), Philostephanus (*FHG* III 31 fr. 13), and Apollodorus (3.182) make Pygmalion a king of Cyprus. In Philostephanus' account, he desires a preexisting cult statue (*simulacrum Veneris, quod sanctitatis apud Cyprios et religionis habebatur antiquae*), not one that he himself made.

ebur: although small dedicatory statuettes were sometimes sculpted in ivory, large statues made from this material depicted the gods (e.g. Zeus at Olympia and Athena Parthenos). To create them, plates of ivory were affixed to a wooden framework; see Lapatin 2001: 7–21; Salzman-Mitchell 2008: 295–297. Although a few ivory statues were made during the Hellenistic and Roman periods that depicted mortals, the intention was probably to link these individuals with divinity; see Lapatin 2001: 120–133. Cf. Dio Cassius 43.45 where the Senate has an ivory statue of Julius Caesar made so that it may join the statues of the gods in a procession in the Circus. Ovid may have had these ivory statues of the gods in mind at 15.792, where *mille locis lacrimavit ebur* during the funeral of Julius Caesar. Ovid speaks of an ivory statue of Venus that was carried in a procession in the circus at *Ars amatoria* 1.147–148.

formamque dedit: Pygmalion is responsible for the transformation of the ivory into an anthropomorphic statue, while Venus is responsible for the metamorphosis of the statue into a woman. He creates the semblance of perfection; she makes it a reality.

248–249 ***qua femina nasci | nulla potest***: the statue had a type of perfect beauty not found in mortals. This implies that the statue represents not a human woman but a goddess, as in the earlier version of the myth. The position of *nulla* at the beginning of line 249 emphasizes the negative.

249–251 These lines explain why Pygmalion is drawn to the statue. It projects, simultaneously, virginal modesty and sexuality.

250 ***credas***: generalizing second-person singular of the potential subjunctive. Orpheus begins to draw the audience into Pygmalion's delusion by suggesting that anyone could have make the same mistake. As at 220 (*roges*), Orpheus is really speaking to a human audience and not to the inanimate objects that he has attracted with his song.

251–276 Many of the details found in this part of Ovid's story also appear in the work of Aristaenetus (2.10), an epistolographer of the fifth century AD who tells the story of an artist who paints a picture of a young woman and falls in love with it. He speaks with the painting, believes that it is alive, kisses it, and urges it to have intercourse with him. Then he places it on a bed and treats it in an erotic manner. Finally the artist, who describes himself as insane, asks Cupid to give him a living woman like the one in his painting. Although the parallels to Ovid's version of the Pygmalion myth are striking, it is unlikely that Aristaenetus was using Ovid as his source, since he appears to have drawn his inspiration only from Greek authors (Lesky 1951: 174–176; Arnott 1973: 197–211). The most likely explanation for the similarities is that both he and Ovid were using Philostephanus' *About Cyprus*. Note that Admetus says that he will have a marble statue of Alcestis made that he will embrace in their bed after her death. See Euripides, *Alcestis* 348–353.

251   ***reverentia***: although this word can denote a sense of shame, it also refers to the religious awe that deities inspire. *OLD* s.v. *reverentia* 1. Therefore this may be another allusion to the identity of the statue as a cult image of Venus. See Knox 1986: 52–53.

   moueri: medio-passive. When used in erotic contexts, *moueri* denotes sexual movement. See *Amores* 2.4.14, 2.10.35; Adams 1990: 195.

252   ***ars adeo latet arte sua***: cf. *Ars amatoria* 2.313: *si latet, ars prodest*; Quintilian 1.11.3: *ea prima est ne ars esse videatur*. It has been suggested that this phrase, and indeed the entire myth of Pygmalion, is a metaphor for Ovid's creative process. See Bauer 1962: 16–17, Sharrock 1991, and Salzman-Mitchell 2008: 304–307.

252–253   ***haurit ... ignes***: cf. 8.325–326: *flammas ... hausit*.

254–255   ***an sit | corpus an illud ebur***: cf. 289: *corpus erat*.

255   ***illud***: this is the last time that the statue is described as an inanimate object. Subsequently the audience is encouraged to see it as Pygmalion does.

   nec adhuc ebur esse fatetur: "he does not admit that it is still ivory." Pygmalion refuses to trust his senses. He no longer views his creation as a statue, but as a woman. According to Anderson 1972: 497, Pygmalion "differs little from the other major psychological characters of Ovid, who live in a world of illusion that gradually replaces reality for them." For hallucinations in antiquity, see Harris 2013: 285–306.

256–257   ***oscula dat reddique putat loquiturque tenetque | et credit tactis digitos insidere membris***: Tarrant 2004 brackets 256 and replaces *et* with *sed* in 257. Hill 1992: 175 argues that "this line violently interrupts Pygmalion's otherwise gradual and subtle progress in his approach to the statue/girl." But surely Pygmalion fears that his enthusiastic embrace (*tenetque*, 256), not the mere act of touching (254), is what will bruise the statue (258). In any case, this line should be retained, since it is integral to Ovid's description of Pygmalion's mental state. Reed 1997: 225 suggests placing it after 258.

258 **metuit pressos ueniat ne livor in artus**: for bruises acquired during erotic encounters, see Ovid, *Amores* 1.7.41–42, 1.8.98, 3.14.34; Horace, *Odes* 1.13.11–12; Tibullus 1.6.13–14; Propertius 3.8.22. The lover of the Aphrodite of Cnidus was said to have left a mark on its thigh when he had intercourse with it; see Lucian, *Amores* 15.

259 **blanditias**: Pygmalion pays the statue compliments as though he were trying to seduce it; cf. 6.685, 7.817; *Ars amatoria* 1.480, 2.159.

259–263 Anderson 1972: 497–498 and Knox 1986: 53–59 argue that these inexpensive gifts indicate that Pygmalion is rejecting the role of *dives amator*, so despised by elegiac poets. Cf. Propertius 3.13.25–32, where the poet yearns for the days when a woman's affections could be won with gifts of colorful flowers, lilies, and birds. See also *Ars amatoria* (2.262–280), where Ovid advises the lover to give fruit, nuts, and birds. See Bömer 1958: 101–102 for other examples. These small gifts recall the inexpensive items that were given as votive offerings to deities; see Kyrieleis 1988: 215–221. Both interpretations are possible and, no doubt, intended.

260 **munera**: for *munera* as a lover's gifts, see 7.740, 7.750, 7.754, 13.831–839. This word can also refer to gifts presented to deities; see *OLD* s.v. *munus* 3. A close parallel is the agalmatophiliac who gave gifts to the Aphrodite of Cnidus with the intent of marrying the statue; see Philostratus, *Vita Apollonii* 6.40; [Lucian], *Amores* 16.

illi: the gender of this demonstrative pronoun is not readily apparent in the dative case. It could refer to the statue (neuter) or to a woman (feminine).

conchas: Ovid mentions Corinna's predilection for shells at *Amores* 2.11.13. For the link between Aphrodite and shells in cult, see Reece 1989: 33–40; Serwint 2002: 328–329. Pliny (*Naturalis historia* 32.5) reports that shellfish were sacred to Aphrodite on Cyprus, which may account for the large quantity of shells from inedible mollusks found in Cypriot sanctuaries; see Reece 1985: 340–371. A large shell found in a tomb at Salamis on Cyprus was inscribed, in the Cypriot syllabary, *a-po-ro-ta-o-i*, indicating that it was dedicated to Aphrodite; see Masson 1961: 314. Callimachus (*Epigram* 5 Pfeiffer) speaks of the dedication of a nautilus shell to Aphrodite. Statius (*Silvae* 1.2.118) mentions Aphrodite's birth in a conch, which is depicted in ancient art; see Grigson 1978: 36–39 and pls. 5–6. Owing to the shape of the openings of clam and conch shells, words that designated them became euphemisms for the vagina, both in Greek (Sophronius 25–26; Aristophanes, *Wasps* 583–589; Henderson 1991: 142) and in Latin (Plautus, *Rudens* 704; Adams 1990: 82).

teretes lapillos: see *Amores* 2.11.13 for Corinna's desire for colored stones from the sea, which would have been polished through the action of the sand and water. Smooth rocks are commonly found in sanctuaries of the goddess in Cyprus, as are beads and stone pendants. See Baumbach 2004: 37.

261 ***paruas volucres***: on women's predilection for birds in Greece and Rome, see 13.833; Theocritus 5.96–97; Catullus 2; Vergil, *Eclogues* 3.68–69; Propertius 3.13.25–32; Ovid, *Amores* 2.6. Aelian (*De natura animalium* 10.33–4 and 10.50; *Varia historia* 1.15) says that small birds were sacred to Aphrodite. She was associated with the dove at Paphos and Eryx. See also Aelian, *De natura animalium* 4.2; Athenaeus 9.394f–395a. Votive statuettes found in Cypriot sanctuaries depict men and women carrying small birds as offerings.

flores mille colorum: for the offering of flowers to deities, see Rouse 1902: 288–290 and 304. Ovid (*Fasti* 4.133–138) says that roses were offered to Venus Erycina in Rome, while Servius (*ad Aeneida* 1.335) says that they were given to Venus at Paphos. See also *POxy* 2688 for Cinyras' offering of roses to a statue of Aphrodite. For Aphrodite wearing flowers, see *Cypria* fr. 6.

262 ***liliaque***: līlĭăquē. *-que* is long, in imitation of a Homeric technique sometimes used in Latin poetry. Only the first *-que* in a pair can be lengthened. Wills 1996: 376–377 notes that most examples of this phenomenon in Latin occur in Vergil and in Ovid's *Metamorphoses*. For lilies as amatory gifts, see Propertius 3.13.29. Lilies were also given as dedicatory offerings, which may have had a connection to fertility. See Baumbach 2004: 118, 140.

pictasque pilas: painted balls are not mentioned elsewhere as a lover's gift. Several explanations have been adduced for its inclusion among Pygmalion's presents to the statue. Eros hits Anacreon with a purple ball at *PMG* 358, and this inspires Anacreon to pursue a girl. While this may be the equivalent of shooting him with an arrow, it does not make the ball a love gift. When a girl made the transition to womanhood, she went to the temple of a goddess and dedicated her toys, balls among them. See *Anthologia palatina* 6.280; Rouse 1902: 249–250. Since Pygmalion is giving balls to the statue, this would imply that he is a prepubescent girl. The popularity of ball games among Greeks and Romans of both sexes has also been noted; see Anderson 1972: 498 and Bömer 1980: 102. These balls were made of different materials and were sometimes colored purple, green, gold, or a combination of hues; see Mau in *RE* 2.2832–2834, s.v. *Ballspiel*. There is another possibility. Venus was sometimes worshiped in the form of a baetyl (an aniconic representation of a deity) on Cyprus. At Paphos, for example, her cult image was a conical stone. See Tacitus, *Historiae* 2.3; Maximus of Tyre 8.8; Philostratus, *Life of Apollonius of Tyana* 3.58. There is evidence to suggest that she was also worshipped in the form of a stone sphere. Painted balls carried by terracotta worshipers from Cyprus provide a parallel to the *pictae pilae* that Pygmalion gave his statue. Like the other objects on Ovid's list of gifts, these may have been votive offerings. See O'Bryhim 1996.

262–265 The addition of these expensive gifts contradicts the theory that Pygmalion is behaving like a poor lover.

262–263 ***ab arbore lapsas | Heliadum lacrimas***: the Heliades produced amber after their transformation into trees; cf. 2.364–366; *Amores* 3.12.37. Amber was also given to Roman brides (2.364–366), so this mention foreshadows Pygmalion's marriage to the statue. On the amber that was dedicated at a sanctuary of Hera, the goddess of marriage, see Baumbach 2004: 37 note 322.

263 ***ornat quoque vestibus artus***: Romans adorned cult statues with clothing and jewelry. Some coins minted in 62 BC depict a bust of Venus Erycina with a diadem, earrings, a necklace, jewels in her hair, and a robe; see Grueber 1910, vol. 1: pl. 47.21; vol. 3: 473. This was also a common practice in Greece; see Romano 1988: 130–133; Baumbach 2004: 36–37.

264–265 Compare the ornamentation of Cyparissus' stag, which was sacred to the nymphs (10.112–116). For gifts of jewelry to cult statues, see Pausanias 1.18.4, 7.23.5; Hyperides 3.24–26; Cicero, *De natura deorum* 3.83; Aelian, *Varia historia* 1.20, *De natura animalium* 10.50; Suetonius, *Galba* 18.2; Lactantius, *Divinae institutiones* 1.17, 2.4; Arnobius, *Adversus nationes* 6.21; see also Kroll 1982: 66, 75; Baumbach 2004: 37–38. Greek inscriptions speak of a specific category of priests, who dressed and ornamented cult images; see Romano 1988: 132 and note 65. During the Veneralia at Rome, women removed jewelry from the cult statue of Venus so that it could be washed. After the bath was complete, the statue was dried, its ornaments were replaced, and roses were presented to it; see Ovid, *Fasti* 4.133–138; Bömer 1980: 215–216; Schilling 1954: 226–233; Fantham 1998: 117. For figurines of a Cypriot goddess wearing jewelry, see Karageorghis 1987: pl. 12, 57 T.170/63; Sophocleous 1985: 98 and pl. 23.1. Naïskoi from Amathus contain models of a cult statue of a goddess covered in jewelry; see Sophocleous 1985: 123–124 and pl. 30.4.

265 ***redimicula***: bands that extend from a headdress to the shoulders. Cf. Ovid, *Fasti* 4.133–138, which mentions golden *redimicula* on a cult statue of Venus at Rome. See also Vergil, *Aeneid* 9.616; Juvenal 2.84; Isidore 19.13.3.

266 ***nec nuda minus formosa uidetur***: Pygmalion's statue is a nude that he himself has dressed and ornamented. He removes its clothing before he lifts it onto a bed in the next line. This is the first time that indisputably feminine adjectives are employed to describe the statue. The audience now sees what Pygmalion sees – a real woman.

stratis concha Sidonide tinctis: purple coverlets were placed on the marriage bed. For the *lectus genialis*, see Catullus 64.47–49; Juvenal 10.334; Hersch 2010: 214–221.

267   **hanc** replaces the ambiguous *illi* (260), leaving us in no doubt that Pygmalion regards the statue as a woman.

268   ***tori sociam***: cf. 1.620, 10.635, 14.678. For *torus* as marriage bed, see 1.353, 6.431, 7.91, 7.709. Pygmalion now has the *thalami consors* whom he previously lacked (246), so he no longer lives *sine coniuge caelebs* (245).

269   ***reponit***: just as Pygmalion places the nude statue onto the marriage bed, Ovid interrupts this erotic scene and jumps ahead, to the festival of Venus, which takes place on the next day.

270   ***festa dies Veneris tota celeberrima Cypro***: Ovid does not name the festival. Strabo (14.6.3) describes an annual procession to Paphos. Given the participation of Pygmalion, a statue, and Venus, it may have been a festival connected with the sacred marriage rite. For this rite on Cyprus, see Young 2005: 28–44.

   tota ... Cypro: *Cyprus* is a feminine of the second declension.

271   ***pandis inductae cornibus aurum***: compare the widely spreading horns of Cyparissus' sacred stag. They are covered in gold, which reveals the animal's sacred nature (109–111).

   aurum: retained (or "Greek") accusative. See Woodcock 1959: §19.iii: "The normal Latin method of expressing these ideas is by the ablative case, whether instrumental or of respect, and the accusative was introduced and developed by the poets in imitation of Greek." See also Courtney 2004: 425–431. *OLD* s.v. *induco* 16b. Cf. 7.161: *inductaque cornibus aurum | victima vota cadit*.

272–273   ***conciderant ictae nivea cervice iuvencae | turaque fumabat***: Tacitus (*Historiae* 2.3.2) says that only fire was permitted on the altar at the temple of Venus at Paphos. Cf. Vergil, *Aeneid* 1.415–417. Animals were killed only for the purpose of divination; and they had to be male. Ovid's description of the ritual clearly contradicts these strictures. Perhaps Orpheus altered the gender of the victim in order to exclude the possibility of sacrificing the transformed Cerastae to Venus (237).

   ictae: sacrificial animals were struck with an ax or a hammer in order to be immobilized before their throats were cut. See Aldrete 2014: 28–50.

   cum munere functus ad aras | constitit: the phrase *munere functus* suggests that Pygmalion is carrying out a duty of a religious nature; cf. Vergil, *Aeneid* 6.885–886; Tacitus, *Annales* 3.2.1. He may be performing the same role as his descendant, Cinyras, who was the priest of Aphrodite at Paphos (Pindar, *Pythian* 2.15–17). According to Clement of Alexandria (*Protrepticus* 2.33, 3.40), Cinyras and his descendants were buried in Aphrodite's temple at Paphos.

274–275 timide: Pygmalion couches his prayer in ambiguous language because he does not want the public to know that he desires the statue.

275–276 "sit coniunx, opto," non ausus, "eburnea virgo": there is no indication that Pygmalion is asking the goddess to make the statue come to life. Rather he is petitioning her for permission to marry an inanimate object. Similarly, Myrrha asks that she be allowed to marry someone "like her father" (364), when she really wants her father. Both seek fulfillment of their unusual desires, although they do not dare to say so openly. Compare Philostratus' agalmatophiliac who wants to marry the Aphrodite of Cnidus at *Life of Apollonius of Tyana* 6.40.

277–278 sensit ... | vota quid illa velint: i.e. that Pygmalion wanted to marry the statue. Venus takes this one step further by transforming the statue into a woman.

277 Venus aurea: cf. 15.761; Homer, *Iliad* 3.64; Vergil, *Aeneid* 10.

278–279 For the omen produced by a fire on an altar, see *Ex Ponto* 4.9.53–54.

278 amici: adjective.

279 ter: the number three figured prominently in Roman ritual. See Lease 1919: 61–62.

280 simulacra: this word can refer to statues of deities; see *OLD* s.v. *simulacrum* 3. For the poetic plural, cf. 7.358.

    petit: "he paid amorous attention to." Cf. 13.755; Sallust, *Bellum Catilinae* 25.3; Horace, *Carmina* 4.11.21; Adams 1990: 212 note 1.

    puellae: "lover." *OLD* s.v. *puella* 3. This sense is common in elegy; see Knox 1986: 54. Its use here indicates that Pygmalion had a romantic relationship with the statue before the latter came to life.

281 incumbensque toro dedit oscula: Pygmalion had placed the statue on the bed before he went to the temple of Venus (267). It is still there when he returns.

    incumbensque: "lying on" rather than "leaning over." *OLD* s.v. *incumbo* 2.

    visa: agrees with *puella*. Pygmalion sees the statue as a woman even before it has been transformed by Venus.

    tepere: "to warm" and "to feel the warmth of love." *OLD* s.v. *tepeo* 1 and 2; 11.225; *Ars amatoria* 2.360.

282 manibus quoque pectora temptat: *temptare* can mean "to test" or "to fondle"; see Propertius 1.3.15; also Adams 1990: 156 note 2. For the fondling of the breasts in erotic poetry, see 8.606; *Ars amatoria* 1.4.3; *Fasti* 2.803–804.

283 mollescit: the more he fondles the statue, the softer it becomes. This is essentially what Pygmalion did at 256–258 and 267–269 without causing a transformation. Venus brought about the metamorphosis at this point to reward Pygmalion for his piety.

positoque rigore: compare Cyparissus' transformation into a tree (*sumptoque rigore*, 139) and the metamorphosis of the Propoetides into stone (241–242).

284 **subsedit digitis ceditque**: what Pygmalion imagined in 257 (*tactis digitos insidere membris*) has now come to pass.

284–286 Ancient artists sometimes created portraits in wax (*Heroides* 13.155; *Remedia amoris* 723–724). They also used wax for encaustic painting, which made statues seem even more lifelike (Pliny, *Naturalis historia* 35.122–123).

284–285 **Hymettia ... | cera**: Mount Hymettus near Athens was famous for its honey.

287 **stupet**: cf. 64, where Orpheus was struck dumb (*stupuit*) when his wife returned to Hades. Pygmalion was shocked by this unexpected event, which suggests that he did not ask Venus to turn his statue into a woman. There is no indication that he was disappointed when he returned home to a lifeless statue. Indeed, he continued to kiss and fondle the statue just as he did before he made his prayer to Venus. The goddess gave him more than he asked for when she transformed the statue into a living woman.

288 **amans**: cf. *vidit amantem*, 294.

vota: "a prayer" or "what he had wished for." *OLD* s.v. *votum* 2a, e.

retractat: this verb is ambiguous. It can mean "to retract"; see *OLD* s.v. *retracto* 4a. If so, then Pygmalion revokes his request to marry the ivory statue because he prefers a living woman. It can also mean "to handle a second time"; see *OLD* s.v. *retracto* 5. According to Adams 1990: 186–187, it can refer to fondling or any number of other sexual acts, including intercourse. After a short break in which he marvels at the miracle of Venus, Pygmalion resumes what he started at 282.

290 **Paphius ... heros**: cf. 50, where Orpheus is *Rhodopeius heros*. Pygmalion has done nothing to earn this title, aside from supporting Orpheus' views on the lustfulness of women. Miller 1988: 208 suggests that this is a nod to an earlier version of the myth, in which Pygmalion was a king.

Paphius: this is anachronistic because Pygmalion's daughter, Paphos, has not yet been born.

concipit: "offer up." *OLD* s.v. *concipio* 12a.

290–291 **oraque tandem | ore suo non falsa premit**: he is no longer kissing a statue (256, 281), but a real woman. In myth, people usually turn into things. Here the process is inverted.

291 **grates**: this word refers to thanks given specifically to deities. *OLD* s.v. *grates*. Compare Hippomenes (681–682), who forgot to give thanks to Venus for her help in securing Atalanta.

tandem: this picks up *diu* and *interea* at 246–247. After living without a wife for a long time and resorting to a statue for sexual release, Pygmalion finally has a real spouse.

291-292   ***oraque tandem | ore sua***: cf. *oscula dat reddique putat* (293).

293   ***sensit***: cf. *tamquam sensura* (269).

erubuit, timidum: contrast the Propoetides, who could not blush because they, unlike Pygmalion's statue, were sexually experienced (241).

ad lumina: the presence of more than one celestial light suggests that this event took place at night, which is when marriages were consummated.

294   ***pariter cum caelo vidit amantem***: this description suggests that Pygmalion and his lover are in a Roman atrium, with its characteristic impluvium open to the sky. This is where the symbolic marriage bed may have been located on the wedding night. See Treggiari 1991: 168; Hersch 2010: 214–216.

295   ***coniugio, quod fecit, adest dea***: it is odd that the marriage gods Juno and Hymenaeus were not present alongside Venus. All three attended the marriage of Iphis and Ianthe in the previous book (9.796). The emphasis on Venus here suggests that the goddess was not merely a substitute for the wedding gods. As the incarnation of the cult statue, she herself was the bride in the sacred marriage rite (Hardie 2002: 190). Note the story about a man from Amathus who puts a ring on a nude statue of Aphrodite, says that he is married to her, and is visited in his bedroom by the goddess, who has intercourse with him (Lavagnini 1963: 322–325).

adest: this verb is used to indicate a divine epiphany. Cf. 4 (*adfuit ille*), where Hymenaeus reluctantly attends the wedding of Orpheus and Eurydice.

297   ***Paphon***: Greek feminine accusative singular. Some manuscripts, however, have *quo*, which would make Paphos a male. Cf. the scholion to Pindar, *Pythian* 2.27a. Note, however, *editus hac* in line 298. Apollodorus (3.14.4) calls her "Metharme."

de qua tenet insula nomen: this information is unique to Ovid; see Reed 1997: 230. Note that the adjective *Paphia* can mean "sacred to Venus." *OLD* s.v. *Paphius* 2.

Cinyras and Myrrha

Myrrha, the daughter of king Cinyras, develops an incestuous desire for her father. Despite his attempts to find a suitable husband for her, Myrrha rejects all her suitors. Although she tries to persuade herself that her lust is sanctioned by nature insofar as many animals have intercourse with their parents, she cannot bring herself to accept that what she feels for her father is proper. Believing that death is the only way out of her situation, she decides to hang herself, but she is stopped at the last minute by her aged nurse. The old woman eventually discovers that the object of Myrrha's affection is her own father. She is horrified, but offers to help Myrrha rather than allow her to die. When the queen leaves the palace for a nocturnal festival, the nurse brings Myrrha to an inebriated Cinyras, who has been told that she is simply a young woman who is in love with him. After they have intercourse in total darkness over a period of several days, Cinyras becomes curious about what his lover looks like. He lights a lamp, discovers that she is his daughter, and chases her from the palace at swordpoint. Myrrha flees to Arabia, where she turns into a myrrh bush and, in due course, produces Adonis, the son of Cinyras.

The story of Myrrha appears in numerous sources whose details vary, especially with regard to the ethnicity of the characters (Atallah 1966: 33–39; Baurain 1980: 277–291; Reed 1997: 231–232). Some say that Myrrha's father was a king named Theias, the son of Belus (see e.g. Antoninus Liberalis 34). Because "Theias" and "Belus" are Hellenized variants of the names of the Phoenician gods El and Baal (Robertson 1982: 351), this version of the myth must have originated in the Levant. Indeed, Apollodorus (3.14.4), Hyginus (*Fabulae* 58, 270), and Oppian (*Halieutica* 3.404–405) make Theias the king of the Assyrians, an appellation that was synonymous with "Syrians" (Dalley 1998: 94). According to Antoninus Liberalis, Myrrha was born on Mount Lebanon, while Strabo (16.2.18) locates the palace of Cinyras at Byblos, where Lucian (*De dea Syria* 9) places the temple of Aphrodite that he built.

There is also a strong connection between Cinyras and Cyprus. According to Apollodorus (3.14.3), Cinyras migrated to Cyprus from Cilicia and married Metharme, the daughter of Pygmalion. Other authors associate him with specific Cypriot cities. The scholiast on Pindar, *Pythian* 2.28 makes him the son of Eurymedon and Paphia (Paphos). Stephanus of Byzantium (s.v. Ἀμαθοῦς) says that his mother's name was Amathousa (Amathus). He produced a daughter named Cyprus and two sons, Koureus and Marieus, who gave their names to the cities of Kourion and Marion. Nonnus (13.452) derives the name of the town Cinyreia from Cinyras. Indeed, Cinyreia may be another name for Amathus, which would link Cinyras to Ovid's Amathusian myths (Baurain 1981: 361–372). Hyginus conflates the Levantine and the Cypriot traditions by making Cinyras king of Assyria and the son of Paphos. Similarly, Ovid makes Cinyras the grandson of Pygmalion and has him chase Myrrha to the Near East. In this way he continues the Cypriot theme at the beginning of the story and then returns Cinyras to the place where his myth originated.

Ovid was almost certainly influenced by Cinna's *Zmyrna*, a popular *epyllion* that earned the praise of Catullus (c. 95). Only three fragments of this poem remain. They deal with Myrrha's devastating passion, the growth of Adonis in her womb, and her sorrow after her father discovers that he was having intercourse with her. Judging from [Vergil], *Ciris* 490–507, *Zmyrna* probably also contained a nurse scene, as did Ovid's version (Lyne 1978: 206–385; Knox 1983: 309–311).

Orpheus draws a sharp contrast between the story of Myrrha and the myth of Pygmalion, which precedes it. Both characters reject potential lovers, but for different reasons: Pygmalion wants the love of a pure woman, Myrrha wants an incestuous relationship with her father. Their unions take place during a religious ritual: Pygmalion honors Venus at her festival, Myrrha defiles the rites of Ceres. Venus legitimizes Pygmalion's union through her presence at the consummation of his marriage, whereas Myrrha's "wedding" is a perversion of the Roman marriage rite. In the end, Pygmalion is rewarded, while Myrrha is punished: the stone statue becomes human, Myrrha becomes wood. Both unions produce children: Paphos enables Pygmalion's line to continue, Adonis brings it to an end.

Despite Orpheus' attempt to make Myrrha into an anti-Pygmalion, she is not an unsympathetic character (Nagle 1983: 301–315). The unwillingness of any deity to take responsibility for Myrrha's incestuous desire suggests that her punishment is an extreme act that would bring disrepute on its divine instigator. Its assignment to one of the Furies exculpates Myrrha from personal responsibility for her feelings: her desire for her father is not due to a character flaw, but to an uncontrollable external force. She is determined to kill herself rather than indulge in behavior that she knows is wrong, but she is blackmailed into having intercourse with her father by the nurse, who threatens to tell him about her attempted suicide (Prince 2011: 59–64). When Cinyras discovers what she has done, Myrrha admits culpability and asks that she no longer pollute the living or the dead. While she does fit Orpheus' theme of "women punished for their illicit lusts," her sexual misbehavior (like that of the Propoetides) was thrust upon her by external forces.

298   **editus hac ille est**: this phrase provides a genealogical transition between the stories of Pygmalion and Myrrha.

298–299   **qui si sine prole fuisset, | inter felices Cinyras potuisset haberi**: lack of offspring would have been disastrous for a king, because he would lack descendants to inherit his throne. This line emphasizes the enormity of the crime that his daughter will perpetrate; it is better for his house to become extinct than for such an atrocity to occur. His line will end with the death of his son, Adonis.

299   **Cinyras**: the son of Paphos and the grandson of Pygmalion. "Cinyras" derives from the name of the Levantine god of the lyre, Kinaru, which accounts for Cinyras' association with the lyre in Greek literature; see Brown 1965: 187–219 and Franklin 2006: 46–47. Cf. Eustathius, *ad Homeri Iliadem* 11.20.

300–303   Once again, Orpheus is not speaking to trees and animals but to a human audience. Barchiesi 2001: 61–62 sees this as a parody of the bard's civilizing mission (Horace, *Ars poetica* 391–398): "Orpheus sings to his audience of animals a theme which *to them* cannot possibly be of any harm."

300   ***procul hinc***: this phrase excludes the polluted from the company of the pure at rituals; cf. 7.255–256; Callimachus, *Hymns* 2; Vergil, *Aeneid* 6.258. Similar phrases also appear in Orphic texts; see Graf 2012: 13–16. Orpheus has inverted this idea by excluding guiltless fathers and daughters from hearing a story about morally reprehensible behavior. Cf. *Ars amatoria* 2.1.3: *este procul, vittae tenues, insigne pudoris,* | *quaeque tegis medios, instita longa, pedes*.

   parentes: "fathers."

301   ***mulcebunt***: "charm." *OLD* s.v. *mulceo* 4. Cf. Vergil, *Georgics* 4.510: [*Orpheum*] *mulcentem tigres*; Seneca, *Medea* 229: *qui saxa cantu mulcet*. Orpheus knows the power of his song. Neither the inhabitants of the underworld, nor nature itself, nor his current audience can resist it. Therefore he must issue the following warning, so that his song may not have an ill effect on them.

303   ***facti ... poenam***: fathers and daughters will be deterred from committing incest by Myrrha's punishment.

304   ***admissum***: "permitted." *OLD* s.v. *admitto* 10.

   natura: compare Iphis, whose lesbianism was against nature (*at non vult natura*, 9.758) and Myrrha, who claims that nature is not opposed to incestuous relationships (*et quod natura remittit*, 330).

305   This line does not appear in several manuscripts. Schrader deletes it, although he admits he has doubts (*haud scio an recte*). The fact that the description in 305–306 progresses from smaller to larger geographical areas argues for its retention.

   gentibus Ismariis: the Cicones, who live on the southern coast of Thrace. Cf. 2: *Ciconumque Hymenaeus ad oras*.

   nostro ... orbi: "our region." *OLD* s.v. *orbis* 13. A larger area of Thrace than just the territory of the Cicones.

306   ***huic terrae***: Thrace in general.

   quod abest regionibus illis | ***quae tantum genuere nefas***: the incest occurred on Cyprus. If Orpheus is drawing a distinction between the West and the luxurious East (Bömer 1958: 118–119; Hall 1989: 189–190), this statement is hypocritical, because the Thracians were known for their drunkenness and lustfulness; cf. 6.438–485, 11.1–43; *Heroides* 5.5; Cornelius Nepos, *Alcibiades* 11.4; Barchiesi 2001: 61–62.

307 **genuere nefas**: cf. the personification of Amathus with *genuisse* (220–221).

nefas: Myrrha will describe her incestuous desire in the same way at 322: *hoc prohibite nefas*.

307–308 **amomo, | cinnamaque costumque suum**: spices from the Near East. For the eastern origin of these words, see Reed 1997: 235.

308 **cinnamaque**: *cīnnămăquē*. Cf. 262 for the epic lengthening of *-que*.

308–309 **sudataque ligno | tura ferat**: probably frankincense. Myrrh is also exuded through the bark. Cf. Vergil, *Eclogues* 8.54: *pinguia corticibus sudent electra myricae*.

309 **floresque alios**: like the spices listed in 307–308, these flowers also produce aromas. Cf. Lucretius 2.417: *Panchaeos ... odores*.

Panchaia tellus: *Pānchāiă*. Vergil (*Georgics* 2.139) calls the region *turiferis Panchaia pinguis harenis*. According to Euhemerus (Diodorus Siculus 6.1), Panchaia is an island in the Indian Ocean. Ovid locates it in Arabia (478). See also Lucretius 2.417.

310 **dum ferat et murram**: clause of proviso. The wealth derived from the spice trade is not worth the ignominy of having produced Myrrha. For the myrrh trade, see Atallah 1966: 44–47; Miller 1969: 104–105.

tanti: genitive of value.

nova ... arbor: the myrrh bush has already been mentioned at 3.555, 4.393, 5.53.

310–337 These lines (310, 314–315, 318, 329–331, 336–337) are punctuated by *sententiae* ("aphorisms") that provide transitions between the various parts of the story. For Ovid's use of *sententiae* and Quintilian's disapproval of them, see Quintilian 4.1.77.

311 **ipse negat ... Cupido**: Cupid will not accept responsibility for Myrrha's illicit desire for her father. Some sources (Plutarch 310f; Oppian, *Halieutica* 3.404–407) say that Venus punished her, but do not specify the reason. Hyginus (*Fabulae* 58.1) says that Venus directed her son to shoot the girl with his arrow because Myrrha's mother had rated her daughter's beauty higher than that of the goddess. The scholiast on Theocritus (1.109A) blames Myrrha herself, who claimed that her hair was more beautiful than Aphrodite's. Apollodorus (3.14.4) says that Myrrha refused to honor the goddess. This implies that she wanted to remain a virgin and that the goddess forced an unnatural lust upon her as a punishment, just as in the myth of the Propoetides (238–242). Ovid's audience, which was familiar with these precedents, knew that Myrrha did not choose to desire her father but was compelled to do so by Venus. Knox 1983: 309–311

believes that Cupid's denial of responsibility is Ovid's signal that he is departing from the traditional version found in Cinna's *Zmyrna*.

312   *faces*: Cupid's primary weapon is the arrow (525–528), but he also wields the torch. See 1.461; Tibullus 2.1.82; Propertius 3.16.16. The Furies, who are blamed for Myrrha's love at 313–314, also carry torches. Cf. 4.481–482: *Tisiphone madefactam sanguine sumit, | importuna facem*.

   tumidisque adflavit echidis: cf. Vergil, *Aeneid* 7.346–348, where Allecto uses a snake from her hair to drive Amata insane.

   isto: this adjective can have a pejorative connotation, which is emphasized by its placement at the end of the line.

314   *e tribus una soror*: according to Apollodorus (1.1.4), they are named Allecto, Tisiphone, and Megara. They usually punish crimes against parents, but here they inspire a crime. The idea is that the motivation for such a hideous act must have originated in the underworld.

315–355   Myrrha's argument for and against her love finds parallels in the stories of Medea (7.11–71), Byblis (9.474–516), Iphis (9.726–763), and Atalanta (611–635).

314–315   *scelus ... scelus*: this *sententia* provides a transition between Orpheus' introduction and the story of Myrrha.

315–316   *undique lecti | te cupiunt proceres*: cf. Antoninus Liberalis 34.1. Myrrha could have chosen a husband from this group of eligible bachelors, but chose her father instead (317–318). Other characters in the *Metamorphoses* had several suitors, too: Daphne (1.478); Narcissus (3.353); Deianira (9.9–10); Atalanta (560–707); Scylla (13.735).

315   *lecti*: this adjective commonly refers to youths who are involved in competitions such as the *thalami certamen* (317). Cf. 8.300, Catullus 64.4, Vergil, *Aeneid* 8.606; see also Reed 1997: 237.

316   *totoque oriente*: Cyprus and the Near East.

317   *ad thalami certamen*: metaphorically here but literally in the case of Atalanta, where the suitors must win a footrace to marry her (560–680). There is no athletic contest for the hand of Myrrha.

317–318   *ex omnibus unum | ... in omnibus unus*: a *sententia* that provides a transition between the competition for Myrrha and her *suasoria* on the topic of incest. Note the nearly identical line endings.

318   *dum ne sit in omnibus unus*: clause of proviso.

319   *foedoque repugnant amori*: compare Byblis, whose resistance to her incestuous desires is minimal (9.509–510). Medea also uses *repugnat* at the beginning of her soliloquy, as she fights her love for Jason (7.11).

320 ***quo mente feror***: cf. Byblis: *quo feror?*, 9.509; *Ars amatoria* 3.667: *quo feror insanus?*

321 ***pietas***: cf. 7.72 for Pietas as a goddess. For perversions of *pietas* among fathers and daughters in the *Metamorphoses*, see Prince 2011: 39–68.

sacrataque iura parentum: cf. 8.499: *pia iura parentum*.

322-323 ***hoc prohibite nefas scelerique resistite nostro, | si tamen hoc scelus est***: all of Myrrha's propositions in her *suasoria* are met with rationalizations and counterpropositions introduced by *si tamen* (323), *sed enim* (323), or *tamen* (331).

nefas: Myrrha agrees with Orpheus' assessment of her incestuous impulse (307).

324-329 When Myrrha's resolution begins to waiver, she resorts to ethical relativism. She adduces parallels, first from the animal kingdom and then from other cultures, to argue that incest is not against nature; see Hall 1989: 189–190. Compare the *exempla* from the animal world that Iphis adduces against lesbianism (9.731–734). Myrrha moves from large to small (horse, goat, bird) to imply that all warm-blooded animals practice incest; contrast Orpheus' movement from small to large in his praise of lands that are free from incest (305–307). For the association of incest with animals, see also 7.386–387: *dextera Cyllene est, in qua cum matre Menephron | concubiturus erat saevarum more ferarum*.

324 ***hanc Venerem***: metonymy that refers to incest here.

pietas: the human *pietas* to which Myrrha appealed at 321 is now defined by animal behavior.

325 ***turpe***: this adjective modifies *ferre* in 326.

326 ***ferre patrem tergo***: this phrase is the subject of *habetur*.

329 ***felices quibus ista licent***: the Greek comic playwright Philemon (fr. 93 CAF) says that animals are happy because they are not burdened by human laws.

329-321 ***humana malignas | cura dedit leges, et quod natura remittit | invidia iura negant***: this *sententia* provides a bridge between animal and human incest. Incest is permitted by natural law, but prohibited by human law. See Feeney 1991: 195–196. Myrrha echoes Byblis (9.551–555) when she rejects laws against incest.

leges ... | iura: written law vs. unwritten conventions.

330 ***cura***: "anxiety."

331-334 In contrast to Byblis, who adduces divine precedents for incest (9.497–501, 554–555), Myrrha resorts to ethnography. For ancient cultures that practiced incest, see Reed 1997: 240.

332–333 ***et nato genetrix et nata parenti | iungitur***: *iungere* can refer to marriage or to intercourse; see Adams 1990: 179–180. For the "noun shift" (dative, nominative/nominative, dative), see Wills 1996: 272–278. Seneca the Elder (*Controversiae* 2.2.9) says that Ovid employed it in his declamations.

333 ***pietas***: having spoken of *pietas* in her own culture (321) and of *pietas* among animals (324), Myrrha now discusses the notion of *pietas* in other peoples.

334 ***me miseram***: this phrase is commonly used by unhappy lovers; see Reed 1997: 241.

335 ***fortunaque loci laedor***: i.e. because she does not live in a culture that permits incest.

quid in ista revolvor? Myrrha began her *suasoria* by shunning her incestuous desire with *quo mente feror? quid molior?* (320). She ends her argument with *quid in ista revolvor*, as she rejects arguments in favor of incest and returns to her senses.

336 ***interdictae***: legal language that recalls Myrrha's earlier mention of *leges* and *iura* (330–331).

336–337 ***dignus ... est***: this *sententia* is a transition between Myrrha's argument in favor of incest and her decision not to pursue it.

338 ***Cinyrae, Cinyrae***: genitive, then dative. Here and at 380, Myrrha prefers to use *Cinyras* instead of *pater*.

339–340 ***ipsaque damno | est mihi proximitas***: cf. Byblis' desire to have been born of a different family than her brother (*omnia, di facerent, essent communia nobis, | praeter avos*, 9.490–491).

339 ***meus est, non est meus***: chiasmus.

340 ***proximitas; aliena***: antonyms. The contrast between these words is amplified by their contiguity.

proximitas: "kinship."

aliena: "unrelated."

341–342 ***ire libet procul hinc | dum scelus effugiam***: like Orpheus' audience (*procul hinc*, 300), Myrrha should leave before she is morally and physically corrupted.

342 ***dum scelus effugiam***: clause of proviso.

343–344 ***tangamque loquarque | osculaque admoveam***: Pygmalion behaves in the same way at 256–258.

344–345 ***ultra. | ultra***: According to Quintilian (9.3.44), the repetition of a word at the end of one line and the beginning of the next is often found in poetry. See Wills 1996: 394–397.

344 **si nil conceditur ultra**: i.e. intercourse with Cinyras, which is rejected as a possibility in the next line.

347 **et matris paelex et adultera patris**: chiasmus.

348 **tune soror nati genetrixque vocabere fratris?** this foreshadows the birth of Adonis, who is both the son and the brother of Myrrha.

349-351 Myrrha fears punishment from the Furies, who have snakes for hair. They punish with insanity those who commit crimes against their parents. Orpheus also identifies the Furies as the cause of Myrrha's incestuous desire for her father (313-314).

350-351 **quas facibus saevis oculos atque ora petentes noxia corda vident**: quas noxia corda vident, petentes oculos atque ora facibus saevis.

352 **nefas**: at the end of her *suasoria*, Myrrha comes back to her original description of her feelings for her father (*hoc prohibite nefas*, 322).

352 **ne concipe**: archaic use of *ne* with the imperative.

352-353 **neve potentis | concubitu vetito naturae pollue foedus**: Myrrha contradicts the argument that she made at 330-331: *quod natura remittit | invidia iura negant*.

354 **velle puta**: supply *te*.

pius: cf. 321, where Myrrha calls on *pietas sacrataque iura parentum*. Cinyras adheres to traditional way of thinking.

memorque est moris: as king, Cinyras must not deviate from the customs of his society. Myrrha supported her argument in favor of incest with examples from foreign cultures, which run contrary to those of her own land.

355 **furor**: "mad passion." OLD s.v. *furor²* 3a, 4a; see Knox 1986: 20-21. Cf. 397: *seu furor est, habeo quae carmine sanet et herbis*.

356 **copia digna procorum**: transferred epithet. Cf. 574, where a crowd of suitors pursue Atalanta.

358 **cuius velit esse mariti**: compare Atalanta, who choses her husband by means of a footrace (568-574).

359 **silet**: Myrrha also remains quiet when questioned by her nurse (*muta silet virgo*, 389).

in vultibus haerens: Myrrha cannot take her eyes off her father.

360 **aestuat et tepido suffundit lumina rore**: *aestuat* describes Myrrha's internal emotional state, while her tears are an external manifestation of it. Cinyras misreads her tears as virginal fear caused by the selection of a husband (361). Here he misunderstands signs; next he will misinterpret words (364).

aestuat: "burns with desire." Cf. Byblis (9.465) and Ianthe (9.765). This word also describes floods and stormy seas, which suggests that Myrrha's emotions are overwhelming.

361   ***virginei ... timoris***: genitive of characteristic.

363–364   ***qualem | optet habere virum***: instead of asking for the name of Myrrha's preferred suitor (357–358), Cinyras now asks more generally about the characteristics that she desires in a husband.

   habere: this word can mean "to marry" or "to have intercourse with." See Adams 1990: 187.

364   ***similem tibi***: cf. Pygmalion's prayer (*similis ... eburnae*, 276), which hid his true desire. Antoninus Liberalis (34) says that Myrrha postponed her decision through trickery.

365   ***non intellectam vocem conlaudat***: Cinyras does not understand Myrrha's ambiguous response. He misunderstands again when the nurse describes his potential lover as *par est ... Myrrhae* (441). The spondees that dominate this line emphasize its ominous import.

366–367   ***esto | tam pia semper***: Myrrha insisted that *pietas* does not condemn incest (324). Now she cannot even look at Cinyras, because she knows that she has perverted this concept (366–367).

367   ***virgo***: note the placement of this word at the end of the line, which may suggest sarcasm.

368–369   ***curasque et corpora somnus | solverat***: zeugma. Note the alliteration, especially the hard "c" followed by the soft "s," which gives the impression of resistance melting away.

369   ***Cinyreia***: Cĭnўrēĭă.

   pervigil: on women who endure sleepless nights because of passion, cf. 6.490–493, 7.185–187 and 634–635, 8.81–84, 9.472; Vergil, *Aeneid* 4.522–532.

370   ***carpitur***: "she is consumed." *OLD* s.v. *carpo* 7b.

   furiosaque: this could be nominative or accusative. If accusative, Myrrha recognizes that her prayers are insane (*furiosaque vota*). If nominative, she herself is insane. Cf. 420, where Myrrha is *furibunda*.

   vota retractat: "she recalls her prayer" (*et o vellem similis furor esset in illo*, 335). Cf. 288, where the same phrase is used for Pygmalion's reaction to the vivification of his statue.

372–376   The tottering tree metaphor is usually applied to a warrior; cf. Vergil, *Aeneid* 4.441–446. Ovid uses it here to describe the emotional vacillation of a girl who is sexually obsessed with her father.

373   ***trabs***: metonymy for the tree.

375   **vario:** "numerous and varied." *OLD* s.v. *varius* 4.

378   **mors placet:** Myrrha prefers to die rather than give in to her incestuous desire for her father. Reed 1997: 246 notes that the attempted suicide does not occur in other versions. By including it, Ovid makes Myrrha a more sympathetic character as she tries to stop herself from committing incest; cf. Euripides' Phaedra at *Hippolytus* 400–401. Hanging is a common method of suicide for mythic women; see Sophocles, *Antigone* 1220–1221, *Oedipus Tyranus* 1264; Euripides, *Hippolytus* 778; Hyginus, *Fabulae* 47 and 130; Nonnus 16.390–394.

379   **zona:** a long strip of material that was wound around a woman's waist. Loosening the *zona* is a metaphor for losing virginity. See *OLD* s.v. *zona* 2b; also Anderson 1972: 509. The bridegroom cuts it on the wedding night; see Hersch 2010: 109–112. Cf. Horace, *Odes* 3.27.58–60, where Europa has the option of hanging herself by her *zona*. By loosening her own *zona* and then killing herself, the woman makes herself (metaphorically) the bride of Hades. Cf. *Anthologia palatina* 7.182, 183, 185, 188, 492, and 547.

380   **Cinyra:** Greek vocative. Here and at 338, Myrrha prefers to say *Cinyras* rather than *pater*. It is difficult to understand how Cinyras would intuit the reason why his daughter killed herself, especially given his propensity to misinterpret evidence (361, 365, 441). Compare Phaedra, who left a note to explain her motivation (Euripides, *Hippolytus* 856–886).

  causam te: cf. Byblis' last words in the letter to her brother: *neve merere meo subscribi causa sepulchro* (9.563).

382   **fidas nutricis ad auras:** this is a transferred epithet for *fidae nutricis ad auras*. Compare the character of the nurse in [Vergil], *Ciris* 220–285, whose reference to Myrrha (238) reveals her pedigree. See Lyne 1978: 85–86; Hollis 2007: 33. The nurse is a stock character in tragedy and comedy, where she tries to assist her *alumna* with her love affair; cf. 14.703–706; Parthenius 21. See Lightfoot 1999: 498; Nicolopoulos 2003: 54–55; Rhode 1900: 174.

383   **limen servantis:** the old nurse guards the door to Myrrha's bedroom and, consequently, protects her virginity. Cf. Tibullus 1.3.83–84: *at tu casta precor maneas, sanctique pudoris | adsideat custos sedula semper anus*. Antoninus Liberalis (34) names the nurse "Hippolyte," perhaps as a nod to the nurse in Euripides' *Hippolytus*, who found herself in a similar situation. For similarities between Ovid's myth and *Hippolytus*, see Thomas 1998: 100–104.

384–388 Note the parataxis and the repeated use of *-que*, which makes it seem as though everything is happening quickly.

384   **anus:** Ovid emphasizes the old age of the nurse several times (391–392, 396, 407, 414, 424–425). Although she is physically weak, she has great influence over her ward. Had it not been for her threats (417–418), Myrrha

would have avoided infamy by killing herself. For the aged in Ovid's *Metamorphoses*, see Nicolopoulos 2003: 48–60.

384–385 **mortisque paratae | instrumenta**: the *zona* and, presumably, a chair that would enable Myrrha to put her head in the noose.

385 **spatio conclamat eodem**: "at the same moment she cries out."

387 **dilaniat**: normally the tearing of hair is associated with mourning. Cf. Ovid, *Amores* 3.9.52: *soror ... dilaniata comas*. Here the nurse shreds the noose instead of her hair.

389 **muta silet virgo terramque immota tuetur**: cf. Myrrha's behavior when Cinyras asks her about a potential husband: *illa silet* (359); *demisit vultus ... virgo* (367).

390 **tardae conamina mortis**: *tarda conamina mortis*, another case of transferred epithet.

391–392 **nudans ubera**: maternal figures sometimes bare their breasts to remind their children of their filial responsibilities; cf. Hecuba at Homer, *Iliad* 22.79–81.

395 **nec solam spondere fidem**: in addition to offering a sympathetic ear, the nurse will help Myrrha in the more tangible ways described in 395–396.

397 **furor**: cf. 355: *et o vellem similis furor esset in illo!*

  quae carmine sanet et herbis: for the use of incantations and herbs in love magic, cf. 14.20–22, *Amores* 3.7.28; Tibullus 1.2.61–62.

398 **sive aliquis nocuit magico lustrabere ritu**: cf. Tibullus 1.2.63: *et me lustravit taedis*. Reed 1997: 249 suggests that the nurse is referring to the evil eye. For black magic, see Bömer 1958: 142.

399 **ira deum sive est**: this may be an allusion to an earlier version of the myth, in which Venus is responsible for Myrrha's love for her father. Note that this line begins and ends with *ira*.

401 **paterque**: the most important word in the sentence is delayed for dramatic effect. Cf. 410, where *pater* again ends the sentence.

405 **propositi tenax**: the nurse will not stop what she has set out to do, which is to find out what is troubling Myrrha.

407 **complectens infirmis membra lacertis**: *infirmis lacertis* surrounds *membra* just as the nurse's arms embrace Myrrha.

408 **sensimus**: cf. 277: *sensit ... | vota quid illa velint*.

  et: in addition to all the areas that she discussed at 395–399, the nurse can help in matters of love as well.

409 **sedulitas**: cf. *non est mea pigra senectus*, 396; *male sedula nutrix*, 438.

409–410 ***nec sentient umquam | hoc pater***: Cinyras was deceived for a while, but he discovered the truth in the end.

410 ***pater***: note the emphatic position of *pater* at the end of the sentence. Cf. 401, where this word appears in the same position and elicits an emotional response from Myrrha.

furabunda: cf. *furiosaque*, 370.

410–419 The description of the characters' movements in this section is reminiscent of stage directions (406–407, 410–413, 415, 419).

410–411 ***torumque | ora premens***: cf. Dido at Vergil, *Aeneid* 4.659: *os impressa toro*.

411 ***pudori***: cf. *pudibundaque ... ora* (421).

412 ***instanti***: the nurse did not obey Myrrha's command to leave (411).

416–418 ***blanditur ... terret***: when coaxing and cajoling fail, the nurse resorts to blackmail.

417 ***indicium***: in a legal sense, "to give evidence against a person." *OLD* s.v. *indicium* 1b. The nurse will tell Cinyras about his daughter's attempted suicide, and he will demand an explanation. Fear of his reaction compels Myrrha to confide in her nurse.

420 ***fateri***: "to make an open avowal of" or "to admit guilt." *OLD* s.v. *fateor* 2, 3.

421 ***pudibundaque***: cf. Ovid's description of Lucretia at *Fasti* 2.819–820: *illa diu reticent pudibundaque celat amictu | ora*. Unlike the Propoetides (241), Myrrha is still able to blush, because she has not yet done anything inappropriate.

422 ***felicem ... matrem***: exclamatory accusative. Myrrha finds a way to tell the nurse about her incestuous desire for her father without saying the objectionable words. Quintilian (9.2.65–66) uses this phrase as an example of *emphasis* or words that have hidden meanings.

423–424 ***gelidus ... tremor***: hyperbaton.

423 ***hactenus***: this transition is common in the *Metamorphoses*; cf. 2.610, 5.642, 7.794, 12.82, 14.512.

gemuit: cf. Myrrha's reactions to the nurse's mention of the word *pater* at 410 (*suspiria*) and 410 (*exsiluit gremio furibunda*).

gemuit. gelidus: the caesura separates Myrrha's veiled confession from the nurse's reaction.

gelidus: for the use of this adjective in expressions of fear, cf. 2.200 (*gelida formidine*), 3.100 (*gelido terrore*).

424 ***sensit***: the nurse finally understands completely. At 408 (*sensimus*), she simply believed that Myrrha was in love.

426–427 **multa ... addidit**: Ovid foregoes the *suasoria* that he could have placed here.

426 **excuteret**: "to shake off." *OLD* s.v. *excutio* 3. Cf. 7.18 and 9.754–756, which refer to women who try to overcome a harmful love.

diros ... amores: cf. 300: *dira canam*.

428 **si non potiatur amore**: subjunctive in implied indirect discourse.

429 **vive ... potiere tuo**: the nurse's response (especially the repetition of *potiri*) indicates that Myrrha did not simply think *certa mori tamen est, si non potiatur amore*, but actually said it.

429–430 **non ausa "parente" | dicere**: cf. Pygmalion at 275–276: *non ausus "eburnea virgo" | dicere*. Now that the nurse knows the object of Myrrha's love, she balks at saying the word "*parente*," as did Myrrha at 422.

430 **numine**: the nurse swears by one of the gods.

431 **festa piae Cereris celebrabant annua matres**: after the nurse agrees to help Myrrha, the scene shifts to a festival of Ceres. Ovid uses the same technique in the myth of Pygmalion (269–270): just as the sculptor is about to have intercourse with the statue, the scene shifts to the festival of Venus (*festa dies Veneris tota celeberrima Cypro venerat*). Reed 1997: 251 notes the irony of having intercourse during a festival that requires abstinence.

piae: the adjective modifies *matres*.

432 **illa**: enjambment. There were other festivals of Ceres, but the one in August had the characteristics listed in 431–435. It is a women's cult in which the worshippers wear white clothes, offer the first of the harvested crops, and abstain from intercourse. See O'Bryhim 2007: 194.

nivea: for the wearing of white clothes during the festival of Ceres, see *Fasti* 4.619–620: *alba decent Cererem: vestes Cerialibus albas | sumite*.

433 **primitias frugum ... suarum**: first-fruit offerings.

spicea serta: an appositive that defines *primitias frugum suarum*. For the crown of wheat worn by Ceres, the goddess of agricultural fertility, see *Amores* 3.10.3 and Tibullus 2.1.4.

434–435 **Venerem tactusque viriles | in vetitis numerant**: for celibacy in the Roman cult of Ceres, see *Amores* 3.10.1–4; Tibullus 2.1.11–13; Spaeth 1996: 110–116.

434 **perque novem noctes**: according to the *Homeric Hymn to Demeter* (47), the goddess searched for Persephone for nine days. This extensive amount of time allowed Myrrha to visit her father's bed repeatedly without her mother's knowledge (471).

Venerem: metonymy for sexual intercourse.

435   **Cenchreis**: *Cēnchrēĭs*. Antoninus Liberalis (34) calls her Oreithyia, while Apollodorus (3.14.3) has Metharme. Reed 1997: 252 suggests that this may be an adjective derived from a toponym; she is the Cenchrean wife of Cinyras.

436   **regis adest coniunx**: *adest* separates the word *rex* from the word *coniunx* just as the festival separates the king and his wife from each other.

436   **arcanaque sacra**: the adjective can refer to mystery religions. *OLD* s.v. *arcana* 3. Cf. Horace, *Odes* 3.2.27: *qui Cereris sacrum vulgarit arcanae*. Men appear to have been excluded from these rites. Conversely, Orpheus established a cult that was originally closed to women; see Conon *FGrHist* 26 F 1 45.4 and Pausanias 9.30.5.

437   **legitima ... coniuge**: the king's true wife, as opposed to Myrrha.

438   **gravem vino Cinyran**: the implication is that Cinyras would not have agreed to have intercourse with a woman sight unseen unless he were drunk; Hyginus (*Fabulae* 164.3) makes this explicit. Nevertheless, Cinyras' suspicion of the nurse's proposition is revealed by the phrase *quaesitis virginis annis* (440). Reed 1997: 253 argues that Cinyras was otherwise faithful to his wife and that alcohol weakened his resolve.

   Cinyran: Greek accusative.

   male sedula nutrix: cf. *Ars amatoria* 3.699: *aliquis male sedulus*. The nurse promised *mea ... sedulitas erit apta tibi* (408–409) before she knew exactly what Myrrha wanted. Now that she is willing to facilitate her union with Cinyras, her *sedulitas* is employed to a bad end.

439   **nomine mentito veros exponit amores**: the nurse has given Myrrha a pseudonym. For the importance of names in this story, see 346, 366, 402. Note the concatenation of *mentito* and *veros*.

441   **"par" ait "est Myrrhae"**: this recalls the ambiguity of Pygmalion's prayer (*similis eburnae*, 276) and of Myrrha's answer to Cinyras (*similem tibi*, 364).

442–443   **gaude ... | vicimus**: For *vincere* in an erotic sense, see 4.356 (Salmacis) and 6.513–514 (Tereus). Clark 1973: 55–56 argues that this is a parody of the runner's report after the battle of Marathon: χαίρετε νικῶμεν. See Lucian, *Pro lapsu inter saltandum* 3. Here the phrase is humorous because the aged nurse is no marathon runner no matter how quickly she returned to Myrrha, nor is her victory a glorious one.

443–445   **infelix ... | laetitiam ... maerent ... | gaudet**: Myrrha is conflicted about her feelings, just as she was in her *suasoria* (370–376).

445   **tanta est discordia mentis**: cf. Byblis, *incerta tanta est discordia mentis* (9.630).

446–464   Nearly every element of Myrrha's procession to her father's bedchamber is an inversion of the Roman marriage ritual. See O'Bryhim 2007.

446–447   **Triones | ... Bootes**: the position of these constellations (Ursa Major and Ursa Minor) marks the time as midnight.

448   **facinus**: legal language. Cf. *sceleri* (460, 468), *crimina* (470), *facinus* (471), *scelus* (474), *confessis* (484, 487), *supplicium* (485). Through his use of such vocabulary, Orpheus ensures that his audience views Myrrha's behavior as a crime.

   suum: the placement of this word at the end of the sentence emphasizes that this is Myrrha's crime. Thus Orpheus exonerates Cinyras and places the blame squarely on a woman whom he depicts as unable to control her passions; cf. 153–154.

448–451   Orpheus' emphasis on complete darkness highlights the shamefulness of the act. The moon and stars refuse to be polluted by witnessing Myrrha's crime.

449   **latitantia**: frequentative. The stars remain hidden and refuse to come out.

450–451   **Icare ... Erigone**: for their story, see *Ibis* 611–614; Apollodorus 3.14.7; Hyginus, *Fabulae* 130; Propertius 2.33.29. Bacchus gave the gift of wine to Icarus, who offered it to a group of shepherds. Having had no experience with this new invention, they drank it without mixing it with water. Believing that Icarus had poisoned them, they killed him. When his daughter, Erigone, found his body, she hanged herself. Icarus became the star Arcturus in the constellation Bootes, while Erigone became the constellation Virgo. Elements of this myth are inverted in the story of Myrrha: Cinyras' intoxication leads to an incestuous encounter with his daughter, and Myrrha attempts to hang herself because of her illicit love for her father. The position of these constellations in the sky (along with the ritual described at 431–435) identifies the festival of Ceres as the *sacrum anniversarium Cereris*. See O'Bryhim 2007: 194; Spaeth 1996: 110–113.

452   **ter pedis offensi signo est revocata**: cf. *Tristia* 1.3.55–56: *ter limen tetigi, ter sum revocatus*. For tripping as a bad omen, see Pease 1920–1923 on Cicero, *De divinatione* 2.84; Valerius Maximus 1.5.2, 1.6.6; Suetonius, *Caesar* 59; Augustine, *De doctrina christiana* 2.20.31; Ogle 1911: 251–254.

   ter ... ter: for the significance of the number three to the Romans, see Tavenner 1916: 117–143; Lease 1919: 56–73.

453   **funereus bubo**: a bird of ill omen, which appears at the wedding of Tereus and Procne (6.431–432); cf. Vergil, *Aeneid* 4.462; also Pease 1920–1923 on Cicero, *De divinatione* 2.84. The presence of the owl is particularly

appropriate here because Nictymene, who committed incest with her father, turned into one (2.594–595).

454   ***it tamen***: Myrrha ignores the omens. Cf. Byblis, who ignores the omen of the dropped tablet in which she revealed her incestuous desire for her brother (9.571–572).

tenebrae minuunt noxque atra pudorem: it must be pitch black so that Myrrha's identity can remain secret. The darkness gives her anonymity, which makes her shameless. Note that Roman marriages were consummated in complete darkness in order to preserve the modesty of the bride; see O'Bryhim 2007: 193.

455   ***nutricisque manum laeva tenet***: the left hand was associated with nefarious acts. Ovid may have used *altera* instead of *dextera* so as to avoid the positive connotation of the right hand; see Wagener 1912: 22–25; 57–58.

456   ***thalami***: the wedding chamber; cf. 245, 317, 469, 571, 620, 703.

tangit limina: the bride must be careful to avoid tripping over the threshold. By touching it, Myrrha has symbolically violated this prohibition. See Ogle 1911: 253; O'Bryhim 2007: 193; Hersch 2010: 180–182.

456–457   ***iam ... iam ... iam***: anaphora and tricolon makes the action more vivid. Cf. 384–388; 9.466–467: *iam dominum appellat, iam nomina sanguinis odit, Byblida iam mavult quam se vocet ille sororem.*

456   ***caecum iter explorat***: cf. Tibullus 2.1.78, which describes an assignation: [*puella*] *explorat caecas cui manus ante vias.*

457   ***ducitur***: this verb can refer to the conveyance of the bride to the wedding chamber. *OLD* s.v. *duco* 5a.

at: her fear exceeds that of a bride, who goes through similar stages in the Roman rite of marriage. See Hersch 2010: 61–65; 251–253.

458   ***poplite succido***: the knee buckles. Cf. *Heroides* 13.25: *succido dicor procubuisse genu.*

458–459   ***fugitque | et color et sanguis animusque relinquit euntem***: as she passes into the wedding chamber, Myrrha undergoes a symbolic death. *que ... que* joins the two clauses, while *et ... et* joins *color* and *sanguis.*

459   ***sanguis***: *sānguīs*.

animus: "courage." *OLD* s.v. *animus* 13b.

460–461   ***quoque ... reverti***: thus far, Myrrha has been a willing participant in the perverted marriage rite. Now she is having second thoughts and must be pushed into completing it by the nurse.

460   ***quoque***: ablative of degree of difference with *proprior.*

suo ... sceleri: cf. *facinus suum* (448).

horret: cf. *horret anus* at 414.

461 ***vellet***: optative subjunctive.

462 ***cunctantem***: Myrrha delays, knowing that what she is doing is wrong. The bride also hesitates before she goes to her husband's house; see Hersch 2010: 144–148.

   longaeva: the nurse plays the part of the young boys of living parents who lead the bride to her husband's house; see O'Bryhim 2007: 192; Hersch 2010: 159–162.

   manu deducit: this recalls the formula *deductio in domum mariti*, which describes the transferal of the bride to her husband's house; see Hersch 2010: 141 note 23.

   alto: "exalted." *OLD* s.v. *altus* 11.

463 ***admotam***: here with the dative. *OLD* s.v. *admoveo* 2.

464 ***devotaque corpora iunxit***: the nurse now plays the part of the *pronuba*, who carries a torch, leads the bride to her groom, and perhaps joins their hands or formally unites them. *corpora iunxit* may reflect the *dextrarum iunctio*, "the joining of the right hands" of the bride and groom. For a discussion of the *pronuba* and her role in the Roman wedding, see Hersch 2010: 190–212.

464 ***tua***: "your lover" or "your daughter."

   devotaque: "accursed." *OLD* s.v. *devotus* 1. Note the use of ominous vocabulary in this section: *devota* (464), *obsceno* (465), *diro* (469).

465 ***obsceno genitor sua viscera lecto***: the word order depicts the couple (*genitor sua viscera*) lying in the middle of the bed (*obsceno ... lecto*).

   obsceno lecto: proleptic. Now that Cinyras is about to commit incest, his *alto lecto* (463) becomes *obsceno*.

   sua viscera: "his own flesh and blood."

466 ***virgineosque metus***: cf. *virginei ... timoris*, 361.

467 ***fortisan***: Orpheus speculates about what happened next in order to make the situation even more uncomfortable for the audience.

467–468 Servius Danielis (*ad Aeneadem* 4.58) says that the words *pater* and *filia* may not be uttered during the festival of Ceres at Rome. Thus Cinyras and Myrrha commit a double crime: incest and the violation of a ritual prohibition. See Lowrie 1993: 50–52.

   aetatis ... nomine: "by virtue of her age."

469 ***plena patre***: "pregnant by her father." *OLD* s.v. *plenus* 2b. Cf. Valerius Flaccus 1.414: *plena tulit quem rege maris*.

470 ***semina fert utero conceptaque crimina portat***: cf. 3.268–269: *manifestaque crimina pleno fert utero*; Cinna, fr. 7 Morel: *at scelus incesto Zmyrnae crescebant in alvo*.

   conceptaque crimina: "fetus conceived through a crime."

471   ***postera nox facinus geminat, nec finis in illa est***: Myrrha was not satisfied with deceiving her father just once. She returned to his bedroom night after night, while her mother was at the nine-day festival of Ceres (434). Cf. 473: *post tot concubitus*. Apollodorus (3.14.4) says that the affair lasted for twelve nights, which indicates that his version was not associated with the *sacrum anniversarium Cereris*. Antoninus Liberalis (34) simply says that it lasted a long time.

472   ***cum tandem Cinyras***: Hyginus (*Fabulae* 58) says nothing about the discovery and subsequent pursuit of Myrrha. In his version, Myrrha becomes pregnant and hides in the woods, where she turns into a tree.

473   ***inlato lumine***: the discovery of a lover's identity by lamplight also occurs at Parthenius 17. At Apuleius, *Metamorphoses* 5.22–23, Psyche takes with her an oil lamp and a weapon when she approaches the bed to uncover Cupid's identity.

473-474   ***vidit ... et scelus et natam***: zeugma. Antoninus Liberalis (34.4) says that Myrrha gave birth prematurely at this point and then Zeus transformed her into a tree.

474   ***verbisque dolore retentis***: this confirms that Cinyras would never have had intercourse with Myrrha if he had known her true identity. According to Antoninus Liberalis (34.5), he killed himself out of shame.

475   ***pendenti nitidum vagina deripit ensem***: Ovid modeled this line on Vergil, *Aeneid* 10.475: *vaginaque cava fulgentem deripit ensem*. Smith 1990: 458–460 observes that both lines appear at 10.475 and argues that Ovid's audience would have noted this. In this context, the phrase may have sexual undertones. While it can mean that Cinyras took the sword from the scabbard, these words also have slang meanings, which imply that Cinyras removed his penis from Myrrha's vagina; see Adams 1990: 20–21. This is reinforced by the word *pendenti*, which may allude to a *vagina diffututa* that has become distended from constant use (here over several consecutive nights of intercourse). See Martial 3.72, 11.21; also O'Bryhim 2012: 152. While it is impossible to know for certain whether this is an intentional *double entendre*, Cicero (*Epistulae ad Familiares* 189 = 9.22.4) says that even an innocent word can have an obscene sense that an audience will notice.

476   ***tenebrisque et caecae munere noctis***: the night is pitch black because the moon and the stars still refuse to shine (446–456).

477   ***intercepta neci est***: "she was saved from death." For the dative, see *OLD* s.v. *intercipio* 2.

478   ***Panchaea***: Ovid mentions Panchaea at the beginning of this story (309). By having Myrrha flee from Cyprus to Arabia, he may be alluding to other

versions of the myth set in the Near East (Apollodorus 3.14.3–4; Hyginus, *Fabulae* 58; Antoninus Liberalis 34). How she crossed the water between Cyprus and Arabia is not explained.

479 **perque novem erravit redeuntis cornua lunae**: the pregnancy has now come to full term. Cf. 295–296: *iam coactis | cornibus in plenum noviens lunaribus orbem*.

480 **terra ... Sabaea**: southwest Arabia (biblical Sheba). For the association of myrrh with Sabaea, see Vergil, *Georgics* 1.57, 2.117; *Aeneid* 1.416–417. According to Miller 1969: 104–105, myrrh was transplanted from the coast of Somalia to the Arabian Peninsula. For the production of spices in Arabia, see Theophrastus, *Historia plantarum* 9.4.2.

481–482 **nescia voti**: "not knowing what to pray for." Myrrha did not know whether to pray for deliverance or death.

482 **mortisque metus et taedia vitae**: chiasmus.

483 **complexa**: "adopt." *OLD* s.v. *complector* 2d.

483–484 **o si qua patetis | numina confessis**: "if any of you gods are receptive to those who have admitted their wrongs."

484–485 **merui nec triste recuso | supplicium**: Myrrha becomes more sympathetic by admitting her error and accepting punishment. Cf. Scylla at 8.127: *nam, fateor, merui et sum digna perire*.

485–486 **vivosque superstes | mortuaque extinctos**: chiasmus.

486–487 **ambobus ... negate**: Myrrha's desire for a transformation that would put her in limbo between life and death recalls the transformation of the Cerastae (222–223), whose punishment lies somewhere between death and exile. For other parallels, see Reed 1997: 260–261.

488 **numen confessis aliquod patet**: cf. *o si qua patetis | numina confessis* (483–484).

488–489 **ultima certe | vota suos habuere deos**: Antoninus Liberalis (34.5) makes Zeus responsible for the metamorphosis. In Hyginus (*Fabulae* 58), it is Venus. Apollodorus (3.14.4) does not specify which god transforms her.

489–498 Cf. Daphne (1.548–552) and Dryope (9.349–362), whose appendages turn into various parts of a tree.

491 **firmamina**: "support." This word may have been coined by Ovid.

492 **agunt**: "to put forth" or "to produce." *OLD* s.v. *ago* 10, 11.

mediaque manente medulla: the marrow becomes the soft pith in the center of the bush. Cf. Pliny, *Naturalis historia* 16.181: *corpori arborum ut reliquorum animalium ... venae, ossa, medulla*.

497–498 ***non tulit illa moram ... mersitque suos in cortice vultus***: Myrrha willingly accepts her metamorphosis. Cf. *Ars amatoria* 1.286: *et nunc obducto cortice pressa latet*.

venientique obvia ligno | subsedit: "meeting the spreading wood, she settled into it."

499 ***amisit veteres cum corpore sensus***: all of her old emotions, including her lust for her father, are now gone. *OLD* s.v. *sensus* 7.

500 ***flet***: compare the sisters of Phaethon, who become poplars and cry tears of amber (2.364–366). Even though Myrrha has lost her emotions, the tree cries. Its tears are myrrh, a resin that flows through slits cut into the bark. Cf. 308–309: *sudataque ligno | tura*; *Fasti* 1.339: *lacrimatas cortice murras*. The practice of cutting the bark to release the resin may be reflected in the versions of the myth in which Theias cuts the tree with his sword (Hyginus, *Fabulae* 164.3; Fulgentius 3.8; Servius, *ad Aeneadem* 5.72). Since he does not do so here, Lucina's assistance is required.

501 ***est honor et lacrimis***: perhaps because myrrh is used in embalming, in religious ceremonies, and in the triumphal crown. See Reed 1997: 164.

502 ***nomen erile tenet***: cf. *Ars amatoria* 1.288: *dominae nomina gutta tenet*.

nulloque tacebitur aevo: Orpheus' implication that the story of Myrrha's incest will always be told as part of the etiology for the myrrh tree undercuts *est honor et lacrimis* (501). She will always be among *inconcessisque puellas ignibus attonitas meruisse libinine poenam* (153–154); see Reed 1997: 264. Hollis 2007: 36 suggests that this is an echo of Cinna's hope for the survival of his *Zmyrna*.

504–505 ***quaerebatque viam qua se genetrice relicta | exsereret***: this may be Ovid's contribution to the story. According to Servius (*ad Aeneidum* 5.72) and Fulgentius (8.8), Cinyras cuts the tree with a sword and Adonis exits through it. Servius (*ad Aeneidum* 5.72; *ad Eclogas* 10.18) preserves yet another version, in which Adonis emerges after a boar cuts the tree with its tusk. In Antoninus Liberalis (34), he is born before Myrrha's metamorphosis.

qua se ... | exsereret: relative clause of purpose.

505 ***tumet***: this verb is used in connection with the fertility of plants. Cf. *Fasti* 1.152: *et nova de gravido palmite gemma tumet*; Propertius 4.2.14: *et coma lactenti spicea fruge tumet*.

506 ***onus***: "unborn child." *OLD* s.v. *onus* 1b.

dolores: the labor pains that Myrrha would have experienced if she had retained her senses (499). Now she is merely *nitenti tamen est similis* (508).

507 ***Lucina***: Roman goddess of childbirth. Parturient women call on her to relieve their labor pains. Cf. 5.303–304, 9.293–323.

voce vocari: figura etymologica. Cf. *voce vocatur* (3).

508 **nitenti**: for *nitor* in descriptions of birth, cf. 2.294, 302.

509 **gemitus ... lacrimis**: the tree's creaking and flowing sap are similar enough to the groans and tears associated with labor to summon Lucina.

510 **mitis**: Lucina is gentle because she assuages the pain of childbirth and assists with delivery.

511 **admovitque manus**: a ritual gesture, especially during childbirth; cf. *Anthologia palatina* 6.244.4, 271.3–4; also Bömer 1958: 168.

verba puerpera: a magical spell that aids in childbirth. For Lucina inhibiting a birth with a spell, see 9.300–301.

512 **arbor agit rimas et fissa cortice**: Myrrha produces Adonis just as the tree produces myrrh through slits in its bark. Cf. Fulgentius (8.8), who says that Cinyras cut the tree with a sword and Adonis emerged through it.

agit: "to put forth" or "to produce." *OLD* s.v. *ago* 10, 11. Cf. 492: *ossaque robor agunt*.

513 **onus**: cf. 481: *vixque uteri portabat onus*.

vivum: a child, as opposed to myrrh.

mollibus herbis: this recalls the placement of dolls on the plants grown in the gardens of Adonis. See the note on 519–523.

514 **Naides impositum lacrimis unxere parentis**: myrrh has antiseptic qualities; see Majno 1975: 215–218. For the use of myrrh to cleanse the uterus and to alleviate pain, see Hippocrates, *De natura muliebri* 358. Mark 15:23 implies that it was administered as an analgesic.

Naides: the presence of water nymphs suggests that the birth occurred at an oasis with a pool, which accounts for the tree and the grass (513).

515 **laudaret faciem Livor quoque**: cf. 6.129–130, where personified envy could not find fault with Arachne's tapestry.

faciem: good looks in general, not confined to the face. *OLD* s.v. *facies* 8a.

515–516 **qualia namque | corpora nudorum ... Amorum**: By equating Cupid and Adonis, her future lover, Ovid continues the theme of incest. As Galinsky 1975: 102 says, "when Venus falls in love with him she continues the pattern of incest which she inflicted on Myrrha, and the outcome of her love will be disastrous also." See also Hardie 2004: 9–10; von Glinski 2012: 43. If Pygmalion's statue represented Venus, then Adonis is her grandson.

516–518 Cupid's attribute was the bow; Adonis used a javelin to hunt boars.

516 **tabula pinguntur**: these are paintings on wooden tablets that often depict erotic scenes. See *OLD* s.v. *tabella* 6; also Clarke 1998: 91–100. Plautus, *Menaechmi* 143–144 refers to such a painting of Venus and Adonis; see O'Bryhim 2010: 636–639.

517 ***discrimina cultus***: "differences in their accoutrements."

518 ***aut huic adde leves aut illi deme pharetras***: the singular *illi* may refer to *Amores* as though they have been reduced to Cupid alone. Anderson 1972: 519 suggests that these demonstrative adjectives agree with an implied *cultui*. Tarrant 2004 favors *huic ... illis*, which appears in some manuscripts as a correction to their predecessors.

leves ... pheretras: Although *leves* and *pheretras* appear in different clauses, they belong to both. Cf. 525: *pharetratus ... puer*.

Venus and Adonis

Orpheus now tells the tale of Adonis, the son of Myrrha and Cinyras. After describing his birth in detail, he skips ahead several years to recount his affair with Venus. Orpheus says that the goddess' love for Adonis was not voluntary; Cupid accidentally grazed his mother with an arrow, which forced her to desire the youth. She is so besotted with love for him that she abandons her favorite cities to join him in the hunt, her skirt hitched up like Diana's. During a break from this strenuous activity, they recline in a *locus amoenus*, where Venus warns her lover against hunting dangerous animals, especially boars and lions. She explains her hatred for the latter by telling the inset story of Atalanta and Hippomenes, who were transformed into lions when Hippomenes forgot to thank her for helping him win Atalanta. After one final warning to avoid dangerous animals, Venus leaves for Cyprus and Adonis returns to the hunt, where he is killed by a boar. When the goddess hears his groans, she returns, mourns for her lover, turns him into an anemone, and establishes a ritual in his honor: the Adonia.

While this character has a long history in the Near East, the Adonis that the Greeks and Romans knew originated in the Levant, where the so-called "Baal Cycle" tells how this god of agricultural fertility struggled against Mot, the god of death. One of Baal's titles, *adon*, passed into Greek as "Adonis." His death near the Adonis River in Lebanon was commemorated annually by women throughout the Mediterranean. The Romans, too, knew of his Near Eastern origin. Cicero (*De natura deorum* 3.59) says that "the fourth [Venus] came from Syria and Cyprus, who is called Astarte and is said to have married Adonis."

The myth of Hyacinthus and that of Adonis have a number of obvious parallels: a god falls in love with a boy, the boy dies in an accident, the god transforms him into a flower, and he establishes a festival in the boy's honor. There are also significant differences. Hyacinthus and Apollo are involved in activities – hunting and athletics – that were thought to help

Athenian youths develop into men. Apollo encourages Hyacinthus' participation. Venus, however, attempts to stunt the young man's development by encouraging him to seek harmless quarry suitable for boys and to avoid the more dangerous animals hunted by youths who are making the transition to manhood (Barringer 2001: 10–59). Both gods abandon their cities and cult places to be with their human lovers: Apollo leaves behind Delphi, while Venus deserts her favorite cities and even Olympus itself. By neglecting his divine duties in order to cavort with his human lover, Apollo becomes almost human himself and loses his ability to heal the boy; even though Venus dresses as the virgin goddess Diana while she hunts with Adonis, she nevertheless retains a strong interest in sexuality, her primary sphere of influence. Both couples find themselves in a *locus amoenus*: Hyacinthus dies there from the blow of an errant discus, but Venus and Adonis enjoy cuddling and storytelling in the shade. In the end, Hyacinthus' demise is a direct result of Apollo's action, while Adonis dies because he ignores the warnings of Venus to avoid danger. The myth of Hyacinthus is, then, the story of a boy who is being guided to manhood by an *erōmenos* but is accidentally prevented from making this transition. Adonis, on the other hand, is a young man whose development is hindered by a lover who tries to prevent him from engaging in hunting practices associated with mature males. Nevertheless, Adonis becomes a symbol of *virtus* on Roman sarcophagi because he hunts the boar even though it will cause his death (Koortbojian 1995: 32–38).

519–523 This description of Adonis' rapid growth may reflect the rapid growth of plants in gardens of Adonis, which play an important role in the Adonia, an annual ritual that was performed all across the Roman Empire, from the Levant to Spain; see Cumont 1927: 330–341. As part of the ritual, women planted seeds in shallow potsherds and placed figures of Adonis on top of the soil. The plants sprouted rapidly and then died quickly, as did Adonis. After mourning him on the rooftops, the celebrants threw their gardens of Adonis into the sea; see Baudy 1986. Ovid alludes to this ritual at *Ars amatoria* 1.75.

519 **labitur occulte fallitque volatilis aetas**: cf. *Amores* 1.8.49: *labitur occulte fallitque volubilis aetas*. This line serves the practical purpose of moving the narrative swiftly from Adonis' birth to his adulthood.

522 **formosissimus infans**: several sources recount an event that occurred during the infancy of Adonis that does not appear here. Apollodorus (3.14.4) says that Aphrodite fell in love with him while he was still an infant because of his beauty. She hid him in a chest, which she entrusted to Persephone. When the goddess of the underworld saw the baby, she refused to return him to Venus. Zeus tried to resolve the goddesses' dispute by dividing Adonis' time

between them. Each goddess got one third of the year, while the final third went to Adonis himself, who chose to spend it with Venus. Hyginus (*De astronomia* 2.7.3) also mentions this dispute, but says that Jupiter made Calliope the arbiter. When Calliope divided Adonis' time equally between the two goddesses, Aphrodite took revenge by causing the death of Calliope's son, Orpheus. This is no obscure variant on the myth of Adonis. Plaques from Locri dating to c. 450 BC show Aphrodite lifting the lid of a box that contains an infant, while a number of vases from the fourth century BC depict Aphrodite and Persephone supplicating Zeus; see Gantz 1996: 730–731; *LIMC* 1.2: 160, plate 5. Because this story is not strictly relevant to Orpheus' theme, and perhaps because of its similarity to the myth of Persephone, which appears in Book 5, Ovid does not include it here.

523   **iam iuvenis, iam vir, iam se formosior ipso est**: tricolon. According to Theocritus (15.129), Adonis was 18 or 19 years old when he began his affair with Aphrodite. Varro (*Menippeae saturae*, fr. 540 Astbury) says that he was just a *puellus*. In Orpheus' account Adonis has passed from youth to man, but has not yet hunted any of the animals that were the quarry of men (537–541).

iam se formosior ipso est: cf. *ars adeo latet arte sua* (252). Adonis' beauty and youth were his main attributes. For Adonis as *formosus*, see Vergil, *Eclogues* 10.18; Propertius 2.13.55.

524   **iam placet et Veneri**: Adonis is so handsome that he is attractive even to Venus, who normally does not have sexual relationships with humans. Cf. *Homeric Hymn to Aphrodite* (45–52, 198–199, 249–251), where Zeus humiliates the goddess by making her have intercourse with Anchises.

matrisque ulciscitur ignes: cf. Hyginus, *Fabulae* 58.3: *natus est Adonis, qui matris poenas a Venere est insecutus*. Myrrha's vengeance upon Venus recalls the version of the myth in which the goddess is responsible for Myrrha's lust for her father; see Apollodorus 3.14.4; Hyginus, *Fabulae* 58.1; Oppian, *Halieutica* 3.404–407; Plutarch 310f. As Hardie 2002: 187–188 says, "an incestuous love would be the most fitting revenge for Myrrha's tragic fate."

525   **pharetratus ... puer**: Cupid; cf. 518.

526–528   Cupid unintentionally scratches Venus with his arrow, which forces her to love a human. Cf. 1.452–472, where he uses his arrows to force Apollo to fall in love with Daphne. Venus, who is well aware of the power of her son's arrows, seeks to avoid a deeper wound by pushing him away. Thus Orpheus relieves Venus of the responsibility for falling in love with Adonis. He does not extend the same courtesy to Myrrha, despite the numerous versions of her myth that blame a deity for her incestuous desire for her father. See the note on line 311.

526   **harundine**: "arrow." Cf. 1.471: *habet sub harundine plumbum*.

527–528 **altius ... specie**: "deeper than it looked."

529–532 After Venus fell in love with Adonis, she left behind her familiar haunts. Apollo behaved in the same way after he fell in love with Hyacinthus (167–171).

529 **Cythereia**: Cÿthĕrēĭă. This epithet of Venus refers to her island of Cythera, which lies just off the southern Peloponnesus.

530–531 **Paphon aequore cinctam | piscosamque Cnidon gravidamque Amathunta metallis**: these cities had famous sanctuaries of Venus. Paphos and Amathus are on Cyprus, while Cnidus is in Caria, which lies off the coast of Asia Minor near Rhodes. According to Pausanias (9.41.2), Amathus had a sanctuary of Venus and Adonis.

530 **Paphon**: Greek accusative.

aequore cinctam: Palaipaphos is bounded by the Mediterranean to the West and by rivers to the North and South.

531 **Cnidon**: Greek accusative.

Amathunta: Greek accusative.

gravidamque Amathunta metallis: cf. *fecundam Amathunta metallis* (220).

532 **abstinet et caelo; caelo praefertur**: chiasmus. The first *caelo* is ablative, while the second is dative.

533 **tenet**: "she holds the attention of." *OLD* s.v. *teneo* 22a. This verb can also mean "to restrain" or "to hold up" (*OLD* s.v. *teneo* 19a–b), an action that reflects Venus' attempt to hold Adonis back from hunting dangerous animals and implicitly to check his development into a mature adult.

533–537 cf. Apollo, who joined Hyacinthus in the hunt (167–168).

533 **adsuetaque ... colendo**: the participle is concessive. Venus was unaccustomed to the outdoor exercise that she had to endure with Adonis. Cf. *sed labor insolitus iam me lassavit* (554). For the topos of the lover accompanying the beloved on a hunt, see Reed 1997: 273.

535 **per iuga**: the same phrase appears in the story of Hyacinthus (172).

536 **fine genus**: "as far as the knee." *fine* is used as a preposition with the genitive. *OLD* s.v. *finis* 3a.

vestem ritu succincta Dianae: cf. *Amores* 3. 2.31: *talia pinguntur succinctae crura Dianae*. The goddess of the hunt hitches up her tunic so as to be unencumbered while chasing animals. Venus is becoming like her polar opposite Diana in some respects, but not in her desire for Adonis.

537–541 At *Fasti* 5.173–176, Ovid says that hares and stags are suitable targets for young hunters, but reserves boars and lions for those with more experience. There is a similar division between safe and dangerous quarry at [Ovid], *Halieutica* 63–65.

538–539 pronos lepores ... dammas: The list of Venus' quarry moves from hares close to the ground (*pronos*) to stags with high horns (*celsum*) to medium-sized gazelles (*dammas*). In other words, animals that are safe to hunt come in all sizes. Grattius, *Cynegetica* 199–201 confirms that the hunting of hares and gazelles is a *leve opus*.

538 celsum in cornua: cf. Manilius 2.246: *Ariesque in cornua tortus*.

539–541 Venus, who is accompanied by wolves, lions, bears, and leopards in the *Homeric Hymn to Aphrodite* (69–74), now avoids boars, wolves, bears, and lions. The first and last animals in the list, boars and lions, are particularly relevant to the myths of Adonis and Atalanta. The boar will kill Adonis and Atalanta will be transformed into a lion.

539 agitat: "she hunts" or "she scours the area for (game)." *OLD* s.v. *agito* 3b, 4.

542 quoque: Venus wants Adonis to fear these dangerous beasts as much as she does.

543 Adoni: Greek vocative.

  esto: cf. *ea lex certaminis esto* (572). The future imperative occurs frequently in legal language, which makes Venus' prohibition sound like an edict.

  fugacibus: dative of reference.

544 audaces: this adjective refers to the dangerous animals at 539–541.

545 parce meo, iuvenis, temerarius esse periclo: "Young man, don't be reckless to my detriment." Venus' tone is almost maternal.

  parce ... esse: poetic usage of *parcere* with the infinitive.

  meo ... periclo: ablative of attendant circumstances.

546 neve ... lacesse: poetic usage of *ne* with the imperative; cf. 352.

546–547 arma ... gloria: dangerous animals are described as though they are armed soldiers. Adonis can win glory by killing them, but no glory comes from attacking animals that flee.

547 stet: "cost." *OLD* s.v. *sto* 23.

  magno: ablative of price.

548 quae movere Venerem: i.e. the physical attractions of Adonis. Cf. *capta viri forma* (529).

  movere: *moverunt*.

549 satigerosque sues oculosque animosque ferarum: although Tarrant 2004 deletes this line, it should stand because it is part of a pattern. In 548–549 Orpheus mentions boars and lions along with other animals. In 550–551 he specifies just boars and lions. At 552 he focuses on lions alone, by way of a transition to the story of Atalanta.

550 **fulmen**: this refers to the swiftness with which boars use their tusks.

551 **vasta**: "awe-inspiring." *OLD* s.v. *vastus* 3a.

552 **invisumque mihi genus est:** Venus' hatred for lions, which is mentioned nowhere else, provides a transition to the story of Atalanta.

   quae causa roganti: *sit* is implied in this indirect question.

553 **monstrum**: "enormity." *OLD* s.v. *monstrum* 5.

554–556 These lines contain many elements of the stock description of the *locus amoenus*: the character is weary, a tree provides shade, a mortal lies on the ground, and an encounter of a sexual nature ensues. For the *locus amoenus*, see Segal 1969.

554 **iam**: Venus has tired quickly because she is unaccustomed to physical labor (533–534).

555 **opportuna**: "convenient." *OLD* s.v. *opportunus* 1.

   blanditur: "seduces." *OLD* s.v. *blandior* 6. This translation is particularly appropriate in light of *datque torum caespes* (556).

   populus umbra: for the poplar as a shade tree, see 5.590–591; Vergil, *Eclogues* 9.41. Cf. 90–105, where Orpheus recounts his tales under the shade of trees, just as Venus does here.

557 **et requievit**: reminiscent of a stage direction.

   pressitque et gramen et ipsum: Adams 1990: 182 notes that this verb is used of the dominant partner in a sexual encounter. Venus, then, is playing the role traditionally associated with the male. For the feminization of Adonis, cf. 578–579, where Venus likens Adonis to Atalanta: *ut faciem et posito corpus velamine vidit, | quale meum, vel quale tuum, si femina fias.*

558 **inque sinu iuvenis posita cervice reclinis**: Venus' head is on the chest of Adonis, who is reclining on the grass.

559 **mediis interserit oscula verbis**: the position of *oscula* between *mediis* and *verbis* reflects the kisses with which Venus intersperses her words.

Atalanta and Hippomenes

After a short time spent chasing small game, Venus warns Adonis against hunting dangerous animals such as boars and lions. When Adonis asks her why she hates lions, Venus tells him the story of Atalanta and Hippomenes.

Atalanta went to Delphi to consult the oracle about a husband, presumably because she had reached marriageable age and had questions about her future.

The god told her to avoid marriage but predicted that she would marry nonetheless, warning with characteristic ambiguity that she would lose herself while she was still alive. The frightened girl fled to the forest, pursued by a throng of persistent suitors. In an attempt to dissuade them, she announced that anyone who wanted to marry her would first have to defeat her in a footrace; the victor would win a bride and the vanquished would lose their lives. Unable to resist her beauty, many accepted the challenge and died. Hippomenes, who happened to be watching one of these races, was astounded by their foolishness until he saw Atalanta run by him unclothed. Then he understood why they put their lives at risk. When the handsome and youthful Hippomenes challenged her, Atalanta waffled between wanting to win and wanting to lose. Just before their race began, Hippomenes asked Venus for help. She gave him three golden apples from her sanctuary at Tamassos on Cyprus and told him how to use them to defeat Atalanta. Each time she passed him, Hippomenes tossed an apple in her path. Twice Atalanta retrieved them and this slowed her progress, but not so much that she was unable to regain her lead. During the final stretch, Hippomenes called on Venus for assistance. The goddess made the final apple heavier than the rest so that Hippomenes could pass Atalanta. He won the race and claimed his prize, but neglected to thank Venus for her help. Determined that he should not set a bad example for future worshipers, she inspired him with an uncontrollable lust for Atalanta as they were passing a rustic sanctuary of Cybele. As they defiled her sacred space, Cybele transformed them into lions.

This myth contains many elements of initiation rites, which normally have a preliminal stage in which the initiate is separated from society, a liminal stage that involves trials and tests, and a post-liminal stage in which the initiate is reintegrated into society in a new role; see Van Gennep 1960: 65–115. First Atalanta leaves her home to live in the woods after she receives the ominous oracle. Then she takes part in the race, where she faces repeated trials. Races for girls are in fact well documented as prenuptial rites, particularly those performed for Artemis at Brauron and for Hera at Olympia; see Barringer 1996: 71–74. Finally, Atalanta's acceptance of Hippomenes' apples signals her acceptance of marriage, since this fruit is given as a love gift in anticipation of wedlock; see Faraone 1990: 230–238; Barringer 1996: 74. Atalanta, however, does not complete the postliminal stage – integration into her new role as a wife in her husband's city. While Greek marriages could take place at the home of the bride or the groom, they were consummated at the groom's house; see Oakley and Sinos 1993: 23 and 26–37. When Venus says, "they were passing by a sacred area and their long journey made them want to rest" (686–688), they were travelling from Atalanta's home in southern Boeotia to Onchestos in the North, where Hippomenes' father lived (Hyginus, *Fabulae* 185.5). On the way,

Venus inspired him with an uncontrollable desire for Atalanta, which led him to have intercourse with her in the sanctuary of Cybele. In retribution for this defilement, the goddess turned them into lions, thereby denying Atalanta the opportunity to complete her rite of passage into adulthood at the home of her father-in-law.

Like Atalanta, Adonis is involved in a rite of passage. According to Greek custom, he must display his *virtus* by killing a dangerous animal in the hunt to become a man; see Barringer 2001: 10–59. Venus objects to this perilous undertaking: "let your glory not come at great expense to me" (*stet mihi ne magno tua gloria*, 547). As a cautionary tale, she relates the story of Atalanta and, by equating Adonis with her physically (579–581), she encourages him to identify with this girl, who is also going to embark upon an ill-fated rite of passage. Adonis ignores her advice and begins the hunt, his own rite of passage, as soon as she leaves his side, only to be killed by a boar. Therefore he can never undertake the responsibilities of a man.

560–563 ***fortisan audieris aliquam certamine cursus | veloces superasse viros***: although the names of the main characters of this story are not revealed until later, this phrase leaves no doubt as to their identities, since there is no other myth about a woman who defeated men in a footrace. When Venus says *audieris*, she admits that she is not the first to tell this story, which invites Ovid's audience to compare this version with others.

560 ***audieris***: syncopated form of the perfect subjunctive *audiveris*.

561 ***superasse***: *superavisse*.

561–562 ***non fabula rumor | ille fuit***: here a *fabula* is a false story. *OLD* s.v. *fabula* 3a. Venus implies that the thought of a woman defeating men in a footrace is so outlandish that no one would believe it.

562 ***superabat***: the imperfect tense is due to the fact that Atalanta defeated a number of suitors over a period of time in the past.

563 ***laude pedum formaene bono***: chiasmus.
bono: for *bonum* as "excellence"; see *OLD* s.v. *bonum* 5.

564 ***scitanti deus huic de coniuge***: apparently Atalanta wanted to marry and was asking the oracle for advice on a husband. This consultation is also mentioned by Servius at *ad Aeneadem* 3.113. Apollodorus (9.3.2) and Hyginus (*Fabulae* 185) say that she wanted to remain a virgin.
deus: Apollo, the god of prophecy.

565 ***fuge coniugis usum***: Atalanta flees marriage, at least for a while, by running (568–570); see Reed 1997: 279–280; Ziogas 2013: 159–160.
tibi: "in your case." The position of *tibi* is emphatic.
usum: "marital relations." *OLD* s.v. *usus* 10; Adams 1990: 198.

566 **teque ipsa viva carebis**: this cryptic prophecy, which is typical of the style of prophecies dispensed at Delphi, foreshadows Atalanta's transformation into a lion.

567 **sorte dei**: at Delphi, prophecies could be delivered by the Pythia or through lots (*sortes*) that provided a "yes" or "no" answer. See *OLD* s.v. *sors* 1b and 3. Ovid has conflated these two methods (cf. 1.368, 4.643). Unlike Daphne (1.486–487), who simply wanted to remain a virgin, Atalanta received from the oracle a compelling reason to avoid marriage.

per opacas innuba silvas: Atalanta resembles the virgin huntress, Diana, who inhabits the woods. Like Venus, who also resembles Diana (535–536), Atalanta has deserted her home in order to roam the forest. But, unlike Venus, she wants to avoid a sexual relationship. The preposition *per*, "throughout," suggests that she had no permanent habitation but ranged throughout the forest like an animal. For Atalanta's sylvan sojourn, see Propertius 1.1.11–14.

568 **instantem turbam ... procorum**: cf. *temeraria turba procorum*, 574. The suitors are intruding upon Atalanta's isolation in the forest. Cf. Myrrha, who also rejected a crowd of suitors, but not so that she could remain a virgin (356–364).

violenta: "savage." *OLD* s.v. *violentus* 1. This adjective often describes dangerous animals and is therefore appropriate for a woman who lives in the forest, eschews the human institution of marriage, and will cause the death of the men who pursue her. Thus she is like the dangerous quarry that Venus warns Adonis to avoid (539–541).

569–572 Apollodorus (3.9.2) says that Atalanta, dressed in full armor, chased her suitors and killed them. According to Hyginus (*Fabulae* 185), an armed Atalanta chased her unarmed suitors, killed them, and then nailed their heads to the stadium. In both versions, Atalanta engaged in more of a hunt than a race.

569 **fugat**: "put to flight." *OLD* s.v. *fugo* 1c.

nec sum potienda: "and I am not a woman to be won sexually." *OLD* s.v. *potior* 2c. Cf. 429 (*potiere tuo ... parente*), where the nurse promises to find a way for Myrrha to have intercourse with her father.

571 **praemia veloci coniunx thalamique dabuntur**: *coniunx thalamique* are in apposition to *praemia*.

thalami: poetic plural for a nuptial chamber.

572 **esto**: this future imperative is reminiscent of legal language, especially when combined with *lex*. It gains force through its position at the end of the line. Cf. *fortisque fugacibus esto* (543).

573 **immitis**: this adjective is also used at 8.110 to describe an uncaring beloved; cf. *violenta* at 568.

574 **ad hanc legem**: "under these conditions."
temeraria turba procorum: transferred epithet.

575–577 The pluperfects indicate Hippomenes' actions and opinions before he sees Atalanta in 578.

575 **Hippomenes**: Apollodorus (3.9.2) calls him "Melanion."

576 **cuiquam**: dative of agent.

577 **damnarat**: syncopated form of *damnaverat*.

578 **posito corpus velamine**: Atalanta ran nude, as was the custom for men in Greek footraces. Only in Sparta did women exercise nude (Euripides, *Andromache* 595–600; Propertius 3.14.1–4; Plutarch, *Lycurgus* 14.3 = 47e). Apollodorus (3.9.2) says that she ran the race in armor, which was an Olympic event for men. Unmarried women raced each other every four years at the games for Hera at Olympia. Their hair was loose, they wore short tunics, and their right shoulders were bare; see Pausanias 5.16.2–8. [Hesiod], *Catalogue of Women*, fr. 9–10 Merkelbach–West seems to say that Atalanta was clothed.

posito ... velamine: cf. *ut stetit ante oculos posito velamine nostros*, *Amores* 1.5.17.

579 **quale meum, vel quale tuum, si femina fias**: cf. *at quam virgineus puerile vultus in ore est* (631). See also the description of Iphis at 9.712–713: *facies, quam sive puellae | sive dares puero, fieret formosus uterque*.

580 **obstipuit**: a compound of *stupeo*, which is used in Book 10 to indicate that a character stops everything because he or she has seen or heard something extraordinary. The personified wheel of Ixion stands still at Orpheus' song (42); Orpheus stops when Eurydice returned to the underworld (64); a man freezes when he sees Hercules dragging Cerberus from the underworld (65–67); Pygmalion stands stock still when his statue becomes living flesh (287). *obstipuit* occurs again at 666, where Atalanta is astonished by the golden apple that lands in her path. For this reaction from a character who falls in love at first sight, see 14.349–350.

tollensque manus: a gesture of prayer.

581 **quos modo culpavi**: "[men] whom I criticized just now."

582 **quae peteretis**: relative clause of characteristic.

584 **insidiasque timet**: this is Shackelton-Bailey's 1981: 334–335 emendation of the manuscript reading *invidiamque timet*. Hippomenes fears that one of the other contestants will come up with a stratagem to defeat Atalanta, as he himself will soon do. Anderson 1972: 423–424, however, retains *invidiamque*

timet, explaining that Hippomenes fears that he may provoke Envy if he praises Atalanta too much. Either is possible.

586 **audentes deus ipse iuvat**: a *sententia*. Cf. *Ars amatoria* 1.608: *audentem Forsque Venusque iuvat*; *Fasti* 2.782: *audentes forsque deusque iuvat*; Terence, *Phormio* 203: *fortis Fortuna iuvat*; Vergil, *Aeneid* 10.284: *audentis Fortuna iuvat*.

588–590   Hippomenes rates her beauty higher than her skill at running. This is his answer to 562–563: *non dicere posses | laude pedum formaene bono praestantior esset*.

588 **Scythica sagitta**: the Scythians were famous for their skill at archery. Reed 1997: 282 suggests that Atalanta is being depicted as one of the Amazons, who were said to have lived in Scythia and to have been accomplished archers.

589 **Aonio**: a poetic term for Boeotia. Cf. 605: *mihi genitor Megareus Onchestius*.

589–590 The placement of *decorem* at the end of both lines increases the emphasis on Atalanta's beauty.

590 **cursus facit ipse decorem**: cf. Daphne at 1.530: *aucta forma fuga est*.

591 **aura refert ablata citis talaria plantis**: "the breeze blows back the fluttering wings on her swift soles."

talaria: the winged sandals that Mercury wears are also called *talaria* (2.736; 4.667, 730). Cf. 587: *passu ... alite*. Anderson 1966: 1–13 believes that Atalanta's *talaria* were ornamental wings attached at the ankle.

592 **eburnea**: white skin was a mark of beauty in a woman. Cf. 3.422 and 4.335; *Amores* 3.7.7; *Heroides* 20.59. Note also the description of Pygmalion's statue at 275.

592–593 **quaeque | poplitibus suberant picto genualia limbo**: "and the bindings with an ornamental border that were below her knees."

genualia: this *hapax legomenon* refers to some sort of binding on her sandals that reached the knee and had a decorated border.

594–595 **inque puellari corpus candore ruborem | traxerat**: "and her body had taken a blush onto its girlish whiteness."

595–596 **super atria ... umbras**: a purple cloth stretched over the impluvium to shade the atrium suffuses the white stone with a reddish hue, just as Atalanta's ivory-white body blushes from her exertion. For an analogous situation in the theater, see Lucretius 4.75–86.

596 **simulatos**: the shade is not natural but man-made.

597 **hospes**: although a stranger would normally fall under the protection of Jupiter, Hippomenes will nevertheless be in danger if he enters the contest for

Atalanta. Compare the *advenae* who were sacrificed at the altar of Jupiter Hospes if they entered his sanctuary at Amathus (224–228).

decursa novissima meta est: "the final turning post was passed." The verb *decurrere* is often associated with racing. *OLD* s.v. *decurro* 8a.

meta: the turning post in a Roman circus; cf. 106, 664.

598 *festa corona*: while Atalanta receives a crown as a prize, as did the winners of events at Greek festivals, this contest, with its *metae* and *carceres*, is reminiscent of a race in a Roman circus (cf. 638, 652, 656–659, 668). Note that footraces and winner's crowns were part of the *ludi magni*, which took place in the Circus Maximus; see Dionysius of Halicarnassus 7.73. For similarities between Ovid's description of the race and Vergil, *Aeneid* 5, see Fortuin 1996: 248–253.

599 *dant gemitum victi penduntque ex foedere poenas*: Ovid omits details of the execution. In Apollodorus (3.9.2) and Hyginus (*Fabulae* 158), Atalanta herself kills the suitors. In Ovid's account someone else kills them, which makes her seem less *immitis* (573). Here the fault lies with the suitors themselves, insofar as they would not leave her alone (568) and they voluntarily agreed to the terms of the race (574). Thus Ovid softens the harsh characterization of Atalanta that appears in other versions of the myth.

601 *vultuque in virgine fixo*: cf. Vergil, *Aeneid* 12.70: *figitque in virgine vultus*. On this echo, see Dyson 1999: 281–288.

602 *titulum*: this refers to the reputation that Atalanta acquired by defeating her challengers. *OLD* s.v. *titulus* 7. It may also allude to commemorative inscriptions such as those erected for victors in athletic contests. *OLD* s.v. *titulus* 2b.

inertes: Hippomenes' suggestion that Atalanta's suitors have been subpar runners is intended to goad her into accepting his challenge and prove her athletic prowess.

603–608 Hippomenes argues that his proposal has no downside for Atalanta. Her reputation will not diminish, no matter the outcome.

603 *mecum confer*: this verb usually takes an object (sc. *te*). Anderson 1972: 525 notes its military tone: "Hippomenes talks like an epic hero challenging a foe to battle." This observation could be extended to his entire address to Atalanta.

603–604 Such sentiments are common in the prelude to single combat in epic; cf. 5.191–192, 9.4–6, 12.80–81; Vergil, *Aeneid* 10.829–830, 11.688–689.

605 *mihi genitor Megareus Onchestius*: in Greece, sons were often named after their grandfathers. Apollodorus (3.15.5) mentions an Onchestian Megareus who was the son of Hippomenes, the grandfather of Ovid's

Hippomenes. Ovid omitted him from his list of ancestors, perhaps to avoid confusion. Since Neptune is Hippomenes' great grandfather, Hippomenes the elder would have been the son of Neptune. Cf. Pausanias 1.39.5, which mentions a Megareus, son of Poseidon.

Onchestius: a town in Boeotia mentioned in the *Iliad*, at 2.505–10.

607   **nec virtus citra genus est**: "and my courage is not inferior to my descent." *OLD* s.v. *citra* 4. Hippomenes does not provide evidence to support this, perhaps because he has had no opportunity to do anything heroic in his short life. This could, however, be a reference to the courage that he exhibited in challenging Atalanta after so many of her previous suitors had been executed.

608   **Hippomene**: the ablative of *Hippomenes*. Since Greek has no ablative case, this form had to be created by analogy with corresponding forms of Latin nouns of the third declension.

609   **molli vultu**: Atalanta gives him a look that betrays her nascent feelings for him. Previously she was *violenta* (568) and *immitis* (573) toward her suitors.

Schoenia: cf. *Cinyreia virgo* (369). The identification of Atalanta as the daughter of Schoenius goes back to [Hesiod], *Catalogue of Women*, fr. 75.12–15 Merkelbach–West, which seems to be Ovid's primary source for this story. She is sometimes identified with the Atalanta who took part in the Calydonian boar hunt. Ovid calls the huntress "the daughter of Schoenius" at *Heroides* 4.99, Apollodorus makes her the daughter of Iasus, and Hyginus (*Fabulae* 173, 175, 244, 246) says that both were daughters of Schoeneus. For an attempt to make sense of these variants, see Hill 1992: 180–181 and Ziogas 2013: 154–164.

610   **dubitat superari an vincere malit**: Atalanta's upcoming speech reflects this uncertainty. She seems to have forgotten the dire prediction of the oracle.

611–635   Atalanta's waffling internal monologue recalls that of Myrrha, who also struggles against feelings of love (321–355). The difference is that Atalanta's love is not illicit.

611–612   **"quis deus hunc formosis," inquit, "iniquus | perdere vult"**: Atalanta speculates that some god, jealous of Hippomenes' beauty, wants him dead and has chosen the race as the mechanism to accomplish this. At 630 she decides that Hippomenes is out of his mind.

613   **hoc**: the emphatic position of *hoc* ("*this* marriage") suggests that Atalanta does not believe that marriage to her is worth Hippomenes' life.

non sum, me iudice, tanti: Atalanta again underrates her worth to a potential suitor. Cf. 618: *tantique putat conubia nostra | ut pereat*; 622: *optari potes a sapiente puella*.

615   **puer**: at 589 and 600 Venus calls Hippomenes *iuvenis*, which can mean "youth" generally or designate, more specifically, a male over the age of 14 who has adopted the *toga virilis*. The word *puer* also describes Amor (1.456), Phaethon (2.198, 198), Narcissus (3.351), Liber (4.18), and Hermaphroditus (4.320, 329). Reed 1997: 284 suggests that Atalanta uses *puer* to emphasize Hippomenes' inexperience.

   non me movet ipse: cf. *non movet aetas | nec facies nec quae Venerem movere leones* (547–548).

616–618   Note the triple anaphora, which is (appropriately) reminiscent of rhetorical speech.

616–619   Atalanta admires Hippomenes' courage, his nobility, and the fact that he values her so highly that he is willing to die for the chance to marry her. Because it is the final element on the list, his love for her carries the most weight. While some of her other suitors may have had these qualities, they may not have had the beauty of Hippomenes, which Atalanta discounts even though she keeps mentioning it (611, 614–615, 621–622, 631).

616   **quid quod**: "what about the fact that."

617   **quartus**: the fourth, counting inclusively, as the Romans did: Neptune, Hippomenes the elder (Apollodorus 3.15.5), Megareus, Hippomenes the younger; cf. 605.

618   **tantique putat conubia nostra**: cp. *non sum, me iudice, tanti* (613).

619   **si me fors illi dura negarit**: i.e. if Hippomenes loses the race. Cf. 634: *nec mihi coniugium fata importuna negarent*.

   negarit: syncopated form of *negaverit*.

620   **hospes**: cf. *dum notat haec hospes* (597).

   thalamos: cf. *praemia veloci coniunx thalamique dabuntur* (571).

620–621   **cruentos | coniugium crudele**: note the harsh alliteration, which reflects the harsh fate that awaits Atalanta's challengers.

621–622   **nubere nulla | nolet**: the hard sound of 620–621 is followed by the soft alliteration in this line, where Atalanta considers the possibility that Hippomenes may find happiness.

   nulla: Hippomenes would be a prize for any woman.

622   **sapiens puella**: "a girl who has sound judgment." *OLD* s.v. *sapiens* 2.

624–625   **viderit! intereat quoniam tot caede procorum | admonitus non est**: Atalanta now tries to see Hippomenes as no different from any other suitor.

624   **viderit**: rare use of the perfect in the jussive subjunctive. "Let him see to himself." Cf. 9.519: *"viderit! insanos" inquit, "fateamur amores."*

625 **taedia vitae**: cf. *inter mortisque metus et taedia vitae* (482).

626 **occidet hic igitur voluit quia vivere mecum**: Atalanta once again softens her attitude toward Hippomenes.

628 **non erit invidiae victoria nostra ferendae**: "our victory will result in unbearable ill-will." Genitive of description. *OLD* s.v. *invidia* 2a. The spectators will feel pity for the handsome young man and blame Atalanta for his death. Cf. *Amores* 3.6.21–22: *non eris invidiae, torrens, mei crede, ferendae*.

630 **demens**: because he stubbornly insists on challenging Atalanta, knowing full well the penalty for losing.

utinam velocior esses: by wishing that Hippomenes were faster, Atalanta hopes that he will win. She again forgets the consequences of a potential marriage. Cf. *aspicit et dubitat, superari an vincere malit* (610).

631 **at quam virgineus puerile vultus in ore est**: Hippomenes looks like a young girl. *OLD* s.v. *virgineus* 1a. Earlier, Venus said that Adonis would look like Atalanta if he were a girl (579). Cf. *cuius erat facies, in qua materque paterque | cognosci possent* (4.290–291); *facies, quam dicere vere | virgineam in puero, puerilem in virgine possis* (8.322–323). In inscriptions, *virgineus* refers to a man who has married a girl who was not previously married. *OLD* s.v. *virgineus* 1c. This would certainly describe the man who marries Atalanta.

puerile: cf. 115. Cp. *puellari* (594).

632 **Hippomene**: Greek vocative.

635 **eras**: "you would deserve to live." Unreal indicative; see Palmer 1954: 316–317.

634 **fata importuna**: fortune does not deny Atalanta the opportunity to marry; it simply imposes consequences on this option. Cf. *si me fors illi dura negarit* (619).

635 **unus eras cum quo sociare cubilia vellem**: unreal indicative.

cubilia: Anderson 1972: 527–528 notes that this word sometimes refers to the lairs of beasts and therefore may foreshadow the transformation of Atalanta and Hippomenes into lions. *OLD* s.v. *cubile* 3.

636 **rudis**: "inexperienced in love."

637 **quid facit ignorans**: "unaware of what she is doing." This is an archaic use of the indicative in place of the subjunctive in an indirect question. A subjunctive could cause confusion if it were interpreted as being deliberative: "not knowing what she should do." This may explain why G emended this phrase to *quod facit*. See Bömer 1958: 210; Reed 1997: 286.

sentit: "recognize." *OLD* s.v. *sentio* 2a.

638 **iam solitos poscunt cursus populusque paterque**: even if Atalanta wanted to stop the race, societal and familial pressure would have forced her to go through with it.

paterque: this word is emphatic as a result of its position at the end of the line. The people desire the race for its entertainment value, but Atalanta's father is perhaps eager for her to be defeated so that she will be forced to marry. Schoeneus has a greater role in establishing the rules of the race in other versions of the story; see [Hesiod], *Catalogue of Women*, fr. 75.12–21 Merkelbach-West; Hesychius 185.2. This suggests that he may have opposed her marriage, possibly because of the threat it posed to his daughter. There is no indication that he is aware of the oracle in Ovid's version.

639 **proles Neptunia**: cf. *Neptunia proles, Cycnus* (12.72). This phrase emphasizes Hippomenes' heroic aspect, which foreshadows his victory. For his ancestry, see 605–606.

640 **Cytherea**: nominative (*Cўthĕrĕă*) and subject of the indirect command; cf. 717.

641 **adsit**: this verb is typically used to indicate that a deity is present. Cf. *adfuit ille* (4, of Hymenaeus) and *coniugio, quod fecit, adest dea* (295, of Venus).

642 **venta ... non invida**: the winds scatter prayers as though they were envious and wanted to destroy them. For this trope, see Reed 1997: 287.

644 **Tamasenum**: sc. *agrum*. This is the adjectival form of Tamassus (or Tamasos), a city in central Cyprus that was closely associated with Venus.

645 **telluris Cypriae pars optima**: for the fertility of its fields and mines, see Strabo 14.6.5.

645–647 These lines describe the dedication of a parcel of land and its proceeds to the temple of Venus, which provided an income for the sanctuary and support for its personnel. For the excavation of the temple of Aphrodite at Tamassos, see Buchholz and Untiedt 1996: 25–31.

645 **quem**: the antecedent is *ager* in 644.

646 **sacravere**: *sacraverunt*.
accedere: "accrue." *OLD* s.v. *accedo* 15.
dotem: "endowment." *OLD* s.v. *dos* 2b.

647–648 **medio nitet arbor in arvo, | fulva comas, fulvo ramis crepitantibus auro**: cf. Ovid's description of the tree that bore the apples of the Hesperides at 4.637–638: *arboreae frondes auro radiante nitentes | ex auro ramos, ex auro poma tegebant*. Aristenetus (1.10) says that Acontius used an apple from a garden of Aphrodite to seduce Cydippe. Buchholz and Untiedt 1996: 29–30 posit a connection with Aphrodite of the Gardens, who was worshipped at Athens

(Pausanias 1.19.2, 1.27.3; Pliny, *Naturalis historia* 36.16) and may have had a sanctuary near Paphos at Geroskipou (ἱερὸς κῆπος). According to Hesychius (s.v. Κάρπωσις), she received an offering of fruit at Amathus. Cf. Strabo (14.381), who mentions a place on Cyprus named Ἱεροκηπίς. For Aphrodite of the Gardens, see Langlotz 1954. Pliny (*Naturalis historia* 19.50) and Varro (*Res rusticae* 1.1.6) made Venus the tutulary deity of gardens. Note the temple of Venus in the Gardens of Sallust (*CIL* VI 32451).

647 ***medio nitet arbor in arvo***: the word *arbor* stands in the middle of this phrase just as the tree stands in the middle of the field.

648 ***fulvo ramis crepitantibus auro***: *fulvo* ... *auro* encloses *ramis crepitantibus* just as the gold encases the branches.

comas: accusative of respect.

crepitantibus: cf. Vergil's description of the Golden Bough at *Aeneid* 6.209: *sic leni crepitabat brattea vento*.

649–654 Apollodorus (3.9.2) says that Hippomenes already has the apples when he challenges Atalanta. Ovid makes him appear braver by having him challenge her before he obtains the help of the goddess.

650 ***aurea poma***: Ovid does not say what Venus originally intended to do with these apples, nor does he specify where Hippomenes put them during the race. Vergil (*Eclogues* 6.61) says that they were the apples of the Hesperides. For apples in amatory contexts, see McCartney 1925: 70–81. According to Faraone 1990: 230–238, apples were used as aphrodisiacs; public acceptance by a woman indicated that she consented to marriage. Compare the story of Hermochares and Ctesylla at Antoninus Liberalis 1.1-2. For apples and marriage, see also Barringer 1996: 74.

nullique videnda nisi ipsi: cf. Homer, *Iliad* 1.197–198, where Athena appears to Achilles, but no one else can see her.

videnda: the future participle expresses intention.

651 ***Hippomenen***: Greek accusative.

quis usus in illis: indirect question with an implied *esset*.

652 ***signa tubae dederant***: for the use of a starting horn at the beginning of a race, cf. Vergil, *Aeneid* 5.113 and 139 and Servius on 5.113, who says that this was *more Romano*.

652–653 ***cum carcere pronus uterque | emicat***: starting gates (*carceres*) for chariot races were employed in Rome, but not for footraces; see Humphrey 1986: 132–174. They were, however, used in Greek footraces; see Balabanes 1999. Both Ovid (*Heroides* 18.166) and Tibullus (1.4.32) speak of Elian *carceres*. Perhaps they use this word to transfer the restlessness and speed of the racehorses to the runners. For the numerous parallels between these lines and the race during the funeral games of Anchises in Vergil, *Aeneid* 5, see Bömer 1958: 214.

652   ***pronus***: they lean forward at the starting line.

uterque: this word confirms that there were only two contestants in this race.

653   ***emicat***: Vergil uses this verb in connection with footraces at *Aeneid* 5.319.

summam celeri pede libat harenam: they were running so quickly that they barely touched the ground.

655   ***et segetis canae stantes percurrere aristas***: cf. Vergil, *Aeneid* 7.808–809 for a description of the speed of Camilla, another virgin who competes with men: *illa vel intactae segetis per summa volaret | gramina nec teneras cursu laesisset aristas.*

655   ***canae***: the wheat is dry and ready for harvest. Since it is now at its tallest and most brittle, they would have to run extremely quickly to avoid damaging the crop.

656   ***clamorque favorque***: the crowd supports the underdog. Reed 1997: 288 suggests that the people are cheering not so much for Hippomenes himself as for Atalanta, because they want her to be wed.

657   ***incumbere tempus***: "buckle down." *OLD* s.v. *incumbo* 6d.

658   ***Hippomene***: Greek vocative.

659–660   ***Megareius ... Schoeneia***: the use of epic nomenclature for both contestants brings them to the same level.

dubium ... dictis: as at 610, Atalanta's infatuation with Hippomenes appears to have made her forget the consequences of defeat.

660   ***virgo ... Schoeneia***: cf. *virgo Cinyreia* (369).

Schoeneia: *Schoenēĭă.*

661–662   ***cum iam posset transire, morata est | spectatosque diu vultus invita reliquit***: Atalanta runs neck and neck with Hippomenes not because she cannot pass him, but so that she may gaze at his face. This slows her down, as will the golden apples (*remorata*, 671).

663   ***aridus e lasso veniebat anhelitus ore***: this refers to Hippomenes, who refrains from using the apples until he is in danger of losing the race. For his panting, cf. [Hesiod], *Catalogue of Women*, fr. 76.23 Merkelbach-West.

meta: cf. 597: *decursa novissima meta est.* The conical turning posts were located at both ends of the divider (*spina*) in the middle of the circus.

665–666   Note the use of dactyls for speed in 665. Ovid switches to spondees in 667 to depict delay. See Emeljanow 1969: 74.

666 ***obstipuit***: this verb is used repeatedly in Book 10 (42, 64, 287, 580) to indicate that something so extraordinary is happening that it compels the beholder to stop whatever she or he is doing. At 580, Hippomenes *obstipuit* when he saw Atalanta; here Atalanta *obstipuit* when she saw the golden apple. Cf. Vergil, *Eclogues* 6.61: *Hesperidum miratam mala puellam*. [Hesiod], *Catalogue of Women*, fr. 76.18 Merkelbach–West compares her to a Harpy in her eagerness to get the apple.

668 ***spectacula***: "the stands." *OLD* s.v. *spectaculum* 3.

669 ***celeri cessataque tempora cursu***: note the word order. Atalanta's swift course is broken up by her delay.

670–671 Ovid uses the same metrical technique as in 665–666: dactyls for speed in 670 and spondees for delay in 671.

672 ***virum***: this is the first time that Hippomenes is called a man rather than a boy (615) or a youth (589, 600).

673 ***"nunc" inquit "ades, dea muneris auctor"***: having used the first two apples ineffectively, Hippomenes asks Venus for her help with his last chance to win the race. This is the second time Hippomenes asks the goddess for assistance. Cf. 640–641.

674–675 ***inque latus campi ... | iecit ab oblique nitidum iuvenaliter aurum***: this time Hippomenes throws the apple diagonally and far to the side of the track, so that Atalanta will have to run farther.

675 ***iuvenaliter***: "with youthful vigor," in contrast to his two prior attempts, which failed to slow her progress sufficiently.

676–678 Atalanta hesitates to pick up the third apple because she knows that this will cause her to lose the race. She did not hesitate to retrieve the first two (664–672), perhaps because Hippomenes threw them earlier in the race and Atalanta thought (rightly) that she had sufficient time to catch up with him. Now they are at the end of the race, when a diversion may cost her the victory. Her hesitation echoes the feelings expressed in her internal monologue (610–635), where she wavers between wanting to win or to lose. Venus must intervene and force her to pick up the apple. Note that the goddess takes credit for this three times: *coegi | tollere, adieci ... pondera, impediique*. If it were not for her intervention, Atalanta may have decided not to endanger her lead. There is no doubt that Venus is responsible for Hippomenes' victory. His lack of gratitude leads to his punishment.

677 ***sublato pondera malo***: Venus places the word *pondera* inside *sublato* and *malo* just as she places extra weight inside the retrieved apple.

678 ***impediique oneris partier gravitate moraque***: zeugma.

moraque: appropriately, "delay" is delayed until the end of the sentence.

679   ***neve meus sermo cursu sit tardior ipso***: Venus does not elaborate on the end of the race. She wants to move on to her purpose in telling this story – to explain why she hates lions (552).

680   ***duxit sua praemia victor***: *ducere* is also used of a man marrying a woman (*ducere in matrimonium*). *OLD* s.v. *duco* 5a. The reward is Atalanta, whom Hippomenes intends to marry.

681–683   The answer to Venus' rhetorical question is obviously "yes." Since Hippomenes did neither of these things, he deserves to be punished.

681–682   ***cui grates ageret, cui turis honorem | ferret***: relative clauses of characteristic.

682   ***nec grates immemor egit***: Hippomenes has violated his contractual obligation to the goddess (*do ut des*), which required him to reward her for her service. Compare Pygmalion (290–291), who gave thanks to Venus immediately after she made the statue come to life.

   turis: cf. Homer, *Odyssey* 8.362–363 and *Homeric Hymn to Aphrodite* 59, which mention the incense offered to Aphrodite at Paphos. The altar of Venus smokes with incense when Pygmalion makes his prayer at 273.

   grates: this word describes thanks given to deities. *OLD* s.v. *grates*.

684–685   Venus fears that, if she does not punish Hippomenes now, she will set a precedent for those who would cheat her in the future.

685   ***exemplo caveo***: "I guard [against scorn] through an object lesson."

   ambos: this seems unfair because Atalanta has done nothing to earn the wrath of the goddess.

686   ***templa***: "sacred precinct." *OLD* s.v. *templum* 1c. Venus describes a rustic sanctuary that consists of a woodland temple, a cave, and wooden cult images (691–694).

   deum Matri: Cybele, a goddess from Asia Minor who was brought to Rome during the Second Punic War. Ovid mentions her at 103–105 and speaks of her love for the boy Attis at *Fasti* 4.223–250.

686–687   ***clarus Echion | fecerat***: Echion was one of the men who sprung from the dragon's teeth that Cadmus sowed at Thebes (3.126). Other versions of the myth locate this event in a sanctuary of Jupiter on Mount Parnassus. See Apollodorus 3.9.2; Hyginus, *Fabulae* 185.6.

687   ***ex voto***: Echion's offerings were made in fulfillment of a vow. He gave thanks to the gods, but Hippomenes does not.

688   ***iter longum***: from the Boeotian home of Atalanta to Onchestus, west of Thebes. [Hesiod], *Catalogue of Women*, 75.21 appears to say that the winner in this race will take Atalanta back to his fatherland. Cf. Hesychius 185.5: *hanc cum in patriam duceret*. According to Strabo (9.2.22), there was a city called Schoinos just north of Thebes. Pausanias (8.35), however, says that Schoeneus was a Boeotian king who migrated to Arcadia, where there were racecourses of Atalanta near a town called Schoeneus. A scholion on Theocritus 3.38d attempts to sort this out by saying that there were two Atalantas, one from Boeotia and one from Arcadia.

688   *iter longum requiescere suasit*: cf. 554–556, where the exertion of the hunt makes Venus want to rest, and this turns into a romantic interlude.

689–690   *illic concubitus intempestiva cupido | occupat Hippomenen a numine concita nostro*: this untimely lust is not the fault of Hippomenes, but the punishment of Venus for his failure to thank her. Nothing is said about the desire of Atalanta, although her attraction to Hippomenes during the race suggests that she may not have been an unwilling participant. Note the shift from the past tense in 688 to the present tense here, which makes the action more vivid. Cf. 695.

691–692   *prope templa recessus, | speluncae similis, nativo pumice tectus*: Ovid describes a perfect lair for lions, which foreshadows the metamorphosis of Atalanta and Hippomenes. For intercourse in caves in Roman poetry, see Segal 1969: 20–23 and Reed 1997: 291.

693   *religione sacer prisca*: cf. *Fasti* 3.264: *antiqua religione sacer*; Vergil, *Aeneid* 8.598: *religione patrum late sacer*.

694   *lignea contulerat veterum simulacra deorum*: the *lignea simulacra* are primitive wooden cult statues that the Greeks called *xoana*. It is fitting that the cult images of the old gods be of archaic workmanship. Hippomenes must have seen these and knew that the area was holy, but he defiled it in spite of this. In the eyes of Cybele, who had no way of knowing that Venus was responsible for his uncontrollable lust, Hippomenes deserved punishment.

695   *vetito temerat sacraria probro*: intercourse pollutes sacred spaces; see Parker 1983: 74–103; O'Bryhim 1990: 75–80. Cf. 4.798, where Medusa is punished for having intercourse with Neptune in a sanctuary of Minerva.

   probro: an improper sexual act, whose character is emphasized by *vetito*.

696   *sacra retorserunt oculos*: cf. 448–451, where the constellations refused to witness Myrrha's incest.

   turrita Mater: Cybele, who wears a mural crown. Cf. *Fasti* 4.219: *turrifera ... corona*; Lucretius 2.606: *muralique caput summum cinxere corona*; Vergil, *Aeneid* 6.785: *invehitur curru Phrygias turrita per urbes*. According to Apollodorus (3.9.2) and Hyginus (*Fabulae* 185.6), Atalanta and Hippomenes defiled a sanctuary of Jupiter, who turned them into lions. Nonnus (12.87–89) says that it was Artemis who transformed Atalanta.

697 ***Stygia sontes dubitavit mergeret unda***: in other words, the goddess is trying to decide whether to kill them. Cf. 232–233, where Venus tries to think of an appropriate punishment for the Cerastae. *sontes* is enveloped by *Stygia ... unda*, which reflects how the offenders would be drowned in the river Styx.

698–704 This description takes the form of a riddle, whose answer is the last word of the sentence: *leones*.

689–689 ***levia ... colla***: "necks free from coarse hair." *OLD* s.v. *levis* 2.

700 ***ex umeris ... armi fiunt***: "the shoulders of animals develop from their human shoulders." *OLD* s.v. *armus* 1a.

701 ***summae cauda verruntur harenae***: cf. 653: *summam celeri pede libat harenam*.

702 ***iram vultus habet***: compare the description of Jupiter disguised as a bull at 2.858: *pacem vultus habet*.

703 ***thalamis***: Hippomenes and Atalanta behaved like animals by copulating in a cave instead of in a bedroom. For the extreme lustfulness of lions, see Pliny, *Historia naturalis* 8.17. According to Hyginus (*Fabulae* 185) and Servius (*ad Aeneidum* 3.113), the gods do not allow lions to mate. Forbes Irving 1990: 75–76 observes that Atalanta began as an untamed virgin living in the wild and ends as a yoked animal.

celebrant silvas: Atalanta frequents the forest at the beginning and at the end of this myth.

704 ***dente premunt domito Cybeleia frena leones***: a pair of lions pulled the chariot of Cybele. Cf. Lucretius 2.601: *in curru biiugos agitare leones*.

dente ... domito: by the bit that they hold in their mouths.

Cybeleia: *Cȳbĕlēĭă*.

705–707 These lines echo Venus' warning to Adonis at the beginning of the myth of Atalanta (543–552).

706 ***terga fugae ... pugnae pectora***: chiasmus.

708 ***iunctisque ... cycnis***: cf. *Cypron olorinis nondum pervenerat alis* (718). Venus is often depicted riding on a swan or in a cart drawn by swans; see *LIMC* 2 s.v. Aphrodite. Bömer 1958: 226–227 and Reed 1997: 293 trace the history of this motif in Italy to the Etruscans. See also *Ars amatoria* 3.809–810; Horace, *Carmina* 3.28.15, 4.1.10; Propertius 3.3.39. Compare Cybele, who travels in a chariot drawn by lions (704).

709 ***sed stat monitis contraria virtus***: Adonis is searching for an opportunity to display his courage. See Barringer 2001: 154–155 on the heroic associations of the hunt. For the boldness of Adonis, see Nonnus 29.135.

710–711 ***forte suem latebris vestigia certa secuti | excivere canes***: the boar is the very animal that Venus warned Adonis to avoid at 539 and 549–550. Sources vary concerning the origin of the boar. Apollodorus (3.14.4) says that Artemis sent it; Servius (*ad Georgicon* 10.18) says that Mars turned himself into the boar, but elsewhere (*ad Aeneidem* 5.72) he says that an angry Mars sent the boar; Nonnus (42.320) blames a jealous Hephaestus. For further variants, see Lightfoot 2003: 319–320.

712 ***Cinyreius***: Cĭnўrēĭŭs. This heroic epithet recalls Adonis' relationship to Cinyras, his father/grandfather. It occurs immediately before the boar kills him, just as the same epithet is applied to Myrrha immediately before she attempts suicide (369).

obliquo ictu: an oblique blow would not sink deeply into the flesh, but would make the animal wounded and angry. Cf. 675, where Hippomenes slows Atalanta's progress by tossing the apple *ab obliquo*. Adonis dies in his contest, but Hippomenes lives. In the end, both undergo a metamorphosis.

713 ***pando ... rostro***: ablative of means rather than ablative of separation.

venabula: poetic plural.

714 ***trepidumque et tuta petentem***: Adonis does not display the *virtus* that he seeks in 709. Compare the behavior of Hippocoon after his leg was gored during the Caledonian boar hunt: *trepidantem et terga parantem* (8.363).

715–716 ***totosque sub inguine dentes | abdidit***: thigh wounds are common in myths of boar hunting; cf. 8.371, 400; Homer, *Odyssey* 19.449–450; Apollonius 2.825; Bion, *Epitaphius Adonidis* 41; Lycophron 487. For the wounding of Adonis, see *Amores* 3.9.16. This is a particularly dangerous injury because it can sever the femoral artery, which supplies blood to the lower part of the body. Usually one tusk pierces the hunter's skin. Here the wound is made by all the boar's teeth, which implies that it is deep and will bring certain death.

716 ***fulva moribundum stravit harena***: cf. Vergil's (*Aeneid* 5.374) description of Dares' defeat of Butes in a boxing match: *fulva moribundum extendit harena*. As Anderson 1972: 533 notes, the boar appears more heroic than Adonis.

harena: Ovid says (710–711) that the hunt takes place in the forest, but Adonis dies on the sand. This may be an allusion to the sand in the arena, where wild animals such as boars were hunted, sometimes as travesties of myth. See Coleman 1990: 44–73. Sand was mentioned twice in the story of Atalanta: Hippomenes' race takes place on the sand (653); and the tails of lions sweep the sand (701).

717–718 ***vecta levi curru ... olorinis***: cf. *iunctisque per aera cycnis | carpit iter* (708–709).

717 ***medias Cytherea per auras***: note the word order. *Cytherea* stands between *medias* and *auras*, which reflects how the goddess is being carried through the midst of the sky. Hill 1992: 194 suggests that this refers to the "intervening air."
  Cytherea: Cȳthĕrĕă.

718 ***Cypron***: Greek accusative. Venus is traveling from the Near East to one of her cult places on Cyprus.

719 ***agnovit longe gemitum***: the same words appear at Vergil, *Aeneid* 10.843, where Mazentius hears the mourning for his dead son from far off.

720–724 For Ovid's model for these lines, see Vergil, *Aeneid* 10.821–825, 11.39–42; Reed 1997: 296.

721 ***iactantem***: frequentative. The wounded Adonis keeps writhing in agony.

721–722 ***pariterque sinum pariterque capillos | rupit et indignis percussit pectora palmis***: these mourning behaviors play a role in the Adonia, where women commemorate the death of Adonis. Venus describes the mourning ritual at 725–727.

721 ***indignis percussit pectora palmis***: transferred epithet. It is her breasts that are unworthy of being beaten. The alliteration reflects the sound of palms striking the body.

722–723 Deities tend to avoid the pollution of death; compare Artemis' behavior in Euripides at *Hippolytus* 1437–1438. Apollo is present while Hyacinthus is dying, but transforms him into a flower before he expires.

724–725 ***questaque cum fatis "at non tamen omnia vestri | iuris erunt"***: note the enjambment. The Fates have the right to claim Adonis, but Venus will find a way to keep his memory alive.

724 ***quaestaque cum fatis***: cf. Orpheus after his failure to retrieve Eurydice: *esse deos Erebi crudeles quaestus* (76).

724 ***cum***: "against." *OLD* s.v. *cum* 13b.
  at: this strong adversative indicates that Venus will not be completely controlled by the Fates.

725 ***luctus monimenta manebunt***: cf. Apollo's mourning for Hyacinthus at 414–413, which also results in the production of a flower.
  monumenta manebunt: Venus says that this memorial will focus on her mourning, which will be reflected in the women's mourning during the Adonia. Ovid uses the phrase *monumenta manebunt* in connection with etiologies at 1.710, 4.161, 11.743 and 794, 15.305 and 621; *Fasti* 2.301–302, 4.709.
  monumentum: a memorial, but not a physical one. *OLD* s.v. *monumentum* 3.

726-727 ***repetitaque mortis imago | annua plangoris peraget simulamina nostri***: this myth provides an etiology for the annual Adonia festival; see Sappho, fr. 140.2 Voigt; Aristophanes, *Lysistrata* 396; Dioscorides in *Anthologia palatina* 5.53.193; Bion, *Epitaphius Adonidis*; Plutarch, *Alcibiades* 18.5, Nicander 13.7; Lucian, *De dea syria* 6. Ovid, *Ars amatoria* 1.75 mentions the Adonia in Rome. Cf. the annual mourning rituals for Hyacinthus (218–219) and Hippolytus (Euripides, *Hippolytus* 1425–1430).

repetitaque mortis imago | annua: "repeated annual reenactment of your death." Cf. the Hyacinthia, which has an *annua pompa* (219).

726 ***Adoni***: Greek vocative.

727 ***plangoris ... nostri***: cf. Apollo, who turned Hyacinthus into a flower that will imitate *gemitus nostros* (206).

simulamina: this appears to be an Ovidian coinage.

peraget: "recount" or "deal with." *OLD* s.v. *perago* 11.

728 ***cruor in florem mutabitur***: this flower is the anemone. According to Bion (*Epitaphius Adonidos* 64–66), Aphrodite's tears become anemones and Adonis' blood becomes roses; see Reed 1997: 298. Compare Hyacinthus, whose blood was transformed into a hyacinth (209–213).

729 ***femineos artus in olentes vertere mentas***: Strabo (8.3.14) says that Menthe was Hades' lover. A jealous Persephone trod upon her and then changed her into the mint plant, which releases its fragrance when crushed. Because Persephone was allowed to transform her rival into a plant, Venus should be allowed to change her lover into a flower. For a somewhat different version of the myth of Menthe, see Oppian, *Halieutica* 3.486–498.

730-731 ***nobis Cinyreius heros | invidiae mutatus erit?*** "will the transformation of the Cinyreian hero be begrudged to me?" Double dative.

730 ***Persephone***: Ovid must use the Greek form of Proserpina at the beginning of this line because it will form a dactyl.

Cinyreius heros: cf. Orpheus as *Rhodopeius heros* (50), Pygmalion as *Paphius heros* (290), and Hippomenes as *Megareius heros* (59).

732 ***nectare odorato sparsit***: in Homer, nectar acted as a divine preservative for dead bodies; see *Iliad* 19.38–39 and 23.185–187. When consumed by mortals, it can bring immortality; see *Homeric Hymn to Ceres* 237; Apollonius 4.870–872; Theocritus 15.108. Here it gives Adonis immortality as a plant that returns every year.

733-734 ***ut fulvo perlucida caeno | surgere bulla solet***: although most manuscripts have *caelo*, Merkel 1897 emends *caelo* to *caeno*. This phrase may refer to the yellow bubbles formed by the methane that is produced in a swampy area full of decomposing organic material, such as the Pontine

Marshes that lay outside of Rome. Boars often favor a swampy habitat. For the creation of new life from slime, see 1.418-419: *caenumque udaeque paludes | intumere*. Anderson 1972: 534-535 argues in favor of keeping *caelo*, which he interprets as an allusion to the yellow Italian sky and supports with Ovid's reference to yellow clouds at 3.273.

735-739 This is a riddle about the anemone, whose name does not appear here; cf. 698-704 for a riddle about lions. The scholiast to Theocritus 5.90 attributes this metamorphosis to Nicander.

734 **nec plena longior hora | fata mora est**: Hyacinthus' metamorphosis happened immediately (209), but the transformation of Adonis took some time.

736 **qualem lento celant sub cortice granum**: this phrase refers to the tough rind that covers the seeds of the pomegranate. Cf. *Fasti* 4.608: *granis, punica quae lento cortice poma tegunt*; *Ex Ponto* 4.15.7: *punica sub lento cortice grana rubent*.

quae: refers to *punica* in 737.

737 **punica**: the pomegranate, an allusion to Persephone, who had to remain in Hades for a portion of the year because she ate its seeds. Cf. 5.534-538; *Fasti* 4.607-608; *Homeric Hymn to Ceres* 372.

brevis est tamen usus in illo: this flower, like the life of Adonis, does not last long.

738 **haerentem ... caducum**: sc. *florem*.

nimia levitate: the fragility of the anemone reflects the fragility of Adonis.

739 **qui praestant nomina, venti**: the anemone derives its name from the Greek word for "wind," ἄνεμος.

praestant: "furnish."

Although the song of Orpheus concludes at the end of Book 10, his story continues into Book 11, where the women of Thrace, whose love he rejected, attack the bard as he sings. At first their weapons have no effect, because these inanimate objects are charmed by his song. When their flutes, drums, and howling drown out his music, their weapons find their mark, and the frenzied Bacchants dismember Orpheus. All of nature mourns as his disembodied head floats down the Hebrus until it comes to rest on the shores of Lesbos. Orpheus' soul descends to the underworld and proceeds to the Elysian Fields, where he finds Eurydice. At last he can embrace her and look back at her without fear, as they stroll through paradise.

Works Cited

Agelarakis, A. 1998. "The Osseous Record in the Western Necropolis of Amathus: An Archeo-Anthropological Investigation." In V. Karageorghis and N. Stampolidis, eds., *Proceedings of the International Symposium "Eastern Mediterannean: Cyprus–Dodecanese–Crete, 16th–6th cent. BC."* University of Crete / A.G. Leventis Foundation: Rethymnon / Nicosia, 217–229.

Adams, J.N. 1990. *The Latin Sexual Vocabulary*. Johns Hopkins University Press: Baltimore, MD.

Aldrete, G. 2014. "Hammers, Axes, Bulls, and Blood: Some Practical Aspects of Roman Animal Sacrifice." *Journal of Roman Studies* 104: 28–50.

Anderson, W.S. 1966. "*Talaria* and Ovid *Met*. 10.591." *Transactions of the American Philological Association* 97: 1–13.

Anderson, W.S. 1972. *Ovid's Metamorphoses, Books 6–10*. University of Oklahoma Press: Norman.

Anderson, W.S. 1982. "The Orpheus of Vergil and Ovid: *flebile nescio quid*." In J. Warden, ed., *Orpheus: The Metamorphoses of a Myth*. University of Toronto Press: Toronto, 25–50.

Anderson, W.S. 1989. "The Artist's Limits in Ovid: Orpheus, Pygmalion, and Daedalus." *Syllecta Classica* 1: 1–11.

Arbel, B. 2012. "Cypriot Wildlife in Renaissance Writings." In B. Arbel, E. Chayes, and H. Hendricks, eds., *Cyprus and the Renaissance (1450–1650)*. Brepols: Turnhout, 321–344.

Arnott, W.G. 1973. "Imitation, Variation, Exploitation: A Study in Aristaenetus." *Greek, Roman, and Byzantine Studies* 14: 197–211.

Atallah, W. 1966. *Adonis dans la littérature et l'art grecs*. Klincksieck: Paris.

Balabanes, P. 1999. *Hysplex: The Starting Mechanism in Ancient Stadia*. University of California Press: Berkeley.

A Student's Commentary on Ovid's Metamorphoses *Book 10*, First Edition. Shawn O'Bryhim.
© 2021 John Wiley & Sons, Inc. Published 2021 by John Wiley & Sons, Inc.

Barchiesi, A. 2001. *Speaking Volumes: Narrative and Intertext in Ovid and Other Latin Poets*. Bristol Classical Press: London.

Barringer, J. 1996. "Atalanta as Model: The Hunter and the Hunted." *Classical Antiquity* 15: 48–76.

Barringer, J. 2001. *The Hunt in Ancient Greece*. Johns Hopkins University Press: Baltimore, MD.

Baudy, G. 1986. *Adonisgärten: Studien zur antike Samensymbolik*. A. Hain: Frankfurt am Main.

Bauer, D. 1962. "The Function of Pygmalion in the *Metamorphoses* of Ovid." *Transactions of the American Philological Association* 93: 1–21.

Baumbach, J. 2004. *The Significance of Votive Offerings in Selected Hera Sanctuaries in the Peloponnese, Ionia and Western Greece*. Archaeopress: Oxford.

Baurain, C. 1980. "Kinyras: La fin de l'âge du bronze à Chypre et la tradition antique." *Bulletin de Correspondence Hellénique* 104: 277–308.

Baurain, C. 1981. "Un autre nom pour Amathonte de Chypre." *Bulletin de Correspondence Hellénique* 105: 361–372.

Beard, M. and J. Henderson. 1998. "With This Body I Thee Worship: Sacred Prostitution in Antiquity." In M. Wyke, ed., *Gender and the Body in the Ancient Mediterranean*. Wiley Blackwell: Oxford, 56–79.

Bernabé, A. and J. San Cristóbal. 2008. *Instructions for the Netherworld: The Orphic Gold Tablets*. Brill: Leiden.

Bömer, F. 1958. *P. Ovidius Naso: Die Fasten*. Carl Winter: Heidelberg.

Bömer, F. 1980. *P. Ovidius Naso: Metamorphosen, Buch X–XI*. Carl Winter: Heidelberg.

Bremmer, J. 1991. "Orpheus: From Guru to Gay." In P. Borgeaud, ed., *Orphisme et Orphée en l'honneur de Jean Rudhardt*. Droz: Geneva, 13–30.

Brown, J. 1965. "Kothar, Kinyras, and Kythereia." *Journal of Semitic Studies* 10: 197–219.

Buchholz, H. and K. Untiedt. 1996. *Tamassos: Ein antikes Königreich auf Zypern*. Paul Åströms: Jonsered.

Budin, S. 2008. *The Myth of Sacred Prostitution in Antiquity*. Cambridge University Press: Cambridge.

Buisson, R. du. 1963. "Origine et évolution du panthéon de Tyr." *Revue de l'Histoire des Religions* 164: 153–162.

Carter, A. 1902. *Epitheta deorum quae apud poetas Latinos leguntur*. Teubner: Leipzig.

Caubet, A. 1989. "Pygmalion et la statue d'ivoire." In R. Étienne, M. le Dinahet, and M. Yon, eds., *Architecture et poésie dans le monde grec: Hommage à Georges Roux*. Maison Orient: Paris, 247–254.

Works Cited

Cazeaux, J. 1980. "Anaxarète et Iphis (Ovide, *Metamorphoses*, 14, 698s) ou la pierre, le lin, le discourse." In M. Yon, ed., *Salamine de Chypre: Histoire et archéologie*. Éditions du Centre national de la recherche scientifique: Paris, 237–247.

Clark, W. 1973. "Myrrha's Nurse: The Marathon Runner in Ovid?" *Classical Philology* 68: 55–56.

Clarke, J. 1998. *Looking at Lovemaking: Constructions of Sexuality in Roman Art, 100 BC–AD 250*. University of California Press: Berkeley.

Coleman, K. 1990. "Fatal Charades: Roman Executions Staged as Mythological Enactments." *Journal of Roman Studies* 80: 44–73.

Connors, C. 1992. "Seeing Cypresses in Vergil." *Classical Journal* 88: 1–17.

Courtney, E. 2001. *A Companion to Petronius*. Oxford University Press: Oxford.

Courtney, E. 2004. "The 'Greek' Accusative." *Classical Journal* 99: 425–431.

Cross, F.M. 1994. "A Phoenician Inscription from Idalion: Some Old and New Texts Relating to Child Sacrifice." In M. Coogan, J. Exum, and L. Stager, eds., *Scripture and Other Artifacts: Essays on the Bible and Archaeology in Honor of Philip J. King*. J. Knox Press: Louisville, 231–237.

Cucchiarelli, A. 2002. "A Note on Vergil, *Aeneid* 12.941–2." *Classical Quarterly* 52: 620–622.

Cumont, F. 1927. "Les Syriens en Espangne et les Adonies a Seville." *Syria* 8: 330–341.

Curtius, E.R. 1954. *Europäische Literatur und lateinisches Mittealter*. Francke: Bern.

Dalley, S. 1998. *The Legacy of Mesopotamia*. Oxford University Press: Oxford.

Dörrie, H. 1974. *Pygmalion: Ein Impuls Ovids und seine Wirkungen in die Gegenwart*. Westdeutscher Verlag: Opladen.

Dyson, J. 1999. "Lilies and Violence: Lavinia's Blush in the Song of Orpheus." *Classical Philology* 94: 281–8.

Edwards, C. 1993. *The Politics of Immorality in Ancient Rome*. Cambridge University Press: Cambridge.

Elsner, J. 1991. "Visual Mimesis and the Myth of the Real: Ovid's Pygmalion as Viewer." *Ramus* 20: 158–159.

Emeljanow, V. 1969. "Ovidian Mannerism: An Analysis of the Venus and Adonis Episode in *Met.* X 503–738." *Mnemosyne* 22: 67–76.

Erker, D. 2011. "Gender and Roman Funeral Ritual." In V. Hope and J. Huskinson, eds., *Memory and Mourning: Studies on Roman Death*. Oxbow Books: Oxford, 40–60.

Fantham, E. 1998. *Ovid: Fasti Book 4*. Cambridge University Press: Cambridge.

Fantuzzi, M. 1985. *Bionis Smyrnaei Adonidis epitaphium*. Francis Cairns: Liverpool.

Faraone, C. 1990. "Aphrodite's ΚΕΣΤΟΣ and Apples for Atalanta: Aphrodisiacs in Early Greek Myth and Ritual." *Phoenix* 44: 219–243.

Faraone, C. 2004. "Orpheus' Final Performance: Necromancy and a Singing Head on Lesbos." *Studi italiani di filologia classica* 4: 5–27.

Farnell, L.R. 1896. *Cults of the Greek City States*. Cambridge University Press: Cambridge.

Feeney, D. 1991. *The Gods in Epic*. Oxford University Press: Oxford.

Forbes Irving, P.M.C. 1990. *Metamorphosis in Greek Myths*. Oxford University Press: Oxford.

Fortuin, R. 1996. *Der Sport im Augusteischen Rom*. Franz Steiner Verlag: Stuttgart.

Franklin, J. 2006. "Lyre Gods of the Bronze Age Musical Koine." *Journal of the Near Eastern Religions* 6: 39–70.

Galinsky, G.K. 1975. *Ovid's Metamorphoses: An Introduction to the Basic Aspects*. University of California Press: Berkeley.

Gantz, T. 1996. *Early Greek Myth: A Guide to Literary and Artistic Sources*. Johns Hopkins University Press: Baltimore, MD.

Gärtner, T. 2008. "Die hellenistische Katalogdichtung des Phanokles über homosexuelle Liebesbeziehungen: Untersuchungen zur tendenziellen Gestaltung und zum literarischen Nachleben." *Mnemosyne* 61: 18–44.

Gee, E. 2013. *Aratus and the Astronomical Tradition*. Oxford University Press: Oxford.

Graf, F. 2012. "Exclusive Singing (*OF* 1a/b)." In M. Jáuregui, A. Cristóbal, E. Martínez, R. Hernández, M. Álvarez, and S. Tovar, eds., *Tracing Orpheus: Studies of Orphic Fragments*. De Gruyter: Berlin, 13–16.

Graf, F. and S.I. Johnson. 2007. *Ritual Texts for the Afterlife: Orpheus and the Bacchic Gold Tablets*. Routledge: New York.

Grigson, G. 1978. *The Goddess of Love: Birth, Triumph, Death and Return of Aphrodite*. Constable: London.

Grueber, H.A. 1910. *Coins of the Roman Republic in the British Museum*. Longmans: London.

Hall, E. 1989. *Inventing the Barbarian*. Oxford University Press: Oxford.

Hardie, A. 1994. *Vergil: Aeneid Book IX*. Cambridge University Press: Cambridge.

Hardie, A. 2002. *Ovid's Poetics of Illusion*. Cambridge University Press: Cambridge.

Hardie, A. 2004. "Approximative Similes in Ovid: Incest and Doubling." *Dictynna* 1: 83–112.

Harris, W.V. 2013. "Greek and Roman Hallucinations." In W.V. Harris, ed., *Mental Disorders in the Ancient World*. Brill: Leiden, 285–306.

Heath, J. 1994. "The Failure of Orpheus." *Transactions of the American Philological Association* 124: 163–96.

Heath, J. 1996. "The Stupor of Orpheus: Ovid's *Metamorphoses* 10: 64–71." *Classical Journal* 91: 353–70.

Henderson, J. 1991. *The Maculate Muse*. Oxford University Press: Oxford.

Hermary, A. 1987. "Amathonte de Chypre et les phéniciens." In E. Lipinski, ed., *Studia Phoenicia V: Phoenicia and the East Mediterranean in the First Millennium BC*. Peeters: Leuven, 375–388.

Hermary, A. and V. Tatton-Brown. 1981. *Amathonte II: Testimonia*. Part II: *Les sculptures découvertes avant 1975*. Éditions ADPF: Paris.

Hersch, K. 2010. *The Roman Wedding: Ritual and Meaning in Antiquity*. Cambridge University Press: Cambridge.

Hill, D.E. 1992. "From Orpheus to Ass's Ears: Ovid, Metamorphoses 10.1–11.193." In T. Woodman and J. Powell, eds., *Author and Audience in Latin Literature*. Cambridge University Press: Cambridge, 124–137.

Hollis, A.S. 1970. *Ovid: Metamorphoses, Book VIII*. Oxford University Press: Oxford.

Hollis, A.S. 2007. *Fragments of Roman Poetry, c. 60 BC–AD 20*. Oxford University Press: Oxford.

Hope, V. 2009. *Roman Death: The Dying and the Dead in Ancient Rome*. Continuum: London.

Hubbard, T. 2013. "Pindar's Tenth Olympian and Athlete-Trainer Pederasty." In B. Verstraete and V. Provencal, eds., *Same-Sex Desire and Love in Greco-Roman Antiquity and in the Classical Tradition of the West*. Routledge: London, 137–171.

Humphrey, J. 1986. *Roman Circuses: Arenas for Charioteers*. University of California Press: Berkeley.

Janan, M. 1988. "The Book of Good Love? Design vs. Desire in *Metamorphoses* 10." *Ramus* 17: 110–137.

Jashemski, W. 1993. *The Gardens of Pompeii*, vol. 2. Caratzas: Yonkers.

Johnson, P. 2008. *Ovid before Exile: Art and Punishment in the Metamorphoses*. University of Wisconsin Press: Madison.

Jones, C.P. 1987. "Stigma: Tattooing and Branding in Greco-Roman Antiquity." *Journal of Roman Studies* 77: 139–155.

Karageorghis, V. 1982. *Cyprus from the Stone Age to the Romans*. Thames & Hudson: London.

Karageorghis, V. 1987. *La nécropole d'Amathonte: Tombes 113–367*. A.G. Leventis Foundation: Nicosia.

Knox, P. 1983. "Cinna, the *Ciris*, and Ovid." *Classical Quarterly* 78: 309–11.

Knox, P. 1986. *Ovid's Metamorphoses and the Traditions of Augustan Poetry*. Cambridge University Press: Cambridge.

Koehl, R. 1986. "The Chieftain Cup and a Minoan Rite of Passage." *Journal of Hellenic Studies* 106: 99–110.

Koortbojian, M. 1995. *Myth, Meaning, and Memory on Roman Sarcophagi.* University of California Press: Berkeley.

Kroll, J. 1982. "The Ancient Image of Athena Polias." *Hesperia Supplements* 23: 65–76, 203.

Kurke, L. 1996. "Pindar and the Prostitutes, or Reassessing Ancient 'Pornography.'" *Arion* 4.2: 49–75.

Kyle, D. 2007. *Sport and Spectacle in the Ancient World.* Wiley Blackwell: Oxford.

Kyrieleis, H. 1988. "Offerings of the 'Common Man' in the Heraion at Samos." In R. Hägg, N. Marinatos, and G. Nordquist, eds., *Early Greek Cult Practice.* Paul Åströms: Stockholm, 215–221.

Lafaye, G. 1904. *Les Métamorphoses d'Ovide et leurs modèles grecs.* Olms: Paris.

Langlotz, E. 1954. *Aphrodite in den Gärten.* Carl Winter: Heidelberg.

Lapatin, K. 2001. *Chryselephantine Statuary in the Ancient Mediterranean World.* Oxford University Press: Oxford.

Lapinkivi, P. 2004. *The Sumerian Sacred Marriage in the Light of Comparative Evidence.* Neo-Assyrian Text Corpus Project: Helsinki.

Lateiner, D. 1990. "Mimetic Syntax: Metaphor from Word Order, Especially in Ovid." *American Journal of Philology* 111: 204–237.

Lavagnini, B. 1963. "L'amore della statua." *Maia* 15: 322–325.

Lear, A. 2013. "Eros and Greek Sport." In P. Christesen and D.G. Kyle, eds., *A Companion to Sport and Spectacle in Greek and Roman Antiquity.* Wiley Blackwell: Oxford, 246–257.

Lease, E. 1919. "The Number Three, Mysterious, Mystic, Magic." *Classical Philology* 14: 56–73.

Lesky, A. 1951. *Aristainetos: Erotische Briefe.* Artemis: Zurich.

Lightfoot, J. 1999. *Parthenius of Nicaea.* Oxford University Press: Oxford.

Lightfoot, J. 2003. *Lucian: On the Syrian Goddess.* Oxford University Press: Oxford.

Lindsell, A. 1937. "Was Theocritus a Botanist?" *Greece & Rome* 6: 78–93.

Liveley, G. 1999. "Reading Resistance in Ovid's *Metamorphoses.*" In P. Hardie, A. Barchiesi, and S. Hinds, eds., *Ovidian Transformations: Essays on Ovid's Metamorphoses and Its Reception.* Cambridge Philological Society: Cambridge.

Lowrie, M. 1993. "Myrrha's Second Taboo, Ovid *Metamorphoses* 10.467–68." *Classical Philology* 88: 50–2.

Lyne, R.O.A.M. 1978. *Ciris: A Poem Attributed to Vergil.* Cambridge University Press: Cambridge.

Maas, M. and J. Snyder, 1989. *Stringed Instruments of Ancient Greece.* Yale University Press: New Haven, CT.

Madvig, J.N. 1873. *Adversaria critica ad scriptores graecos et latinos*, vol. 2. Hegel: Haunia.

Maier, F.G. and V. Karageorghis. 1984. *Paphos: History and Archaeology*. A.G. Leventis Foundation: Nicosia.

Majno, G. 1975. *The Healing Hand: Man and Wound in the Ancient World*. Harvard University Press: Cambridge, MA.

Makowski, J. 1996. "Bisexual Orpheus: Pederasty and Parody in Ovid." *Classical Journal* 92: 25–38.

Mannack, T. 2001. *The Late Mannerists in Athenian Vase Painting*. Oxford University Press: Oxford.

Masson, O. 1961. *Les inscriptions Chypriotes syllabiques*. E. de Boccard: Paris.

McCartney, E.S. 1925. "How the Apple Became a Token of Love." *Transactions of the American Philological Association* 56: 70–81.

Merkel, R. 1897. *P. Ovidius Naso*, vol. 2: *Metamorphoses*. Teubner: Leipzig.

Miller, J.I. 1969. *The Spice Trade of the Roman Empire*. Oxford University Press: Oxford.

Miller, J. 1988. "Some Versions of Pygmalion." In C. Martindale, ed., *Ovid Renewed: Ovidian Influences on Literature and Art from the Middle Ages to the Twentieth Century*. Cambridge University Press: Cambridge, 205–214.

Miller, J. 1999. "The Lamentations of Apollo in Ovid's *Metamorphoses*." In W. Schubert, ed., *Ovid: Werk und Wirkung: Festgabe für Michael von Albrecht zum 65. Geburtstag*. Peter Lang: Berlin, 413–421.

Müller, M.-P. 1988. "Pygmaion, Pygmalion und Pumaijaton: Aus der Geschichte einer mythischen Gestalt." *Orientalia* 57.2: 192–205.

Nagle, B. 1983. "Byblis and Myrrha: Two Incest Narratives in the *Metamorphoses*." *Classical Journal* 78: 301–15.

Newby, Z. 2005. *Greek Athletics in the Roman World: Victory and Virtue*. Oxford University Press: Oxford.

Nicolopoulos, A. 2003. "*Tremuloque gradu venit aegra senectus*: Old Age in Ovid's *Metamorphoses*." *Mnemosyne* 56: 48–60.

Oakley, J. and R. Sinos. 1993. *The Wedding in Ancient Athens*. University of Wisconsin Press: Madison.

O'Bryhim, S. 1990. "Ovid's Version of Callisto's Punishment." *Hermes* 118: 75–80.

O'Bryhim, S. 1996. "The Deities on the Kotchati Sanctuary Model." *Journal of Prehistoric Religion* 10: 7–14.

O'Bryhim, S. 1999. "Ovid's Myth of the Cerastae and Phoenician Human Sacrifice on Cyprus." *Rivista di Studi Fenici* 27: 3–20.

O'Bryhim, S. 2007. "Myrrha's 'Wedding' (Ov. Met. 10.446–470)." *Classical Quarterly* 58: 190–195.

O'Bryhim, S. 2010. "Phoenicium in the Wax (Pl. Ps. 20–37)." *Mnemosyne* 63: 635–639.

O'Bryhim, S. 2012. "Malodorous Aemilius (Catullus 97)." *Classical Philology* 107: 150–156.

O'Bryhim, S. 2015. "The Economics of Agalmatophilia." *Classical Journal* 110.4: 419–429.

Ogle, M. 1911. "The House-Door in Greek and Roman Religion and Folk-Lore." *American Journal of Philology* 32: 251–254.

Ohnefalsch-Richter, M. 1893. *Kypros, the Bible, and Homer.* Asher: London.

Otis, B. 1966. *Ovid as an Epic Poet.* Cambridge University Press: Cambridge.

Pagan, V. 2004. "Speaking before Superiors: Orpheus in Vergil and Ovid." In I. Sluiter and R. Rosen, eds., *Free Speech in Classical Antiquity.* Brill: Leiden, 368–389.

Palmer, L.R. 1954. *The Latin Language.* Bristol Classial Press: London.

Palmer, R. 1989. "*Bullae insignia ingenuitatis.*" *American Journal of Ancient History* 14: 1–69.

Parker, R. 1983. *Miasma: Pollution and Purification in Early Greek Religion.* Oxford University Press: Oxford.

Parry, H. 1964. "Ovid's *Metamorphoses*: Violence in a Pastoral Landscape." *Transactions of the American Philological Association* 95: 268–282.

Pease, A.S. 1920–1923. *M. Tulli Ciceronis: De divinatione, I–II.* University of Illinois Press: Urbana.

Pettersson, M. 1992. *Cults of Apollo at Sparta: The Hyacinthia, the Gymnopaidiai and the Karneia.* Komers: Stockholm.

Piacente, L. 1978. "Per la simbologia del cipresso nell' antica Roma." *Athenaeum* 56: 387–390.

Pöschl, V. 1960. "Der Katalog der Bäume in Ovids Metamorphosen." In H.R. Jauss and D. Schaller, eds., *Medium Aevum Vivum: Festschrift für Walther Bulst.* Carl Winter: Heidelberg, 13–21.

Powell, J.U. 1925. *Collectanea alexandrina.* Oxford University Press: Oxford.

Power, E. 1929. "The Ancient Gods and Language of Cyprus Revealed by the Accadian Inscriptions of Amathus." *Biblica* 10: 138–148.

Prince, M. 2011. "The Ties that (Un)Bind: Fathers, Daughters, and *Pietas* in Ovid's *Metamorphoses.*" *Syllecta Classica* 22: 39–68.

Ragette, F. 1980. *Baalbek.* Chatto & Windus: London.

Reece, D. 1985. "Shells, Ostrich Egg Shells and Other Exotic Faunal Remains from Kition." In V. Karageorghis and M. Demas, eds., *Excavations at Kition,* vol. 5.2: *The Pre-Phoenician Levels.* Department of Antiquites: Nicosia, 340–371.

Reece, D. 1989. "The Cassid Lips and Helmet Shells." *Bulletin of the American Schools of Oriental Research* 275: 33–40.

Reed, J.D. 1997. *Bion of Smyrna: The Fragments and the Adonis.* Cambridge University Press: Cambridge.

Rhode, E. 1900. *Der griechische Roman und seine Vorlaufer.* Georg Olms: Leipzig.

Roberts, H. 1980. "The Technique of Playing Ancient Instruments of the Lyre Type." In T.C. Mitchell, ed., *Music and Civilisation*. British Museum Publications: London, 43–77.

Robertson, N. 1982. "The Ritual Background of the Dying God in Cyprus and Syro-Palestine." *Harvard Theological Review* 75: 313–359.

Romano, I. 1988. "Early Greek Cult Images and Cult Practices." In R. Hagg, ed., *Early Greek Cult Practice*. Paul Åströms: Uppsala, 127–133.

Rouse, W. 1902. *Greek Votive Offerings*. Cambridge University Press: Cambridge.

Salzman-Mitchell, P. 2008. "A Whole Out of Pieces: Pygmalion's Ivory Statue in Ovid's *Metamorphoses*." *Arethusa* 41: 291–311.

Scanlon, T. 2002. *Eros and Greek Athletics*. Oxford University Press: Oxford.

Schilling, R. 1954. *La religion romaine de Vénus depuis des origins jusqu'au temps d'Augustus*. E. de Boccard: Paris.

Segal, C. 1969. *Landscape in Ovid's Metamorphoses: A Study in the Transformations of a Literary Symbol*. Franz Steiner Verlag: Wiesbaden.

Serwint, N. 2002. "Aphrodite and Her Near Eastern Sisters: Spheres of Influence." In D. Bolger and N. Serwint, eds., *Engendering Aphrodite: Women and Society in Ancient Cyprus*. American Schools of Oriental Research: Boston, 325–350.

Shackelton-Bailey, D.R. 1981. "Notes on Ovid's *Metamorphoses*." *Phoenix* 35: 332–337.

Sharrock, A. 1991. "The Love of Creation." *Ramus* 20: 169–182.

Sichtermann, H. 1956. "Hyakinthos." *Jahrbuch des Deutschen Archäologischen Instituts* 71: 97–123.

Smith, R. 1987. *Poetic Allusion and Poetic Embrace in Ovid and Vergil*. University of Michigan Press: Ann Arbor.

Smith, R. 1990. "Ov. *Met.* 10.475: An Instance of 'Meta-allusion.'" *Gymnasium* 97: 458–460.

Solodow, J. 1988. *The World of Ovid's Metamorphoses*. University of North Carolina Press: Chapel Hill.

Sophocleous, S. 1985. *Atlas des représentations chypro-archaiques des divinites*. Paul Åström: Göteborg.

Spaeth, B. 1996. *The Roman Goddess Ceres*. University of Texas Press: Austin.

Stackelberg, K. 2009. *The Roman Garden: Space, Sense, and Society*. Routledge: London.

Starr, R. 1992. "Silvia's Deer (Vergil, *Aeneid* 7.479–502): Game Parks and Roman Law." *American Journal of Philology* 113: 435–439.

Tarrant, R.J. 2004. *P. Ovidi Nasonis: Metamorphoses*. Oxford University Press: Oxford.

Tavenner, E. 1916. "Three as a Magic Number in Latin Literature." *Transactions of the American Philological Association* 47: 117–143.

Thomas, M. 1998. "Ovid's Orpheus: Immoral Lovers, Immortal Poets." *Materiali e discussioni per l'analisi dei testi classici* 40: 99–109.
Treggiari, S. 1991. *Roman Marriage*. Oxford University Press: Oxford.
Van Gennep, A. 1960. *The Rites of Passage*. University of Chicago Press: Chicago, IL.
VerSteeg, R. and N. Barclay. 2003. "Rhetoric and Law in Ovid's Orpheus." *Law and Literature* 15: 395–420.
Vian, F. 2003. *Les argonautiques orphiques*. Les Belles Lettres: Paris.
von Albrecht, M. 2014. *Ovid's Metamorphosen: Texte, Themen, Illustrationen*. Carl Winter: Heidelberg.
von Glinski, M. 2012. *Simile and Identity in Ovid's Metamorphoses*. Cambridge University Press: Cambridge.
Wagener, A. 1912. *Popular Associations of Right and Left in Roman Literature*. Johns Hopkins University Press: Baltimore, MD.
Warden, G. 1983. "Bullae, Roman Custom and Italic Tradition." *Opuscula Romana* 14: 69–75.
West, M.L. 1983. *The Orphic Poems*. Oxford University Press: Oxford.
Williams, C. 2010. *Roman Homosexuality*, 2nd edn. Oxford University Press: Oxford.
Wills, J. 1996. *Repetition in Latin Poetry*. Oxford University Press: Oxford.
Woodcock, E.C. 1959. *A New Latin Syntax*. Bristol Classical Press: Bristol.
Young, P. 2005. "The Cypriot Aphrodite Cult: Paphos, Rantidi, and Saint Barnabas." *Journal of Near Eastern Studies* 64: 23–44.
Ziogas, I. 2013. *Ovid and Hesiod: The Metamorphosis of the Catalogue of Women*. Cambridge University Press: Cambridge.

Index

adon. 108
Adonia   55, 108–109, 131–132
Adonis and Venus   108–113, 129–133
Aeneas   34, 37, 44, 57
Amathousa   87
Amathus   64–70, 82, 86, 87, 90, 111, 119, 124
Amyclae   58, 64
Anaxarete   71
anemone   108, 132, 133
Aphrodite of Cnidus   78, 80, 84
Aphrodite of the Gardens   123–4
Apollo Amyclaeus   58, 64
apples   114, 117, 123, 126, 130
arena   62, 130
Aristaeus   33–35, 38, 41
Astarte   55, 65, 71, 77, 108
Atalanta   47, 85, 91, 94, 108, 112, 130
Atalanta and Hippomenes   113–129
atrium   86, 118
Attis   48–49, 50, 127
Augustus   1–2, 4

Baal   67, 87
Belides   41
Belus   41, 87

boar   55, 106, 108–109, 112, 115, 120, 130
branding   62
bull masks   65–66
bull sacrifice   69
Busiris   68
Byblis   34, 55, 91–93, 95–96, 100, 102
Byblos   68, 87

Calais   46–47
Calliope   30, 47, 53, 57, 110
carmen et error   2
Cerastae   64–69, 72, 83, 105, 129
Cerberus   34, 36–38, 44, 117
Ceres   45, 88, 99, 101, 103–104, 132–133
Charon   36, 45
Cinyras   70, 72, 75–76, 81, 83
Cinyras and Myrrha   86–108
Cinyreia   87, 95, 120, 125
circus   49, 78, 119, 125
Cnidus   78, 80, 84, 111
constellations   101, 128
Cupid/Amor   3, 38–39, 79, 90, 107–108, 110, 121
Cybele   48, 114–115, 127–129

A Student's Commentary on Ovid's Metamorphoses *Book 10*, First Edition. Shawn O'Bryhim.
© 2021 John Wiley & Sons, Inc. Published 2021 by John Wiley & Sons, Inc.

Cyparissus   49–52, 60, 82–83, 85
cypress   47, 49, 52, 61
Cythera   68, 111

discus   57–58, 60–62, 109

eagle   55–57, 59
El   87
Elysian Fields   30–31, 43, 53, 133
Enkomi   66
erastes   57, 59
eromenos   59

Fates   38–40, 131
festival of Ceres   99, 101, 103–104
Furies/Eumenides   40, 42, 88, 91, 94

Ganymede   54–59
gardens   61, 124
gardens of Adonis   107, 109
Giants   54

Hades   30, 34, 36–43, 85, 96, 132–133
Hebrus River   30, 34, 133
Hercules   36–37, 40, 44, 50, 68, 117
Hippomenes   85, 108, 113–129, 130–132
Hippomenes and Atalanta   113–129
horns/antlers   50–51, 66, 69, 76, 83, 112
human sacrifice   67
hunt   47, 55, 57–59, 107–108, 111–112, 115–116, 120, 128–130
hyacinth   58, 61–63, 132
Hyacinthia   58, 64, 132
Hyacinthus   52, 57–68, 108–109, 111, 131–133
Hymenaeus   31–32, 35, 86, 89, 123

Icarus and Erigone   101
Ida   45
Idalion   67, 72–73

incest   89, 91–96, 102–103, 106–107, 128
initiation rites   114
Iphis   31, 34, 71, 86, 89, 91–92, 117
ivory statues   74–5, 78, 85
Ixion   40–41, 117

Jupiter Hospes   65, 119

Kinaru   88
Kition   65, 77
Koureus   87
Kourion   87

Lethe   36, 47, 52
lion   112, 116
locus amoenus   51, 60, 108, 109, 113
lyre   33, 42, 50, 53, 54, 88

Marieus   87
Marion   87
Medusa   38, 128
Megareus   118–121
Melkart   65
Menthe   132
Metharme   86–87, 100
mourning   32–33, 45–46, 49, 52, 63, 97, 109, 131–132
myrrh   87, 90, 105–107
Myrrha   54, 69, 84, 86–108, 110, 116, 120, 130
Myrrha and Cinyras   86–108

nurse   87–88, 94–100, 102–103, 116

Orphic Mysteries   30–31
Orphic   39, 43, 45, 52–54
oxhide ingot   67

paintings   57, 107
Panchaia   104

Paphos 67–68, 75–76, 81, 83, 85–88, 111, 124, 127
pederasty 30–31, 46, 49, 53–60, 63, 65, 77
Persephone/Proserpina 30, 34–45, 99, 109–110, 132–133
Phoenicians 64, 67, 79
plectrum 53–54
Pluto 30, 35–45
prophecy 38, 59, 63, 115–116
Propoetides 64–5, 67, 69–74, 77, 85–86, 88, 90, 98
purple dye 63
Pygmalion 43, 50, 64, 74–89, 99, 117, 127, 132

Reshef 65
Rhodope 33, 47

sacred marriage rite 76, 83, 86
sacred prostitution 70
Salamis 65–66, 71, 80

Silvia 51
Sisyphus 40–41
sorcerer 42, 53
Styx 36, 41, 45, 129
suasoria 35–36, 91–94, 99, 100
symposium 57

Taenarus 60
Tantalus 40–41, 55
tattooing 62
Thamyris 46, 57
Theias 87, 106
Thrace 31, 33, 35, 57, 89, 133
Thracians 32, 89
Tityos 40–41
Tomis 2, 4–5
tophet 67
torches 32, 91

Zephyrus 49, 57–58, 60
Zmyrna 87–88, 91, 106